THE FEMALE VOICE IN SUFI RITUAL

The Female Voice in Sufi Ritual

DEVOTIONAL PRACTICES OF PAKISTAN AND INDIA

by Shemeem Burney Abbas

Foreword by Elizabeth Warnock Fernea

UNIVERSITY OF TEXAS PRESS

AUSTIN

Printed in the United States of America

First edition, 2002

♾ The paper used in this book meets the minimum requirements of ANSI/NISO Z39.48-1992 (R1997) (Permanence of Paper).

LIBRARY OF CONGRESS CATALOGING-IN-PUBLICATION DATA

Abbas, Shemeem Burney, 1943–

The female voice in Sufi ritual : devotional practices of Pakistan and India / by Shemeem Burney Abbas ; foreword by Elizabeth Warnock Fernea.

p. cm.

Includes bibliographical references and index.

ISBN 978-0-292-72592-8

1. Music—Religious aspects—Sufism. 2. Sufi music—Pakistan. 3. Sufi music—India. 4. Sufism—Rituals. 5. Muslim women—Pakistan—Religious life. 6. Muslim women—India—Religious life. I. Title.

BP189.65.M87 A22 2003

297.4'38'0820954—dc21 2002008288

Dedicated to

the musicians who speak here

and

all those who supported this research

Contents

TRANSLITERATION OF CONSONANTS

Follows transliteration system for Urdu and Pakistani languages

ب	b	ڑ	ṛ		ک	k
پ	p	ز	ze		گ	g
ت	t	ژ	zh		ل	l
ٹ	ṭ	س	s		م	m
ث	s	ش	ś		ن	n
ج	j	ص	s	Panjabi retroflex nasal as in jāṇā	ڻ	ṇ
چ	c	ض	z		و	v
ح	h	ط	t		ھ	h
خ	<u>kh</u>	ظ	z	as in khā e	ء	
د	d	ع	ʿ		ی ے	y
ڈ	ḍ	غ	<u>g</u>			
ذ	z	ف	f			
ر	r	ق	q			

TRANSLITERATION OF VOWELS

a	as in **bas**	**i**	as in **bichānā**
ā	as in **ām**	**ī**	as in **dīvānī**
ā̃	as in **ā̃gūr**	**ī̃**	nasalized "ī" as in **nahī̃**
ā̃	nasalized version of **ā** as in **kahā̃**	**ū**	vowel as in **oo**
e	as in **hue**	**ū̃**	nasalized "u" as in **hū̃**
ɛ	as in **hɛ**	**o**	as in **ho**
ẽ	nasalized "e" as in **mẽ** which is "I," and also the preposition for "in"	**õ**	nasalized **"o"** as in **hathõ**

Author's Note: Translations, Transliterations, and Conversation Analysis Transcript Notation

All the translations and transliterations (see opposite page) are mine unless otherwise indicated. The translations are not a literal rendering of the text; rather, they are done to convey the mood of the Sufi poems so that the reader can enjoy the emotion of the lyrics as they are sung.

CONVERSATION ANALYSIS TRANSCRIPT NOTATION

In order to represent some of the *qawwālī* and *sufiāna-kalām* contexts, I have adapted the conversation analysis transcript system,[1] which enables readers to follow the transmission of live speech. I further adapt the system to transcribe the interviews with the musicians. In some of the *qawwālī* contexts discussed in the earlier part of the study, I adapted the conversation analysis system to capture the turn-taking among the *qawwāls*.

Letters such as A, B, and C represent the different *qawwāls*, and lines are numbered according to the pauses in the musicians' narratives and where semantically I find the end of the line. A Panjabi *qawwālī* sung by Ustad Nusrat Fateh Ali Khan and his ensemble in England in 1984 is represented thus:[2]

10	C	Sir devī te vafā na mang ī-ehī pīr Farīd dā dase
11	A	Palak palak pardesī-ā̃ kāran--merī akhīā̃ ne savāṇ lāe
12	B	Palak palak pardesī-ā̃ kāran--merī akhīā̃ ne savāṇ lāe
13	A	Allah jāne—
10	C	Give thy head, expect no loyalty in return—
		O, this is Farid, the Saint's wisdom

11 A For the one who went have my eyes shed a monsoon of tears--
12 B For the one who went have my eyes shed a monsoon of tears--
13 A O, God alone knows—

In the transliterations, punctuation is not used to mark conventional grammatical units; rather, the marks attempt to capture characteristics of speech delivery. Thus, I use the following symbols:

// Slash marks represent overlapping utterances in the *qawwālī* performance, such as when the Sabri Brothers sang a *qawwālī* in England in 1981 using Mira Bai's voice where she expresses her devotion for Khawaja Muinuddin Chishti of Ajmer:[3]

32 A ū̃ncī beṛī mere *Kh*āja kī-ī-ī-ī-ī-ī-ī-ī-ī-ī
B // ī-ī-ī-ī-ī-ī-ī-ī-ī-ī-ī-ī-ī-ī-ī-ī-ī
32 A O, mighty is my Khaja's abode
B // ī-ī-ī-ī-ī-ī-ī-ī-ī-ī-ī-ī-ī-ī-ī-ī-ī-

-- Hyphens between the long "ī"s represent Mira Bai's melismatic cry or other such occurrences in *qawwālī*. Otherwise a hyphen indicates a short, untimed pause within a sentence.

: Colons indicate an extension of the sound of the syllable they follow:

co: lon Kubra : we we: re going

Allāh ho - Nabī:: O ::O[4]	God ho - Prophet:: O : O
Allāh ho - Nabī:: O :: O	God ho - Prophet:: O : O
Allāh ho - ho Nabi :: O : O	God ho - ho Prophet:: O : O

In the *sufiānā-kalām* contexts where a solo singer chants, such as Abida Parvin's performance at the Open University auditorium in 1985 that is cited below,[5] the lines are numbered and the performers are marked with letters. The audience interaction is represented through the overlap symbols (slashes), such as:

A 98 Ik harf iśq dā na paṛh jāṇan
A 99 Bhulan phiran bicāre hū
B // th /th /th /th [audience claps][6]
A 98 They can't read a word of love

A 99 The poor souls are lost
B // th /th /th /th [audience claps]

The conversation analysis system was adopted only in the earlier performances that I studied between 1985 and 1992. I do not follow it in the performances that I transliterated after 1992, although I use some conventions from the system in the interviews with the musicians.

Foreword

Western scholars have described Islam as a "male" religion, a characterization that continues to be repeated well into the twenty-first century. As evidence for this position, commentators state and restate that no women are observed in the mosque for prayers, that only boys appear to be students in the Quranic schools, and that female participation is lacking during the major religious feasts (the Iid al Fitr which follows Ramadan, and the Iid al Adha, or feast of sacrifice). If this is actually the case, how could Islam be seen as other than male-focused? This view arises from several misconceptions.

Primary among these is the early scholars' need to compare Islam to a familiar system, i.e., Christianity. Such a comparison ignores a central fact: the mosque is not, like the Christian church, the center of religious observance. The focus of Muslim practice, like the focus of Judaic religious practice, lies in the home. The home is where the rituals marking the religious year take place and where women have tended to pray. And girls have always attended Quranic schools and received religious education, though often in private settings separate from boys. Further, early Western studies of Islam were text-based, rather than being the result of on-the-ground research and fieldwork in Muslim countries. The absence of a common language has also contributed to an ethnocentric view. Until very recently, knowledge of Arabic, Persian, Turkish, Urdu, and other languages spoken by Muslims around the world was minimal in the West. Muslim scholars themselves only began to write in English, French, and German after the nineteenth-century incursions by Western colonial powers.

Ethnocentrism also affected scholars' recognition of the importance of different categories of religious behavior that might not be present to the same degree in Christian practice. Here I speak of Sufism, or Islamic mysticism, and the far-flung series of lodges that the Sufi brotherhoods and sisterhoods have established over the centuries throughout the Islamic world. Sufi lodges, or *zawiyas*, are found from Morocco across the Fertile Crescent to Turkey, South Asia, and the Gulf States. (They are not found, of course, among Wahhabi adherents in Saudi Arabia.) Sufism, however, has always been regarded with some ambiguity by Muslim *imams* and *mullahs*, who see the rituals of the Sufi *tariqas* (organizations) as less than orthodox. But as is the case with all religious institutions, the way in which a belief is formally stated and the way in which it is expressed often differs among believers. Thus, just as the rise of holy figures and the pilgrimage to shrines such as Lourdes, Ste. Anne de Beaupré, and Our Lady of Guadalupe arouse controversies within the orthodox hierarchy of Christian Catholicism, so do the activities of the regional cults or organizations evoke mixed feelings among the theologians of Islam.

But the Sufi brotherhoods and sisterhoods have persisted, despite religious disfavor and government attempts to curtail their practices. In Libya, during the Italian colonial period, it was the chain of Sufi Senussi lodges that kept Islamic learning alive and served as a rallying point for Muslims objecting to Italian occupation. Mustafa Kemal outlawed the Sufi lodges in Turkey in the 1920s, believing that they had a deleterious influence on his country's modernization program, and also perhaps posed a political threat to his new republican government. In Morocco and Algeria, young survivors of the French colonial period saw the shrines as evidence of backwardness, and a program to discredit them began among the newly independent citizens. But the Sufi groups survived, and they continue to prosper throughout the Islamic world. Similar organizations are found in South Asia.

Sufi rituals vary from country to country and from rural to urban areas. In some, the lodge is an adjunct to the local mosque, and the activities are closely related. In others, the lodge is a separate building and organization. The organizations embrace both men and women in the rituals, sometimes separately, sometimes together in congregational settings. French ethnographers in North Africa noted early the *marabouts* (shrines) scattered through the countryside as well as the cities, shrines dedicated to *walis* (holy men), which are the focus of annual *moussems*, or celebrations of the lives of the holy men and women for whom the shrines are named. But the French ethnographers seldom mentioned the women auxiliaries of these same *marabouts*. It is only in the work of indigenous social scientists, such as the Tunisian anthropologist Sophie Ferchiou, that we find accounts of women's participation in annual rituals, and their daily or monthly visits (*ziārat*) to the shrines. And almost nothing has been published in English about men and women in South Asian Sufism.

Given these gaps in western scholarship about Islam, then, it is a great pleasure to introduce the book that follows: *The Female Voice in Sufi Ritual*, by Shemeem Abbas. Dr. Abbas is a native of Pakistan who has lived and studied in the West over a period of several years and holds advanced degrees from both British and American universities. Dr. Abbas' first interest in South Asian Sufis focused on the linguistic and performance aspects of their regular rituals. For her doctoral dissertation, she documented performances and linguistic variations within Pakistani communities. She attended sessions not only in her native land, but also in England and the United States, where Pakistanis far from home were developing their own versions of traditional rituals.

Now Dr. Abbas has built upon her earlier research to give us the following work. She has set down events in the ritual cycle in which both men and women are participants. Through her work in historical archives, she has discovered early examples of women's roles as participants, performers, and creators of texts. In travels throughout Pakistan, she visited village and city groups, recorded local variants of rituals, and interviewed not only the Sufi singers (both men and women), but also members of the audiences and local critics. This was possible because of her command of local languages, which allowed her access to local oral traditions. She has translated many of the texts in a fluid and accessible style. Dr. Abbas' research and insight has allowed her to integrate this new material into a South Asian case study, an in-depth view, in English, of women's role in Sufism.

The Female Voice in Sufi Ritual will come as no surprise to Muslim readers. But for Western audiences, it offers an introduction to an area of religious expression—that of women—which has been largely ignored and which is important to all people in the diverse world of Islam.

Elizabeth Warnock Fernea

Map 1. Landmarks of Sufi shrines in the subcontinent, adapted by the author from Saiyid Athar Abbas Rizvi, *A History of Sufism in India*, vol. 1 (New Delhi: Munshiram Manoharlal Publishers, 1978), 16–17.

Preface

WOMAN'S PLACE IN SUFISM

This book documents the place of women in Sufi practice in the subcontinent of Pakistan and India. *Samāʿ*, or the context where devotional Sufi poetry is sung and heard,[1] is almost unknown in the West but is widespread in the Muslim cultures of South Asia and the Middle East. Although it is a significant dimension of Sufi Islam, *samāʿ* is poorly documented and scarcely understood among the wider scholarly audience. Women's contribution to this is even less known. Despite the strong gender component of Sufi ritual discourse, the role of women has been ignored in scholarly work. It is very much a part of the living Sufi traditions in countries like Iran, Iraq, Turkey, Lebanon, Egypt, Syria, Morocco, Afghanistan, and Pakistan and India.

In the Islamic world, the mosque is primarily an arena for male activity, with little visible participation of women in the rituals. In the major mosques in Pakistan, for instance, there is a small space where women can go and pray on Friday or on religious festivals such as the Eid.[2] In the local *mohallā* mosques there is no possibility for a female to offer her ritual prayers. The domain is exclusively for male participation. Thus, the important spheres of religious and spiritual participation for women are the Sufi shrines. There, women's input is visible and they are significant participants in events.

The field has never been the subject of investigation by either native or western male scholars for a number of reasons. Among native scholars the area is ignored despite the fact that women have done much to educate the renowned male Sufis. Women are only referred to as mothers or sisters or spouses of the members of a Sufi *silsilā* (order).[3] A researcher of Amir Khusrau has stated,

> We do not know whether Khusrau had any sisters, for the eastern philosophers generally do not bother themselves about the female relatives of a person; they are considered to be either too insignificant to be mentioned or too sacred and inappropriate to be brought into the glaring and unholy light of publicity.[4]

Western male scholars have ignored the field because, as men, they cannot access the female domains of participation. They cannot enter the culturally close-knit networks among women in the ritual participation at Sufi shrines or at the community festivals, called *melās*, where much activity takes place. Furthermore, they have been handicapped due to their lack of knowledge of the indigenous languages. They cannot fathom the nuances of the discourse in which the ritual linguistic play of Sufi poetry is carried out but in which the illiterate yet informed audiences of the events are fully proficient through oral instruction.

I bring my own understandings and experiences of the culture that I portray. I convey the intuitions and subtleties of an oral culture where information is passed through word of mouth, from person to person and from family to family. I am still astonished, though, when I hear housecleaners and daily-wage workers at car washes in Pakistan recite Waris Shah's Panjabi poetry from memory, or when the technicians at the Institute of Sindhology educate me in the female myths of Shah Abdul Latif's poetry.

When I make certain references, such as to child-marriage or widow-marriage, the western reader may not find scholarly references to the same subjects. When I transcribe Hazrat Amir Khusrau's lyric about child-marriage, the intepretation is novel because there is no documentation of the subject in the literature. There is scant literature on child-marriage, and it is only recently that nongovernmental organizations in the subcontinent started to address the issue as an object for social reform. To a native researcher like myself, such events are endemic in the contexts in which I work. Although no one has examined the material in the particular way I propose, my approach is within the accepted ideas and practices of the indigenous culture that I represent. There is little scholarly evidence available.

I investigate the rituals at the Sufi shrines in Pakistan and look at female participation and the female voices in the ceremonials. My research is a linguistic anthropological study of discourse and poetry used in devotional settings. I apply a range of theories to interpret the data in the book: I have utilized the ethnography of speaking.[5] In addition I have applied the conversation analysis system wherever appropriate to the context.[6] The transliteration of live speech and its context in the performances is based on a conversation analysis scheme with adaptations, especially in the turn-taking among *qawwāls*. I am aware that there are a number of theories about speech and performance, but I use only those that relate to my work. The field is broad and the research expansive. Therefore, I use references that I can link with the study.

Many contexts and linguistic codes that I use are familiar to native scholars in Pakistan and India, but there are some features in the songs in the indigenous languages that western scholars may not understand. Thus, I bridge the gap between the East and the West in this book by giving a contextual interpretation of the lyrics in the translations. I have avoided a word-for-word translation but have made sure that the text is an authentic rendering of the poetic narrative that communicates the sophistication of the mood in which the musician sings. I transmit the flavor of languages such as Panjabi, Siraiki, Sindhi, and Urdu to the reader.

I studied Sufi practices at the shrines of Bulle Shah in Kasur, Bibi Pak Daman, Data Ganj Bakhsh Hujwiri, Shah Hussain, and Hazrat Mian Mir in Lahore, Hazrat Lal Shahbaz Qalandar and Shah Abdul Latif in Sind, and Hazrat Bahauddin Zakariya and Rukunuddin Shah Alam in Multan. At these shrines I observed the rituals that both women and men performed. Some rituals were common to all shrines, and some were particular to just that shrine. For example, women participated actively in the support services at the Lal Shahbaz Qalandar shrine in Sehwan: a female *muridīānī* gave water to the devotees. A woman was the caretaker of the tombs of Shah Abdul Latif's female relatives who were buried in a compound of the shrine. Among the rituals that I observed was one in which women devotees held up glasses of water to seek ritual blessings from the *guluband* or heart-shaped necklace that belonged to Hazrat Lal Shahbaz Qalandar and that hung over his tomb in Sehwan. The glasses of water were then shared with their kinswomen and men. To orthodox Muslims this may seem to be a fetish, but devotees draw strength from the ritual.

My guide to Hazrat Lal Shahbaz Qalandar's shrine was a senior librarian at the Institute of Sindhology at Sind University in Jamshoro, Hyderabad. Although an orthodox Muslim, he was a devotee of the Sufi saint. Many like him go to the shrines because they look upon the spaces as venues for meditation and worship. There is tolerance among individuals like him for the rituals that devotees perform. In recent years, with the coming into power of orthodox Islamic governments in Pakistan, there has been a trend to extend and renovate the shrines of Sufis such as Hazrat Data Ganj Bakhsh Hujwiri[7] in Lahore into mosques and places of worship. Data Darbar has been extended to almost ten times its original size and has been remodeled with the most expensive Italian marble. Huge congregations of devotees perform the Friday prayers in the shrine courtyard. I noticed the same feature at the Hazrat Mian Mir (d. 1635 AD) shrine in Lahore, which I visited this summer. The shrine had fallen to pieces almost a decade ago. It has been recently restored and is also used as a mosque.

The audiences at the shrines come from a variety of socioeconomic backgrounds. Gender plays a role as can be seen in the discussions and the photographs in this book. Women come in large numbers. The majority of participants are rural peasants, factory workers, housewives, and middle-class devotees. A large number who come are illiterate but well versed in the oral culture. The shrines fulfill devotional needs and provide outlets from the chores of daily life. There are many affluent and well-to-do devotees at the shrines who go there for prayer and meditation and also to make a *mannat* (a vow). When that vow is fulfilled, they go to the shrine to make an offering—usually food or charity that they give in cash.

Women's participation in singing *sufiānā-kalām* or Islamic mystical poetry is noticeable in the shrines, at the *melās*, in concerts, and in the larger domains of female domestic life. Although the main body of my research was directed toward the musical traditions, in the course of my fieldwork I was able to identify the following areas of female participation in Sufism and its rituals:

- Women as mystics in Sufi practices.
- Women as creators of Sufi poetry.
- Women who have influenced male Sufis in their roles as mothers, daughters, nurses, and mentors.
- Women as ethnographers and patrons of male Sufi mystics, such as the Mughal princess Jahan Ara, daughter of Shah Jehan.
- Women as singers/musicians/participants of Sufi songs, sometimes even called the *faqīrīanī* in the Sindhi shrines.
- Women as preservers and guardians of Sufi discourse or lore, such as Mai Naimat, a maidservant of Shah Abdul Latif, from whose memory his entire *Risālo* is said to have been reconstructed.
- Active "female" participants at the shrines, known as the *hijṛās* or eunuchs. They have been identified as *k͟hawājāsarā* in earlier shrine traditions during the rule of the Muslim kings in India.
- The aesthetics of the female voice, a poetic device in which the speaker is the female, even in the narratives of male musicians. The musicians play with the syntactic and semantic structures of the languages to speak as though they were females.

- Singing in the falsetto, even by male musicians, to impersonate a female voice, as is done by the *faqīrs* or musicians at Shah Abdul Latif's shrine in Bhit Shah. They mimic the heroines of Shah's poetry.
- The myths of female lovers, such as Sassi, Sohni, and Hir, used as aesthetic devices to speak of broader social, political, caste, and gender issues.

In this study, concentrating on the oral culture of the subcontinent, I have found a common thread that runs through each myth, though Sufi poets may use the myths according to their own intention. Male protagonists in the myths are discussed, but in the oral traditions romance is created through the aesthetics of female voices. Male musicians whom I interviewed confirmed this. Although I focus on female voices in this study, there is substantial discussion of male participation as well. I bring in references to Amir Khusrau and his lyrics, to Ustad Nusrat Fateh Ali Khan, the Sabri Brothers, Shaikh Ghulam Hussain, and Alan Faqir. A large number of the lyrics analyzed in the book are the compositions of male Sufi poets. Whether or not the Sufi poets of the subcontinent wrote in empathy for women is an area of research in itself. The lyrics do have strong female voices, and I leave the field open for further exploration.

The scope of this study is limited to its present undertaking as it is not possible to include every dimension of Sufism here. I do not discuss different versions of the female myths, or delve into male rituals, or bring in every theory or study that a scholar has done on Sufism. I document research in my own field for an informed, educated audience interested in the female dimensions of Sufism in the Pakistan-India subcontinent.

I interviewed a wide range of female and male musicians of Sufi performances in Pakistan between 1992 and 1999. My first interview was with Ustad Nusrat Fateh Ali Khan in 1992 at the Marriott Hotel in Islamabad. Although the interview was a formidable undertaking, I was able to solicit responses to questions. My key questions to him were about singing in the gendered voice of Hir or Sassi. His responses are documented in this book. Within a month after my meeting with Khan, I was able to interview Abida Parvin and her musician husband, Shaikh Ghulam Hussain. I received valuable responses from both musicians and discuss them in this study.

Although contacting key musicians was always a challenge and rather stressful, it was quite rewarding in the end when I transcribed the interviews. Alan Faqir even shared with me the politics of singing the female myths embedded in the poetry of the Sufi poets.

I did additional fieldwork at the Sufi shrines and recorded women's input into the rituals that are performed on a day-to-day basis and during the *'urs* or *melā* that celebrates the death anniversary of the Sufi saint.[8] Major databases in this book are my own field recordings of performances. There is input from professionals such as music directors, producers, archivists, and scholars in Pakistan who are linked with the singing of ritual Sufi discourse at the shrines, in concerts, and in the media, especially the radio. The radio seems to ensure the continuity of this tradition in the popular culture among the speech communities.

Although this book has developed from the fieldwork that I did in Pakistan between 1992 and 1999, it gains from the methodology that evolved during the first part of the research between 1985 to 1992, when I worked on my dissertation at the University of Texas at Austin. I depended on archival materials that were a comprehensive collection of multimedia resources from Pakistan, India, the United Kingdom, France, the United States, and Canada. The key archives from which I collected the materials were the Institute of Folk Heritage and the Allama Iqbal Open University in Islamabad and the Institute of Sindhology in Hyderabad, Sind. I obtained other materials from the School of Oriental and African Studies at the University of London and Oriental Star Agencies in the United Kingdom.

Between 1985 and 1992, I focused on the musicians' speech samples and transcribed them meticulously. I saw the same patterns emerge in Urdu, Purbi, Hindi, Panjabi, Siraiki, and Sindhi poetry that the musicians sang. I found references to mothers and daughters, sisters and brothers, and generally to kin relationships with women. There were allusions to the mystic veil, to women's work, such as husking, grinding, spinning, and weaving, and most fascinating of all to bold female lovers like Hir, Sohni, Sassi, Layla, Mira Bai, and many more. In addition to singing devotional poetry that paid homage to the prophet Muhammad, his family, and his *azwāj* (wives) the musicians further recited the Prophet's *hadīth* (sayings). They invoked bridal imagery to speak about the *mi'rāj* (the Prophet's ascension) and the Prophet's meeting with the deity, when the veil is lifted or the state of *kaśf* is attained. They sang about the Sufis of the Muslim world and about gender, class, color, and caste. Their discourse challenged the patriarchy and the establishment through the device of the female speaker; even in the metalanguage of the mystic ecstasy, the musicians spoke as females. These findings and the musicians' poetry sung to the mesmerizing percussion in the music became the impulse of the study.

Most importantly, in the same period in the eighties when this study was maturing, world music was claiming Ustad Nusrat Fateh Ali Khan, and his *qawwālīs* resonated in the concert halls of the West.[9] He infused a new life into the *qawwālī* by integrating the vibrancy of the Panjabi *qawwālī ang* (style) with experimentation in musical forms, especially the subtle use of saxophone for instrumentation. His Panjabi *qawwālī*s of the time are fascinating for the versatility of the linguistic resources, which portray the many female voices and which inspired the second phase of this study, focusing on the female speakers of Sufi poetry. He was able to infuse a subtle humor through language play in the *qawwālī*, which is traditionally serious mystic discourse.

Within the same time frame, Oriental Star Agencies in the United Kingdom was promoting musicians who sang Sufi poetry in concerts for the Pakistani and Indian expatriate speech communities. Invariably, the charismatic female voices in the musicians' narratives lent the performances elegance. I wonder if they were aware of it, or did they too suffer from the "paradox of familiarity" as I did? At home in Pakistan during this very period, Abida Parvin, a female musician, was framing her critiques of the orthodox establishment in public concerts, using the poetry of the Sufis of the subcontinent. It was at this time that I did substantial data collection of multimedia sources in Pakistan and the United Kingdom.

I have created a large repertoire of transliterations from Sufi songs that I recorded at the shrines. Some transliterations produced from archival multimedia sources are documented. These are in Urdu, Purbi, Hindi, Panjabi, Siraiki, and Sindhi and include an engaging use of dialect by the musicians to communicate with their audiences. Some of the Panjabi dialects that portray the female speakers would be stigmatized by purists, but they give the flavor of popular speech, and that makes them unique. These are the dialects of the old walled city of Lahore from where I trace the ancestry of my maternal family and where I have my roots. These are the dialects of Gujranwala, Faisalabad, and Sahiwal, which are the heart of the Panjab. I found them in Ustad Nusrat Fateh Ali Khan's narratives, and now in Mehr Ali and Sher Ali's *qawwālī*s.

There are sections of *qawwālī*s and *sufiānā-kalām* where the musicians switch to elitist codes like Persian and Arabic or they switch codes intralingually, between, say, Siraiki, Sindhi, Panjabi, and Urdu. There is evidence of turn-taking among the *qawwāl*s. These collections, together with my poetic "transmogrifications," are the data that speak. The many female voices form the basis of this study, and there is much more that speaks to an ethnographer; the material establishes its own authenticity. The transliterations verify the metalanguage of ecstasy; the *cakkī-nāmā*s and the *carkhī-nāmā*s demonstrate the discourse of women's work at grinding and weaving. I found many linguistic and thematic variables in these databases that can be explored for future research.

I stated earlier that I do not try to fit this book into any theoretical frame. I apply the ethnography of speaking and the conversation analysis frame. I let the musicians speak about the female voices, about themselves, about their linguistic resources, and about their songwriters. They are the ones who tell about the roving minstrels and answer the host of questions that the research generates.

As I developed this study, I claimed my own roots. I had listened to the narratives of older women in the family as they talked about my maternal family's descent from Hazrat Bahauddin Zakariya (d. 1267 AD) and Rukunuddin.[10] My family's elder women further spoke about a connection with Hazrat Shams Tabriz.[11] They spoke about the lineage that came from Iran and what is now the Middle East and Central Asia. They further affirmed that my ancestors were appointed as Muftis (religious scholars) of the city of Lahore in the reign of the Muslim slave king Shamsuddin Iltutmish, who ascended to the throne of Delhi after the death of his master, Qutubuddin Aibek, in 1210 AD. Qutubuddin Aibek was himself a slave king. I found this evidence in M. Wahid Mirza's study of Amir Khusrau:

> Shamsuddin, a brave and generous monarch, welcomed to his capital many unfortunate people driven from their homes by the Mongols. "Towards men of various sorts and degrees, Qadis, Imams, Muftis and the like, and to darweshes and monks, land-owners and farmers, traders, strangers, and travelers from great cities, his benefactions were universal. From the very outset of his reign and the dawn of the morning of his sovereignty in congregating eminent doctors of religion and law, venerable sayyids, maliks, amirs, sadrs, and (other) great men, the Sultan used, yearly to expend about ten millions; and people from various parts of the world he gathered at Delhi."[12]

Kanhyalal affirms the information.[13]

My mother, like other Muslim women in the subcontinent, had a home education and was proficient in reading and writing Persian, Arabic, Urdu, and English literary texts.[14] She was a writer for *Ismat,* a leading women's journal, which I read as an adolescent and which made me proficient in Urdu. Muslim women among the elite, including Mughal princesses such as Jahan Ara Begam, daughter of Shah Jehan, were educated at home with erudite female mentors who were related to distinguished male doctors of medicine, letters, sciences, history, and the arts. These women were accomplished in classical Arabic and Persian texts and could recite them mnemonically.

Interestingly, I have found evidence in the same source from M. Wahid

Mirza[15] about my paternal ancestry, which is claimed from Ziya'al Din Barani (1285–1361 AD). He was the author of *Tarikh-e Firuz Shahi*, a history of the Muslim monarch Firuz Shah Tughlak (1351–1388 AD), who was probably of Turko-Mongol stock and came from Khorasan during the reign of the Khilji sultans.[16] Barani's history of the Delhi sultanate in the thirteenth and fourteenth centuries is additionally a major source to study the Muslim ethnomusicology of the time. A substantial portionof Mirza's study of Amir Khusrau used Barani for a resource.

I was born in Pakistan and raised in the North Indian and Bengali traditions of ethnomusicology and poetry, which I further claim from my father, who was an architect educated at Rourkee and Aligarh.[17] I grew up in Bangladesh, which was then East Pakistan and had, immediately after partition, a strong musical tradition. The context was all around me. My father was posted there to build Comilla cantonment. He was a connoisseur of music who played the *tabla* with articulation. My mother played the *sitar*. I can now see the gradual evolution of the present study from a multicultural background: the Panjabi and Siraiki Sufi literary, musical, and linguistic traditions from the maternal side; they were the Muftis and Gardezis who belonged to Lahore and Multan. Among the paternal roots is the Burney lineage from which I inherit the North Indian cultural, musical, and linguistic traditions of "UP," now Uttar Pradesh, of Buland Shehr[18] near Meerut.

I shall now let the musicians of Sufi melodies speak for themselves. My role is that of the interpreter of the culture.[19]

NOTE: Readers who would like to learn more about the music discussed in this book are urged to acquire the CD (with accompanying explanatory material) *Troubadours of Allah: Sufi Music from the Indus Valley*, available from Weltmusic Wergo, Postach 36-40 D-55026 Mainz DDD LC 06336, ISBN 3-7957-6072-0.

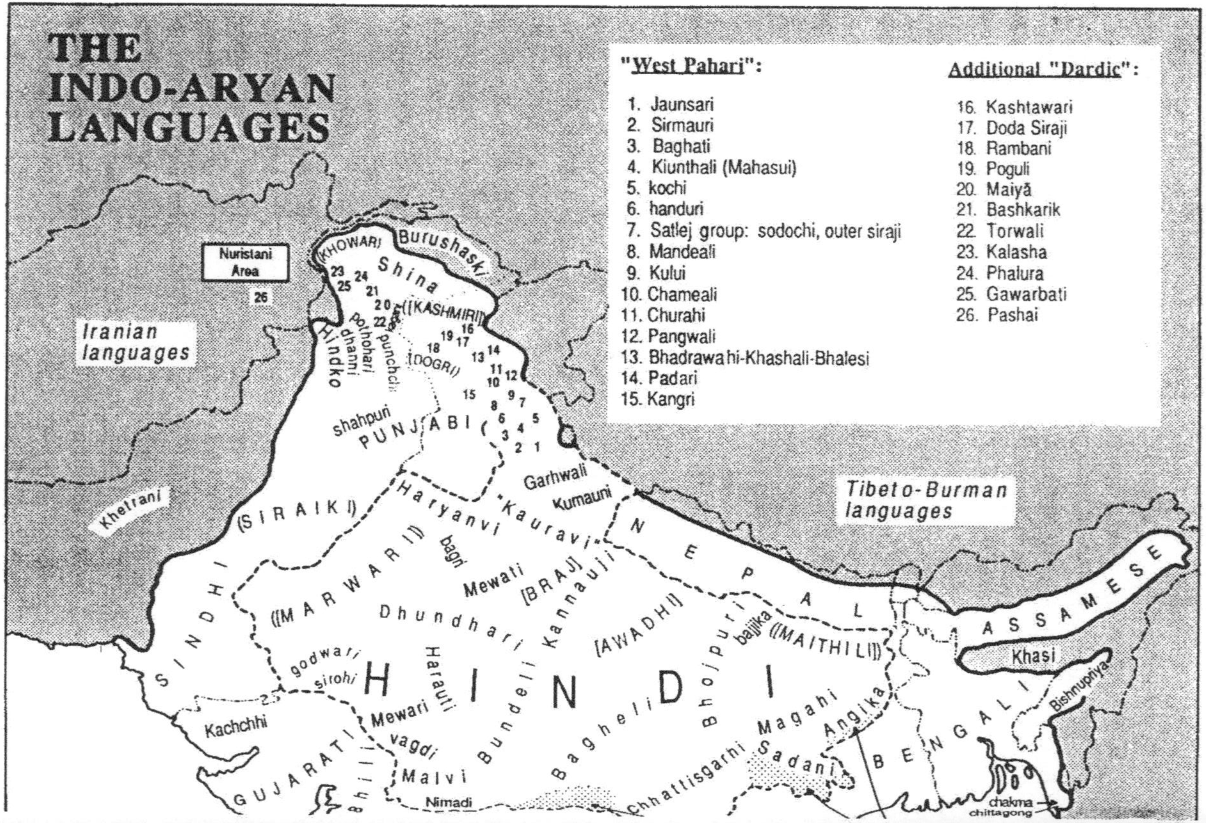
THE INDO-ARYAN LANGUAGES
"West Pahari":
1. Jaunsari
2. Sirmauri
3. Baghati
4. Kiunthali (Mahasui)
5. kochi
6. handuri
7. Satlej group: sodochi, outer siraji
8. Mandeali
9. Kului
10. Chameali
11. Churahi
12. Pangwali
13. Bhadrawahi-Khashali-Bhalesi
14. Padari
15. Kangri
Additional "Dardic":
16. Kashtawari
17. Doda Siraji
18. Rambani
19. Poguli
20. Maiyã
21. Bashkarik
22. Torwali
23. Kalasha
24. Phalura
25. Gawarbati
26. Pashai
Nuristani Area
Iranian languages
Tibeto-Burman languages
Khetrani
KHOWAR
Burushaski
Shina
(KASHMIRI)
(DOGRI)
Hindko
pothohari
dhanni
punchchi
shahpuri
PUNJABI
(SIRAIKI)
Haryanvi
"Kauravi"
Garhwali
Kumauni
NEPALI
ASSAMESE
Khasi
Bishnupriya
(MARWARI)
bagri
Mewati
[BRAJ]
Kannauji
Dhundhari
[AWADHI]
bajjika
(MAITHILI)
SINDHI
godwari
sirohi
HINDI
Harauti
Bundeli
Bagheli
Bhojpuri
Magahi
Angika
Sadani
Chhattisgarhi
BENGALI
Kachchhi
Mewari
vagdi
Malvi
Nimadi
GUJARATI
Bhili
chakma
chittagong

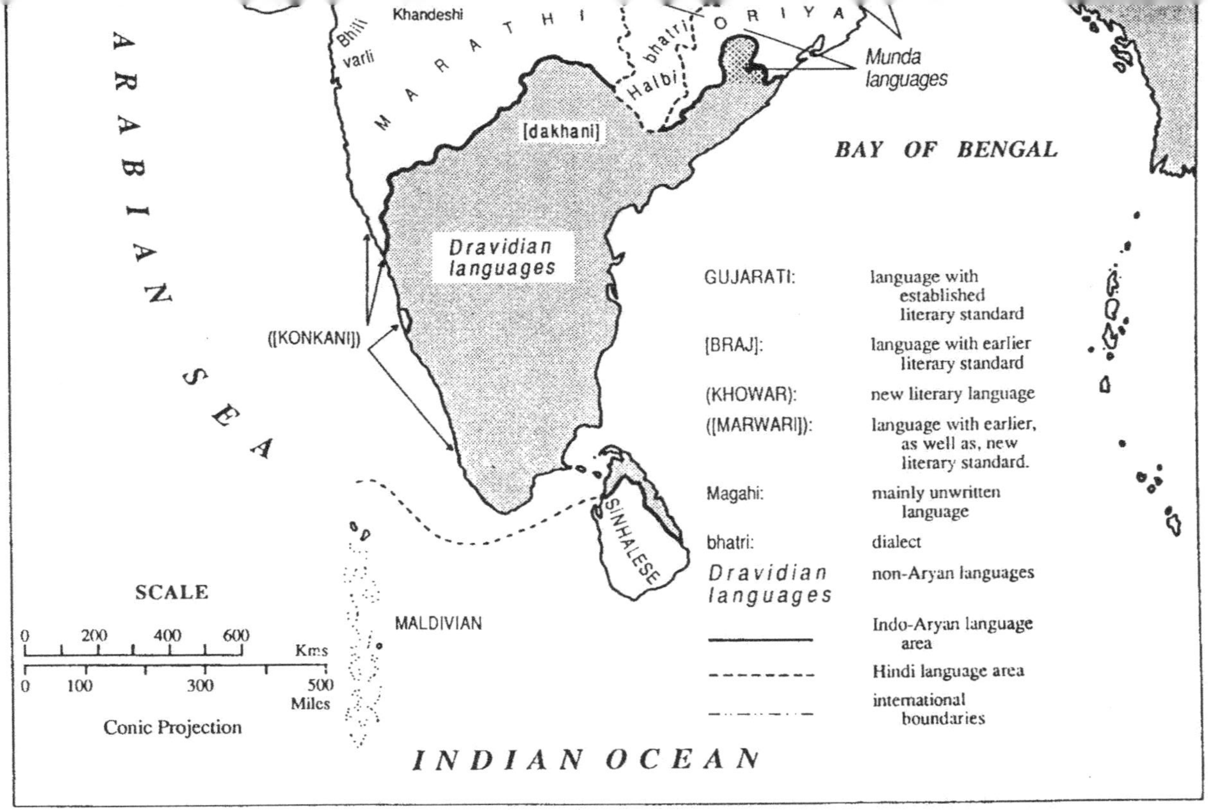

Map 2. Linguistic regions of the subcontinent, from Colin P. Masica, *The Indo-Aryan Languages* (Cambridge: Cambridge University Press, 1991), 10–11. Reprinted with permission of the publisher.

Acknowledgments

I acknowledge the musicians who speak here and those who supported this research. Elizabeth Fernea had faith in the subject of this book and patiently read several versions of the manuscript. Joel Sherzer read the manuscript and gave valuable feedback in addition to arranging my affiliation with the University of Texas at Austin. Gail Minault gave insights on the historical material and supported my nomination to the American Institute of Pakistan Studies Lecture Series. Patrick Olivelle and Peg Syverson provided access to computer facilities. Herman van Olphen guided the phonetic notation of Pakistani and Indian languages. Yildray Erdener clarified the terms. Jim Magnuson, John Ruszkiewicz, Annes McCann-Baker and Kamran Agahie steered me through difficult situations.

Val Daniel, Carl Ernst, Miriam Cook, Jonathan Kramer, Guy Welbon and Wilma Heston hosted me for the American Institute of Pakistan Studies Lecture Series. The United States Educational Foundation in Pakistan gave me a Fulbright Travel Grant.

My colleagues at the Institute of Educational Technology at the Allama Iqbal Open University in Islamabad prepared the multimedia materials. Dr. Latif Mughal, Dr G. A. Allana, Gul Muhammad Umrani, Qasim Makha, Syed Qalandar Shah and Gul Muhammad Mughal organized the data collection in Sind. Khalida and Jaleel Naqvi participated in the fieldwork in Lahore and Kasur. Maria Gillard, Khaula Mahmoud, Yasmin Jehangir and Zakia Malik were always there for me.

Lorraine Sakata, Regula Qureshi, Amy Catlin, Nazir Jairazbhoy, Helene Basu, Amy Maciszewski and Anita Slawek shared materials and insights.

John Bordie, the late Edgar Polomé and Robert Hopper directed the earlier stages of the research.

At the University of Texas Press Jim Burr provided immense support as did his team of editors, designers, marketing specialists and print-production staff; Leslie Tingle coordinated the editing with care. My copyeditor, Carolyn Russ, persevered with the aesthetics and conventions of the transliterations, conversation analysis, translations, and discussion in the manuscript. The reviewers gave valuable feedback.

To all, I am deeply grateful.

CHAPTER I

History and Economy of Women in Sufi Ritual

INTRODUCTION AND HISTORICAL CONTEXT

Although there is a long history of women's participation in the many dimensions of Sufi life, that is, in the traditions of Islamic mysticism, there has been no adequate documentation of it in the literature. In general, little ethnographic investigation of rituals at Sufi shrines, where both women and men participate, has been done. It is only in recent years that some studies have been published,[1] and even in these studies, focus is on male participation. Qureshi discusses the Qawwāl Bachche, a lineage of male *qawwāl*s (performers of Sufi music and poetry) in the subcontinent of Pakistan and India.[2] Schimmel has covered areas of the female voice in the subcontinent, but hers are literary and theoretical studies.[3] Likewise, Smith has researched Rabiʿa al-ʿAdawiyya and some other women mystics of Islam, but neither she nor Schimmel has investigated women's rituals from an ethnographic or performance perspective.[4] This applies as well to other research works that are either literary, theoretical, or historical investigations.[5] No researcher has examined the sociolinguistic aspects of the female voice or some of the performance fields that I have identified in my study, such as the female musicians who sing at the Sufi shrines or who sing the poetry of Sufi poets or texts about Sufi saints and their supernatural powers.

In this chapter I discuss how women who sing Sufi poetry have traditionally supported themselves as singers. I further investigate how community attitudes toward women's work changes depending on class and women's marital status, as becomes evident in my interviews with the Sidi musicians that took place in Hyderabad, Sind. I analyze the economy where female musicians participate in various community festivals and make a living by

1.1 Shrine of Hazrat Lal Shahbaz Qalandar in Sehwan, Sind. Courtesy Hakim Center, Karachi.

singing devotional poetry that I call "Sufi" because its content is about the Sufi saints of the Muslim world, as well as the life of the prophet Muhammad and his family. Most of these women also sing at the Sufi shrines such as Hazrat Lal Shahbaz Qalandar in Sehwan, where they make a living. Here, they find an audience at any time of the night or day that pays them for their performance.[6] Generally, they sing at shrines during the annual *ʿurs* celebration or on Thursday evenings, the eve of the Muslim sabbath on Friday.[7] They are free to sing there at any time except during the prayers. However, due to state control of Sufi shrines, the areas where they can sing may at times be confined to the female sections.

In Islamic societies that integrate religion into almost every aspect of social life, these women and men acquire the skills to earn a living that matches the devotion of their patrons and their audiences. Thus, in family contexts they create devotional settings wherever necessary, be it a birth, a wedding, or an initiation ritual such as a male child's circumcision. Their lyrics invoke Muhammad and his family, and within these frames they add references to Sufi saints. All of this becomes evident in my interviews with both women and men performers. Male musicians' perception of females in their family performing at community rituals is also evident in the interviews. In addition to the traditional orthodox Muslim view of Sufism as peripheral to the larger community practice, men and women who sing Sufi poetry take into consideration the way in which local communities view the place of women in public performances, as well as their need to earn a living from those performances. I point out these considerations in my interviews with the musicians.

Female musicians thus make a living by singing in the feudal households and within their own communities. They sing at the shrines and are paid by the devotees. In addition to singing at Sufi shrines, women musicians perform on the radio or television. Female musicians in the cities sing at ceremonies such as births, weddings, *aqīqā* celebrations, and circumcisions.[8]

Taj Mastani, a female folk singer who also sings some Sufi lyrics, informed me that, although her hometown is Sehwan Sharif, where the renowned Lal Shahbaz Qalandar shrine is located, she moved to Hyderabad because it is a large urban center. She affirmed that in Hyderabad she can earn a living from the radio. She can further negotiate business contracts with television stations and her clients from the affluent feudal households in Sind, who can reach her for ritual ceremonies. She said that Lok Virsa, the Institute of Folk Heritage in Islamabad, contacted her through Radio Pakistan in Hyderabad. Through Lok Virsa she was able to go to international concerts in the Middle East and Europe; as a state organization, Lok Virsa could afford to pay for her trips abroad. On her own she does not have the resources to travel overseas with her entourage. It is through international travel that world music discovered her and other musicians such as Ustad Nusrat Fateh Ali Khan.[9]

The interest of world music in the Sufi variety has provided financial opportunities for female musicians like Taj Mastani. However, earnings of women such as Abida Parvin and Reshma are not regular, and they depend on the whims of recording companies abroad. Sometimes, the female musicians do not have managers able to negotiate with recording companies overseas. Compared with female performers, male musicians such as Nusrat Fateh Ali Khan and the Sabri Brothers have done much better as a result of their international networks of male professional and community contacts. Female musicians have fewer direct contacts with male organizers and sponsors overseas. For all three female musicians that I discuss here, namely, Abida Parvin, Taj Mastani, and Reshma, their husbands functioned as negotiators. Due to cultural norms, female musicians have limited access to their male patrons and therefore their earnings are much less.

Although the female performers have made some capital from concerts in the Middle East, Europe, and North America, their earnings are small

1.2 Abida Parvin in concert. Courtesy Institute of Sindhology, Sind University, Jamshoro.

compared to those of their male counterparts, for example, Nusrat Fateh Ali Khan or the Sabri Brothers. This is in part because they sing *sufiānā-kalām* and not the more popular *qawwālī* that is sung in the classical traditions of North Indian music.[10] Their skills are considered more in line with folk music. As a result, Abida Parvin, who is trained in the classical music traditions, has lately adopted a *qawwālī*-like style while she sings *sufiānā-kalām*. Since the early nineties she has tried to establish an identity comparable to that of the male *qawwāls* by singing the traditional *qaul*, "Mun kunto Maulā fā Alī-un Maulā," in a call-and-response pattern with one of her instrumentalists.[11] Like the male *qawwāls* she has added a formidable repertoire of Amir Khusrau's Sufi lyrics in her performances.[12]

For the female musicians that I discuss here and the lesser-known ones in the rural areas and the urban centers, the cassette culture has provided a source of income.[13] For instance, within areas such as Hyderabad or Faisalabad the local recording companies have assisted women musicians in earning a living from recording their Sufi lyrics with music. Their songwriters are male relatives or men in the community. In fact, this small industry has become a source of income for many women and men. For example,

Rehmat Gramophone Company in Faisalabad provides female musicians with a livelihood by recording their songs during Milad-ud Nabi, which celebrates the Prophet's birthday. In popular culture, people love to hear their songs. Their recordings are played on the local buses, in the restaurants, and on the radio. Rehmat Gramophone Company releases special audiocassette editions in which female and male performers narrate the tragedy of Kerbala (680 AD) during the annual Muharram mourning rituals. These elegies,

1.3 Reshma of Mast Qalandar

1.4 Taj Mastani with spouse

called *nohās* and *marsiyās*, lament Hussain's martyrdom and that of the male members of his family. The lament tradition is expressed in the voices of the women who survived Kerbala, mainly Hussain's sister Zainab and his daughter Sakina. The musicians who chant these narratives can therefore make a living through the local recording companies.

The terms Sufi and Sufism belong to the world of Islam. There are many definitions of the term Sufi in the literature mentioned in this chapter. Briefly, Sufism is associated with the Islamic traditions of metaphysical thought and practices. Sufis believe in intuition and creativity and less in the fundamental and literal interpretation of the holy scriptures. A Muslim is a follower of Islam, the religion given to the Muslim world by Muhammad the Prophet (d. 632 AD). The Quran revealed to the prophet Muhammad is the core of Islam.

Many in the Muslim world object to the rituals at the shrines. However, the Islamic world is diverse. There are close to 1.2 billion followers of Islam in the Middle East, North Africa, and the countries of South Asia, and six million Muslims in North America. The majority of Muslims live in South Asia, including Pakistan, India, Bangladesh, Malaysia, Indonesia, and China.[14] Indonesia has the largest Muslim population in the world, and religious practice there is integrated into the indigenous practices and beliefs. Islam is diverse and has a local color in each geographical region.

Mystical performances originated in Sufism in the eighth century in the Arabian peninsula. The Quran occupied a central position in the life and works of the Sufis. They relied on excerpts from the Quran, for example, "He loves them and they love Him" (Sura 5:53) to develop a particular kind of attachment that shows the love between man and God.[15] According to the Sufis, words have a *zāhir* (overt meaning) and a *bātin* (covert meaning) that can be used to alter the consciousness through *zikr,* which is based on deep, disciplined breathing exercises in which the devotee incessantly repeats God's many names from the Quran. Additionally, short verses from the Quran can be used. *Zikr* is central to the *samā*ʿ practice, to the extent that a state of ecstasy is reached. These concepts are built into both the *qawwālī* and *sufiānā-kalām* traditions, with the result that a competent musician aims to induce this state among the listeners through the boundaries of music, speech, and song.

Sufi poetry in the high tradition was written by Sanaʾi, Attar, and Mansur Hallaj, the famous martyr of love who was crucified in 922 AD for his free-thinking beliefs and his famous doctrine of *anāʾl-Haqq,* which means "I am the truth." Mansur Hallaj was a master of word play and a favorite person in the lore of musicians of mystical poetry in the subcontinent.[16] Additionally, in the high tradition, al-Ghazzali wrote his famous *Book on the Right Usage of Audition and Trance* in the Middle Ages. These are the names of only a few of the leading Sufis, for the list is long and their *silsilās* (lineages) are countless in the Islamic societies.

Sufi poetry outside the high tradition of the *samā*ʿ was used in the eleventh century in Iran. From there it spread to Turkey and gradually into the Pakistan-India subcontinent, where it became popular in the thirteenth and fourteenth centuries. Jalaluddin Rumi (d. 1273 AD) founded the Mevlevi order of the whirling dervishes at Konya in Turkey. He wrote exquisite mystical poetry in Persian and became a strong influence for the Sufis of the subcontinent. Sufi poets and musicians adapt his Persian poems in their compositions to establish the authenticity of their narratives.

The present study focuses on the Sufis of the subcontinent whose poetry musicians sing today not only in Pakistan and India but also in England, France, Canada, the United States, Japan, and the Gulf States. Not only were the poets immersed in the centuries-old Islamic written and oral discourses such as the Quran, the *Sharīʿa,* and the prophet Muhammad's *hadīth;* they were able as well to interpret the texts for application to religious and practical matters. Because of their scholarly wisdom, even monarchs and functionaries in power sought the Sufi scholars' guidance.[17] As missionaries they undertook the dissemination of Islam through an oral medium whose basis was the written religious discourses. The Sufi *khanqahs* (monasteries) were institutions of learning where both men and women were involved in several levels of activities and continue to be so in present times.[18] The female voice has always been important in these rituals.

Sufi poetry emerged for centuries while the subcontinent was ravaged with strife between the different Muslim and Hindu factions. Later, civil wars between other religious groups aggravated the conflict. Dissent was also generated within the Muslim factions between the obscurants and the freethinkers or mystics who absorbed the wider spiritual and intellectual influences around them.

Furthermore, there were external onslaughts from various Central Asian neighbors coveting the riches of the Indian plains. Tamerlane, an ancestor of the first Mughal emperor Babar, led such an attack. The Mongols of Central Asia ravaged the Indian subcontinent and took the famous Sufi poet and musician Amir Khusrau (1253–1325 AD) as prisoner to Balkh. He remained there for two years and wrote one of his finest *marsiyās* (lament poetry) for Prince Muhammad, Sultan Ghiasuddin Balban's son, who was killed in the Battle of Multan. Amir Khusrau also wrote mystical poetry that had strong female voices, which I will discuss later.

In Pakistan and India, Hazrat Amir Khusrau largely popularized *qawwālī*, especially the singing of sacred text such as the *hadīth* (the sayings of the prophet Muhammad). He was a pupil of the famous Chishti saint, Hazrat Nizamuddin Auliya of Delhi (d. 1325 AD). The *qawwālī* in the subcontinent is associated with the Chishtiyya order of Sufi saints whose founding member, Hazrat Muinuddin Chishti (d. 1236), hailed from Iran and settled in Ajmer. The Qawwal Bachche are singers of Sufi lore who trace their lineage to Amir Khusrau.

The singing of Sufi discourse to music is rooted in the Sufi practice of *samā*ʿ (musical concert) that goes back to the middle of the ninth century—references to this event are found in Baghdad. In this setting verses were recited to music accompanied by a whirling dance.[19] The context is based on a *qaul*, which in Arabic means a famous saying. The singer of such discourse is called a *qawwāl*, someone who speaks well.[20] In the subcontinent of Pakistan and India, the institution of *qawwālī* and *sufiānā-kalām*, the singing of mystical poetry, is based on verbal art that is central to the Sufi theory of *tauhīd*, which declares God as one.

Qawwāli is essentially a male genre, usually sung by professional musicians, who come from a line of *qawwālī* singers, and consists of a team of five to twelve musicians who take turns singing a single narrative. They sit during the performance. Two or three main vocalists lead the group. *Qawwālī* performances are characterized by the use of rhythm, created through the percussion of drums and handclaps, together with the melodies. The percussion and the handclaps create the ecstasy in the performance and to a large extent depend on the interaction between musicians and listeners. The socioeconomic status of the listeners and the degree of their involvement in a particular context generate the structure of the event. No two performances are expected to be identical. The performance contexts define the emerging nature of the lyrics and the isomorphisms of language, culture, and society.

Sufiānā-kalām, on the other hand, is mystical poetry usually sung by a solo musician to minimal instrumentation.[21] Women's input in this tradition is significant. Sometimes, two or more singers will perform in a chorus. In Sind this form of choir singing is called *sūng.* However, whether it is a monologue or a chorus, it does not have the structured, classical, turn-taking dialogue found in the *qawwālī.* The musician generates body language to engage the audience in the performance. The audience, in turn, complements the performance with strong, appreciative, linguistic cues. The audience additionally communicates through body language. Male singers of *sufiānā-kalām,* such as Alan Faqir, would dance as they held a stringed instrument in one hand. Usually *sufiānā-kalām* is sung to a *capṛī* (castanets) or a *tambūr* or *yak-tārā* (stringed instruments). Folk singers like Alam Lohar and his son Arif Lohar would use the *cimṭā* (long tongs) to create the percussion, and their vigorous body language almost resembles a dance. I have seen male Baluchi musicians dancing to the rhythm of the *rabāb* (a small stringed instrument) while singing mystical poetry. Sometimes a *ghaṛā* (large clay pot) is used for percussion to sing the *sufiānā-kalām.* Women called *loṭevālī,* or *ghaṛevālī* or *challevālī,* use a small aluminum pot on which they create percussion with the ring on the middle finger while they sing mystical poetry.[22]

By and large, *sufiānā-kalām* seems to be associated with the mobile, indigenous mystical traditions. As part of popular culture it was sung among roving minstrels at the shrines during the *ʿurs,* the *melā*s (folk festivals), and on Thursday evenings. Unlike the *qawwālī,* where the musicians have to have rigorous training in the genre, the singing of *sufiānā-kalām* requires less rigid training. An average singer of *sufiānā-kalām* can get by using indigenous folk melodies and songs. The singers pick them up from the shrine environments or from the folk festivals. Now, of course, radio, television, and the cassette culture are an aid for the musicians, both as venues and as models for their performance.[23]

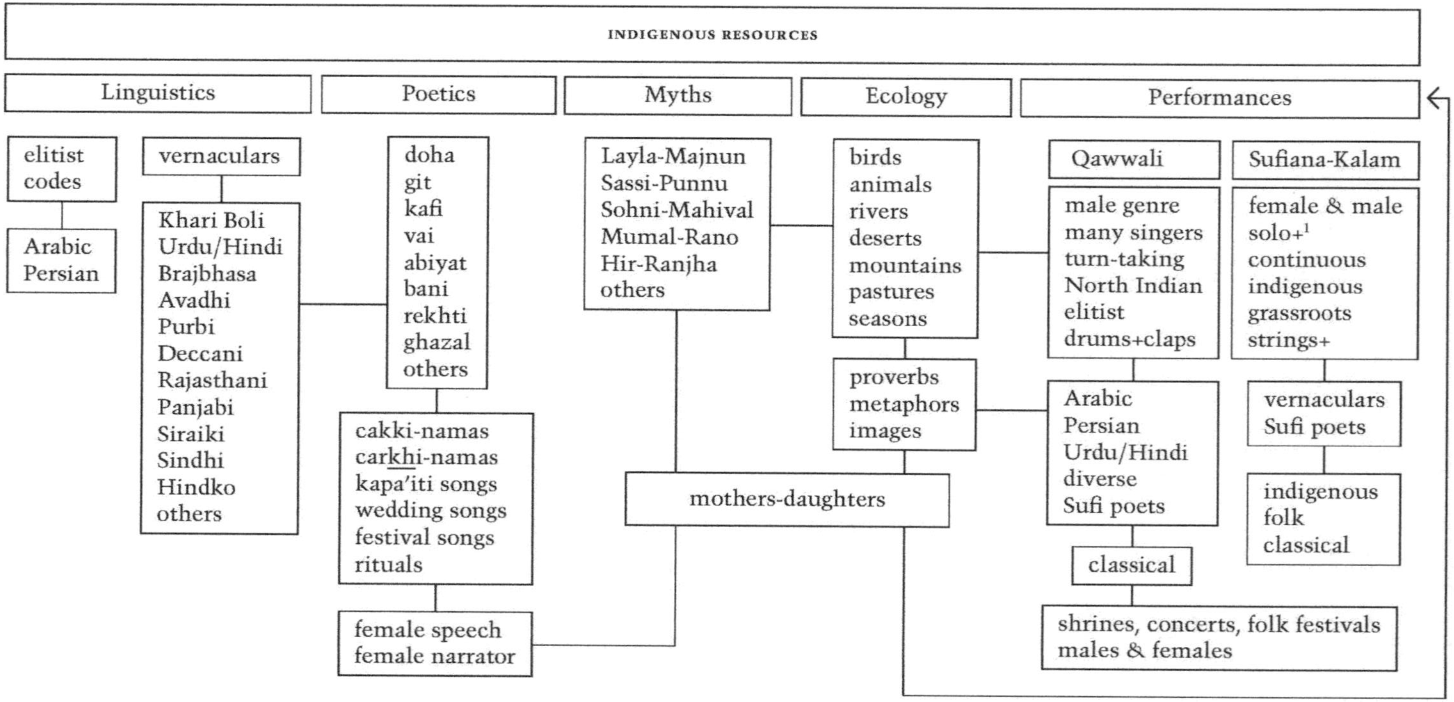

1.5 Comparative model: *Qawwālī* and *Sufīānā-Kalām*

1. Sometimes there can be more than one singer.

Sufiānā-kalām evolved at the same time as *qawwālī* within the framework of the oral mystical traditions in the subcontinent in the thirteenth and fourteenth centuries. The purpose of *qawwālī* and *sufiānā-kalām* is to make a spiritual experience available to the people in an idiom they understand. The use of vernacular languages in *qawwālī* and *sufiānā-kalām* repertoires entails the singing to music of Quranic texts, the *hadīth*, and the wisdom of the Sufis. Such an approach enables the mystics to teach the core of religion without the intervention of the clergy.

Qawwālī and *sufiānā-kalām* are performed at the shrines of the Sufi saints and in public concerts. At the shrines they are performed on Thursday evenings in anticipation of the Muslim sabbath and during the celebrations of the death anniversary of the saint. A public concert, on the other hand, may be held at any time. At some shrines, such as Bulle Shah, Hazrat Lal Shahbaz Qalandar, Shah Abdul Latif at Bhit Shah, Bahauddin Zakariya, and Rukunuddin Shah Alam, *qawwālī* is performed every evening after the prayers. Musicians as well as audiences prefer evening performances that continue well past midnight. The musicians expect to attain a *maqām*, the spiritual station that enables them to create ecstasy among the listeners.

The performers interact among themselves and with their audiences in a cultural and religious context, which may be inside a Sufi shrine or in a concert hall. Although there is a marked difference between a shrine performance and one in concert, the former being more traditional and the latter somewhat secular, the key musicians that I interviewed affirmed the sanctity of both contexts. Abida Parvin categorically affirmed that she sang her poetry with veneration even at public concerts. Whether inside a Sufi shrine or in a concert hall, the musicians uphold the purity of the context. During a *qawwālī* performance in Rawalpindi in 1974, I witnessed the Sabri Brothers request the then–federal minister for education and his entourage not to clap during the event. Almost all the Sufi musicians with whom I spoke insisted on the distinction between sacred and secular contexts even in concert settings. They state that their performance in concert is sacred and not secular, because of the text they sing, and that the text cannot be trivialized. They also assert that their poetry is not folk, but devotional and ritualistic, as they perform with the utmost sanctity (*adab*).

A typical performance of *qawwālī* ritual begins with a *qaul* or *hadīth* in Arabic. Alternatively, it may begin in Persian, which is considered the language of higher intellectual thought. To establish the authenticity of their texts, the musicians recite the initial verses in Arabic or Persian and then switch to the vernacular. This can be either Urdu, Hindi, Purbi, Brajbhasha, Sindhi, Siraiki, Panjabi, Hindko, Baluchi, or any other code depending on the audience and the speech communities involved in the event. The dialect of the performers themselves is significant as they switch codes and use many linguistic and musical improvisations to communicate with their listeners.

Whereas the devotees who visit the shrines do not claim to be Sufis, who in their perception may be associated with great spiritual achievements through rigorous discipline, they firmly believe that they are Muslims and belong to the *ummah* of the Islamic world. The Wahabi followers of Islam disdain the Sufi practices at the shrines as a form of *biddat* (dissent). However, in the Iranian, Turkish, Middle Eastern, and South Asian versions of Islam, the practices have become indigenized with the aboriginal practices. The Bhakti movement (800–1700 AD) meshed with it, and many devotional movements emerged at this time where poetry written in the vernacular was sung to music—these movements emphasized a personal and emotional relationship with God. The poetry of Kabir and Nanak in the fifteenth century was an outcome of these movements and led to the founding of Sikhism. Therefore, a musician who sings *qawwālī* or *sufiānā-kalām* or the poetry of the Sufi poets does not claim to be a Sufi but only a transmitter of Sufi discourse or poetry. This poetry glorifies God, His prophet, Muhammad, Muhammad's family, and the great mystics of Islam in the Muslim world.

Samā' in the Pakistan-India subcontinent is generally understood as the *context* in which Islamic mystical texts are sung and heard, whether in the shrine or in a public context. I found the word used in other contexts as well, especially in the vernacular languages. To create the *samā'* also means to create the context. A grassroots Panjabi musician, Dai Haleema, used the word this way:

> When the musicians and audience sing together there is a lot of peace in the assembly. It creates a nice *samā'*, and you involve more people. This is better than singing alone. And, when we sing it is with full force and passion.

Thus, the terms used in this book are from scholarly literature as well as from the popular culture: These are the beliefs of the participants of the speech events and the grassroots musicians.

Terms like *samā'*, *maqām*, *wajd*, *kefiat*, *hāl*, *zikr*, and *qaul* have meanings according to the context, and they are applied across a broad spectrum in the literature on Sufism. Musicians such as Nusrat Fateh Ali Khan (1992), Abida Parvin and Shaikh Ghulam Hussain (1992), and Surraiya Multanikar (1995) have given them various meanings. Researchers have defined the terms in context.[24] For instance, Shaikh Ghulam Hussain, a music director and Abida

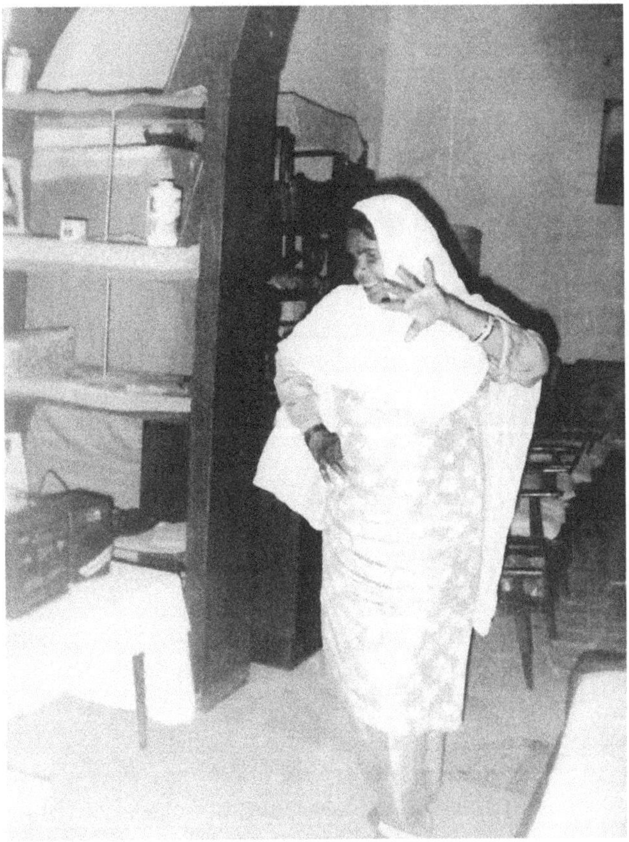

1.6 Grassroots musician: Dai Haleema, Talagang

Parvin's late husband, used the word *kefīat* as a state of altered consciousness. In my interview with him I understood *kefīat* as a refined state of spiritual awareness, induced through the combination of Sufi poetry and music. Shaikh Ghulam Hussain made this clear when he demarcated the boundaries of speech, song, and music and said that there is a fine line between the ecstasy of *kefīat* and what is vulgar. "Vulgar," he said, is when words or music trespass the fine balance and violate finesse or refinement. He elaborated by using the example of rock 'n' roll, which he considered the opposite extreme of Sufi music that produces *kefīat.*

When I interviewed Sikandar Baloch and Naseer Mirza at Radio Pakistan in Hyderabad, they defined the word *maqām* as a hierarchical movement toward ecstasy in a Sufi concert. They explained the term while discussing the Sufi musical concert at Shah Abdul Latif's shrine in Bhit Shah. Because of the diverse linguistic codes, cultures, and contexts of the subcontinent, the word *maqām* is polysemous.

The term *wajd* (trance) may seem pejorative to orthodox Muslims or to someone in the West. *Kefīat* and *hāl* are states of ecstasy in the same mystical experience, although there is a difference in degrees of expression.[25] *Hāl* is a state of arousal outside the control of self.[26] *Kefīat* is subtle and covert although it involves ecstasy. Even singers are involved in the *kefīat,* and there is no *samā*ʿ (context) without interactional *kefīat* between listeners and singers. These are the subtle dynamics of a performance. The musicians who sing the lyrics or the listeners who attend the speech events perceive the state in its manifold aspects. Among some participants it is a desired state that the musicians create. For the musicians it is an indication of the success of their performance: They have succeeded in creating a spiritual ambience through language and music if some among their audience have reached *kefīat* or *hāl.* They are obligated to continue singing until the affected overcome the state of ecstasy.[27] For the audience that experiences this state, it is an expression of devotion or perhaps even temporary spiritual escape.

Sufism and its practices evolved over centuries and at the grassroots level: there are many in the Muslim world who pay homage to the Sufi masters who interpret and present Islam to the average unread individual in simple terms. In the subcontinent of Pakistan and India the hegemony of a clerical order was perhaps not encouraged because the Sufi saints, who were sometimes also poets, simplified the Quranic texts for the masses. Orthodox Islamic zealots are known to have executed Sufi adherents such as Mansur Hallaj (d. 922 AD) and Sarmad (d. 1661 AD).

Sufi Islam was brought to the subcontinent by the Chishtiyya saint Hazrat Muinuddin Chishti. The hallmark of the Chishtiyya order of Sufism in the subcontinent of Pakistan and India was the use of music to sing devotional texts. Ustad Ghulam Haider Khan, a *qawwāl,* reports that when Hazrat Muinuddin Chishti, originally a resident of the town of Sanjar in Iran, came to Ajmer in India, he studied the Hindu style of worship.[28] He found that music was a significant component of worship, and the Brahmins sang *aśloks, śābāds*, and *bhajans* with percussion and wind instruments. Hazrat Muinuddin Chishti adapted the same practice, and thousands of Hindus converted to Islam. Ustād Ghulam Haider further claims that *qawwālī* or *samā*ʿ is centuries old. It came from Khurasan in Iran where the nomads sang lyrics accompanied by drums and handclaps. Thus, according to the musician, Hazrat Muinuddin Chishti integrated Iranian practices into native Indian devotional rituals.[29]

Until recently, the *samāʿ* performances of the male Sufi groups in countries like Iran were secret rituals in which ordinary uninitiated persons were not allowed to participate. Women's entry was even more difficult. Perhaps the Pakistan-India area is one of the few places where the performances are held in the public contexts of the shrine, the folk festival, and the concert. Now the ritual concert is performed among the expatriate speech communities in the West and the Gulf States, where it has evolved within the frames of world music though still retaining the devotional speech forms and ethnomusical content. In all the public contexts women are active participants, thus making it possible for the ethnographer to study the speech events.

MUSICIANS' NARRATIVES AND ROVING MINSTRELS

"Manam Ahn Koolee	ʿĀšiq-e-sanam divāne"
I am that gypsy	A lover and crazy

is a Persian Sufi song that I heard Mohammad Firozee sing in Austin, Texas, at the Rumi Festival in the fall of 1999. The Texas audience was mixed, consisting of members of diasporic communities interested in Sufism and the local population who also were interested in Sufi music. Mohammad Firozee himself was from Iran and had been in the United States for more than two decades. The term "Koolee" that I heard repeatedly in the musician's repertoire was similar to that applied to female peasants I had seen during my fieldwork in Sind in 1999, especially at the shrine of Shah Abdul Latif in Bhit Shah, who were known as Kolhi. The women wore colorful long skirts and were draped in large, equally colorful veils. They had fine features and dark skin that they highlighted by wearing intricately crafted silver jewelry: thick silver bangles almost up to their elbows and ivory bands that covered their arms. They also wore large silver nose rings and several earrings around the earlobes.

The Kolhis are the indigenous peasant communities of Sind who are sometimes migratory. Usually they are temporary farm laborers in the large feudal holdings. They are non-Muslims, and together with the Bhils they are the native inhabitants of the Sind-Rajasthan continuum. Their women are ardent devotees at Muslim shrines such as those of Shah Abdul Latif at Bhit Shah. They go there primarily because the shrine is located in Hala, the heart of a fertile agricultural belt, where they can make a living working on the large feudal farms. Secondarily, Shah's *jamālī* (aesthetic) poetry, written in a syncretic context and sung in falsetto by his *faqīr*s who imitate the female voices of his heroines, draws non-Muslim populations to his shrine. Shah's

1.7 Non-Muslim Kolhi women: Shah Abdul Latif's shrine, Bhit Shah, Sind

sūrmīs (heroines) such as Sassi, Sohni, and Marvi are drawn cross culturally from the centuries-old pre-Islamic myths of the region that he blended into the Islamic mystical framework. He made his *sūrmīs* into representations of the pining soul in search of the beloved. And since Shah wrote his poetry in the Sindhi vernacular, the Kohli and Bhil male and female peasants can understand and relate to it; they can read their own sufferings in the narratives of heroines like Sassi or Marvi.[30] The Bhil and Kolhi women can identify with Shah's heroines, thus, they are ardent devotees of his shrine.[31]

After the concert in Austin, I spoke to Mohammad Firozee, trying to make the connection between the "Kolhis" in Sind and the "Koolee" or gypsy in his lyric. Firozee explained that his poem was about a heart that was a gypsy moving from place to place in its restless passion for the beloved. I was able to relate his mystical lyric in Persian to Shah Abdul Latif's Sindhi mystical poetry that also describes gypsies or roving mendicants.[32] Shah's poetry evolved through his experiences as a roving minstrel. I address this evolution in my interviews with Abida Parvin and her husband later in this chapter.

Firozee's lyric established more connections when I met with ethnomusicologists who had researched the Kacch-Rajasthan-Sind-Baluchistan continuum.[33] The mystical lore of the region that includes Sind, Baluchistan, and the coastal belt of Iran shares myths, melodies, and linguistic codes.[34] Among the melodies are the famous "Mast Qalandar" *dhun*, which most female and male minstrels sing to the popular text that pays tribute to ʿAli, the fourth caliph of Islam and the spiritual mentor of a large number of Sufi *silsilās* (lineages). The "Mast Qalandar" is a theme about the ecstatic mendicant who gives up the material world and roves from place to place in search of divine wisdom. Firozee's Persian lyric was very much in the roving-minstrel tradition that he called the "Koolee" or gypsy. Such poetry is about the *faqīrs* and mystics whose restless souls make them rove from place to place.

The roving-minstrel traditions of Sufi poems, speech, and song evolved from the indigenous, grassroots oral culture in the subcontinent perhaps in the thirteenth and fourteenth centuries. About this time there was a religious renaissance in the subcontinent, and Central Asian Sufism influenced the local Bhakti movement in Hindustan.[35] Reformers and mystics like Kabir (b. 1440) and Guru Nanak (b. 1469 AD) were certainly influenced by Sufism.

1.8 Kolhi women's performance. Courtesy Institute of Sindhology, Sind University, Jamshoro.

To this day some of Shaikh Fariduddin Ganj-e Shakar's (d. 1266 AD) best Sufi poetry in Panjabi is preserved in the Gurmukhi script in the sacred texts of Sikhism.[36] In the syncretic religious environment of the time, when India was ruled by the Mughal emperor Akbar (1556–1605 AD), Tulsidas (d. 1623 AD), Surdas (d. 1563 AD), and Mira Bai (b. 1498 AD) were writing devotional poetry in the vernacular languages. Mira Bai wrote in Hindi and Gujrati, and I discuss her later in the study. Earlier Amir Khusrau (d. 1325), who was both a poet and musician, wrote some of his Sufi lyrics in the Braj dialects such as Hindawi and Purbi, in addition to writing in Persian, which was considered an elitist language. Khusrau's Hindawi poetry is sung in *qawwālī* compositions to this day, together with his Persian texts, and is now claimed by the female musician Abida Parvin, who sings it with improvisation in the *sufiānā-kalām* tradition. This is a grassroots oral tradition where performers sing in the vernacular languages and not an elitist tradition like the *qawwālī*, which is based on the Perso-Arabic traditions established by Hazrat Amir Khusrau.

The great religious and spiritual renaissance in India that started around the fourteenth century reached its peak under the Mughal emperor Akbar in the sixteenth century. He patronized the fusion of Sufi mystical Islam with the indigenous practices of the subcontinent, and he himself was an ardent devotee of Shaikh Saleem Chishti, a Sufi mystic who, according to legend, prayed for him so that he would have a son. His prayers were answered when Saleem, later known as Jehangir, was born and succeeded Akbar to the Mughal throne.

Thus the mystic poetry of India, including that of Sufism in the fourteenth and fifteenth centuries, was emotional and expressed the devotees' love toward a personal God. The movements that emerged at this time challenged hegemonic religious authority, caste boundaries, gender inequity, and the exclusive use of elitist languages in religion.[37] In South Asian Islam, the trend appeared in Sufism and particularly in the *sufiānā-kalām* traditions that used poetry written in the vernaculars by the Sufi poets. As stated earlier, since this model was an indigenous one that required minimal musical skills and resources, women's input in the singing of this poetry is visible. Mira Bai, the Rajput princess who "disappeared" among the people and whose *bhajans* (devotional poems) are sung among the minstrels in India, is a telling example of the roving-minstrel tradition.

Since the *sufiānā-kalām* tradition of singing mystical texts in the vernaculars was based on the roving-minstrel culture, there are indigenous devotional elements in them. In this form of worship the emphasis is on the repetition of God's name.[38]

In the Sind region Shah Abdul Latif (d. 1752 AD) and other Sufi poets composed poetry in the vernacular languages and dialects in which they sang as roving mendicants within an Islamic framework. For fear of the clergy mystic poetry sung to music remained confined to the minstrel class.[39] That is why the *sufiānā-kalām* traditions are strong among this class of roving musicians who sing in the indigenous languages such as Siraiki, Sindhi, Baluchi, and the regional dialects of Pakistan. This further explains why the non-Muslim Kolhi and Bhil communities are devotees of Shah Abdul Latif's shrine in Bhit Shah, Sind: his poetry is linguistically diverse and is tolerant of other beliefs.

The Sufi mystical traditions came to the subcontinent of Pakistan and India through the Sind province with the coming of Islam in 708 AD when Muhammad bin Qasim conquered the region. Muhammad bin Qasim was an Arab general of the Ommayad dynasty who came to Sind through the land route from Iran. After his conquest, a long line of Sufi mystics came to the region through Baluchistan, Mekran, Multan, and Sind itself. In the province of Sind alone there are said to be more than a hundred thousand Sufi shrines. Sufi mystics additionally came through the northern routes to the subcontinent. They came from Arabia, Iran, Iraq, Turkey, Afghanistan, and the entire region that is now the Middle East and the Central Asian Republics.

The Sufi version of Islam in Pakistan and India was based on syncretism and reconciled differing beliefs. It was holistic as it blended in with the beliefs of local cultures and populations who were Davidians, Aryans, Hindus, Buddhists, and all native creeds. At that time in India many converted to Islam because it offered relief from caste oppression. Thus, through Sufism, an indigenous model of Islam evolved in the subcontinent. Since some of these cultures were "matrimythical"[40] and used the indigenous female myths, the Sufi poets creatively blended the female voices from these myths into their poetry that they sang to music. The purpose was mainly aesthetic and devotional.

The best example of such synthesis is the work of the Sufi poet Shah Abdul Latif, for he was both a poet and a musician; his compositions in the local Sindhi vernaculars appealed to his devotees. And even today when his *faqīrs* (mendicants) sing the daily mystical concert at his shrine, they chant in the falsetto that imitates the female voice. It is precisely for this reason that his shrine is known as the *jamālī* (aesthetic) shrine.[41] Furthermore, both Muslim and non-Muslim devotees venerate Shah Abdul Latif's shrine because he was a Syed, who claimed descent from the prophet Muhammad through his daughter Fatima and son-in-law and cousin 'Ali ibn Abi Talib.

Thus, it is not surprising that when poets like Shah Abdul Latif reconstructed and reframed the existing folk legends about female heroines (*sūrmīs*) into mystical texts and sang them with music, they won many devotees. And, because the myths had a pre-Islamic, indigenous origin, non-Muslim devotees had no problem putting the female myths into their own devotional schemas or worldviews. Shah's *Risālo* is a poetic narrative of several heroines where the protagonist of the discourse is a woman such as Sassi, Sohni, or Marvi.[42] Additionally, the female heroines in his *Risālo* invoke references to God and the hereafter that are linked to the Quran.[43] Among musician communities in the Sind, Shah's *Risālo* is treated with great respect because of its sacred Quranic context, and the book is not allowed to lie around on the floor.

Furthermore, in Shah's *Risālo*, especially in the section called "Sūr Rām Kalī," there are innumerable references to mendicants (*faqirs*) who are ascetic with slit ears and who wear large rings in their ears.[44] They travel from place to place in search of divine wisdom and wear colored robes. This tradition evolved in relation to the other existing mendicant traditions such as those of the Bhakti, especially Mira Bai, who herself "disappeared" as a roving mendicant. Her poetry is sung in the regions discussed here. She also belonged to the Sind-Rajasthan continuum. I discuss her later as a subject in the poetry of the Sabri Brothers' *qawwālī* concert in the United Kingdom.

The model (see Fig 1.5) will enable the reader to understand that *sufiānā-kalām* was sung among the roving mendicants who could sing simple mnemonics as solo performers to their audiences with sometimes only a *yak-tarā* (a one-string instrument). They would travel from place to place and camp wherever the night came. I interviewed Abida Parvin and her late husband Sheikh Ghulam Hussain about this tradition:[45]

> A:[46] Can you tell us of the times when the Sufis were both poets and musicians—they would go from place to place and sing mystical discourses—I believe this is the *banjārā* [roving-minstrel] tradition?[47]
> H: In the case of Shah Latif you will find at least fifty places where he used to spend the nights. Audiences would come there and sit there at night—there would be a *paṛāo* [a camp]—they would make a fire—and they would have a *mehfil*—and when he sang his narratives, there would be *faqīrs* and dervishes with him—so like the Shah, these dervishes would also wander around the areas—and when night fell—they set up their camps—burnt the fires—came together to sing mystical texts—
> P: And they would do this

H: The same is true of Bulle Shah—

P: They were mobile people—you don't get anything by just staying in one place—it is only when you leave the home—that you achieve something—the wisdom—you have to wander like the dervish or the *faqīr*—you have to fill your cloak with the wisdom—the pearls of wisdom—that you gather from mobility—you see, this universe is for us to learn—you can even learn from the stone—this wall can teach you something—it is said of Shaikh Sadi that he would greet a wall every day as he went past it—every time he would do it—until people asked him, "Sir, there is nothing there—why do you bend yourself every day as you greet this wall?" Sadi replied, "Really, there is nothing—but once upon a time there was something very wise inscribed on this wall—which enriched my knowledge—"

While Abida Parvin spoke, I saw the performer in her speak as she would to her audience, in a concert:

P: The universe teaches you everything—nature teaches you—and then He is the greatest teacher—and this is the way the Sufis learnt—they would go to the people—and adopt their language—and why is it that today we cannot read that language?

A: You understand it better—

P: This is a great point—for instance, Shah Abdul Latif—he went to Rajasthan—and the person there is a Rajasthani—the Shah took very simple words from him . . . and although the individual from this region is not literate—the Shah acquired great wisdom from him—from the people—

A: You mean from the oral tradition?

P: Those people were roving bards—there are very few Sufis among "educated" people—the educated man is sitting where he was—look at the folks in the universities—every person who is coming out of there is uneducated—like the husk—they have no spiritual connections—education only teaches you to become slaves—the educated man denies the truth—but the Sufi is the slave of truth—he is the slave of the true God—the slave of the true God.

I have reinforced the musicians' interview with written sources about the roving-minstrel traditions in which Shah Abdul Latif was immersed. He evolved as a Sufi poet within this heritage. I have especially looked at the creation of his female narrators and the mendicants whose ears are slit and who wear rings in their ears. Somehow Shah's *jogīs* are closely interlinked with his female voices, and there is hardly a *sūr* (a melody) in his *Risālo* where there is not a reference to one or the other. The Sindhi terms that Shah used for the *jogis* in his *Risālo* are *jājak, maganhār, atāi, pān, chaṛan, rāgī, baraṭ,* and *rabābī.*[48]

Shah Abdul Latif's poetry emerges from his own experiences as a wandering minstrel. He writes about these ascetics in "Sūr Ram Kali" in Sindhi:[49]

Kanna kaṭā kāpaṭā kāpṛī kana jɛ kaṭāīn	This community of *jogīs* who have their ears slit and lobed
Lāhutī Latīfu cāī māgu nā maṭāīn	These Lahutis, according to Latif, do not alter their goal
Jɛ khudī khɛ khāīn halo tā takīa pāsõ tinjā	Let us go and visit the dwelling place of these ascetics, who have consumed their ego completely

Latif further says:[50]

> Let us visit the abodes of these ascetics who are in trance
> O sisters, I am extremely beholden to these lobed *jogīs*
> Their patronage has reformed my heart

Abida Parvin has sung Shah Abdul Latif's poetry in Sindhi and has risen to international fame for her performances. When I asked her about the female voices in the Sufi poetry that she sang, she said,

P: Male and female does not even come into it—what you call Allah is one—God is the *mehver* [center] of everything—you make a roundabout and whatever way it goes—it is in that direction—it is as if you have put up a clock tower, and every passage will go through it—it will go to it—it really does not matter whether it is male or female—in fact we can really say that in the Sufi's terminology—if someone is not a male—he is called a female—

A: I don't quite understand this—

P: In the Sufi thought [*khayāl*] you say:

Masjid ḍha de, mandir ḍhā de	Demolish the mosque, demolish the *mandir*
Dhā de jo kuch ḍhānā	Demolish all that can be demolished

> There is only one God, and there is his temple in each individual—God is in you—He sits in you—His *majlis* [company] is in you—the Sufi propagates God's message and for this he utilizes song—it is a *kefīat*—a state of ecstasy that draws him to God—Allah—and in the end it is His name—and the tranquility that comes from singing His name—time will stop—this circulation continues—the day is timeless—the same day—and then—wherever you sit—it is the moment—what is the year then—and what the age then? Time will stop—the Sufi man is separate from other folks—and every man who sings is not a Sufi—and until I understand what you mean—how can I sing it? You know that Sufi spirit—every one cannot get into it—we all have the Sufi in us—when someone is born—we say he has God's face—the Sufis never got out of this circle—and there were mystics like Baba Bulle Shah—the Sufis never come out of this canvas.

I asked Abida Parvin to explain the *kefīat* (ecstasy) that is induced through Sufi speech and music. She explained it as a state produced or transmitted through *zikr*. This is repetitive chanting of devotional *kalimāt* (phrases) in Arabic:

> P: It is not customary to sing Sufi discourse—*wajd* [ecstasy]—the rhythm of Sindhi music has never been in the West—the Sufi tranquillity—there is a great connection between *words* and *music*—we can't become the Sufi—but we can try to become like him—his *tarz* [music] together with his *words* draws us to purity—there is a purity in music—there is a state of *wajd*—of *kefīat* that is the state of being—of prayer—so that apart from prayer—there is another state of being [*kefīat*]—of ecstasy—of intoxication—*fiqr*—he who is tied to prayer five times a day is not a Sufi—the Sufi is always in *zikr* of God—there is a *lagan* [devotion] in us—there is a purity in us—in every one of us—and we are divorced from that purity in us—We only sing the *kalām* of the Sufia—as no one can express a *khayāl* [thought] like them—I sing Shah Hussain, Bulle Shah, Mian Muhammad Bakhsh, Hazrat Khawaja Ghulam Farid, Sacchal Sarmast, Baba Farid, and Guru Nanak—the *banis* of Guru Nanak—there is Baba Farid's *kalām* in the Guru Granth Sahib—God has said that the more knowledge you acquire—the more you should say that you don't know enough—there is fun in being stupid—a lot of fun indeed . . . why should we say we are wise—when there is no fun in it?

Abida Parvin's account was reinforced with another interview that I had with Sikander Baloch and Naseer Mirza at Radio Pakistan in Hyderabad in 1999.

The radio in Pakistan has played a significant role in identifying musicians and providing them a livelihood. Baloch and Mirza both affirmed that women musicians like Abida Parvin are immersed in the *rūh* (spirit) of Sufi poetics and music and can create the contexts (*racāo*) of that discourse. They used the indigenous term *sūng* for the practice in the Sufi poetics and music where the lover woos the estranged beloved through a serenade on the *capṛī* (wooden castanets).[51] The speech and song create ecstasy, which is a very special context of some shrines in Sind. Abida Parvin's evolution, they said, has been within these grassroots mystical traditions, later to be enhanced through her training in the semiclassical and classical traditions of music through her father, Ustad Ghulam Haider, and her tutors Ustad Nazakat Ali Khan and Ustad Manzur Hussain. Baloch and Mirza reported that since she was trained within the male traditions her style is exceptional. She uses the *ḍohra* or the *bait,* short two-line verses, within the main body of her narrative, a style she imbibed from her male mentors, including her late husband, Shaikh Ghulam Hussain. They claim that no other woman musician in the Sind has this style, which is essentially a unique male style. The fact that now Abida Parvin has introduced the *qaul* in the *sufiānā-kalām* tradition fits in with this assertion. The *qawwālī* genre of Sufi music is essentially a male domain.

In the officially organized *'urs* celebrations in Pakistan commemorating the Sufi's death anniversary at his shrine, key musicians are invited to sing.[52] In the Sind, performers like Abida Parvin are invited to sing at Shah Abdul Latif's shrine.[53] Although she does not belong to the roving-minstrel tradition, she does sing lyrics related to the tradition, at the shrines and in concert. I have transcribed a mystic text about a female mendicant (*joganī*) that the musician sings in Urdu. The lyric was composed by Hakim Nasser around the eighteenth or nineteenth century AD and is one of Abida Parvin's popular concert compositions.[54] I find allusions to the Layla-Majnun myth in the discourse, where Majnun has become a madman for love of Layla. People in the streets ridicule him and throw stones at him:

Je. . . Je . . . .na . . .na. . .	Je. . . Je . . . .na . . .na. . .
Nadī kināre	The river's bank
Dhuā̃ uṭhe	Arises some smoke, some fire smolders
A . . . .A . . .	A . . . .A . . .
Nadī kināre	The river's bank . . . .

Nadī kināre . . uṭhe	The river's bank . . arises
Dhuā̃ uṭhe . . .	Arises smoke . . .
Mẽ jānū̃ kuch ho..e	I wonder something happens ther..e
Jis karān mẽ jogan banī	For whom I became the female mendicant
Kahī̃ vohī nā jaltā ho--e	Has he ignited himself--e
Nainā tumhī bure ho	O eyes, thou are wicked
A . . tumhī bure ho	A . . thou art wicked
Tum sā burā nā ho . .e	None can be worse than thee . . e
Aāp hī prīt kī āg lagāī	Thou started this fire of love
Aāp hī beṭha ro..e	Now you sit there weeping . . e
A . . .ā. . . ā. ā	A . . .ā. . . ā. ā
. . . .	. . . .
Jab se tune mujhe	Since thou made me
Divānā banā rakhā hɛ	A mad one
Sang har sakhs ne	A stone every person
Hathõ mẽ uṭhā rakhā hɛ	Carries in their hand

In the song there is the metalanguage of one who is "possessed" or has become a *divānā*. Additionally, there is subtle humor in the verses when the musician sings of the smoldering fire. The speaker who is the female mendicant is fearful that it is perhaps the one she loves who has set himself on fire. Such discourse is rarely sung in the *sufiānā-kalām* traditions in the regional languages, but I selected it for its uniqueness and humor.

RESHMA AND MAST QALANDAR

In this section I explore some aspect of the personal histories of women musicians who sing devotional Sufi poetry. Their histories, told partly by themselves and partly by others, show how the melodies that they sang at Sufi shrines became marks of their personal identities. I present some performative contexts.

During my fieldwork in Sind at the Hazrat Lal Shahbaz Qalandar shrine in 1999, I studied women roving minstrels who sing devotional narratives to the Sufi saints. I looked for them at this shrine because Reshma, who was once a roving gypsy woman, rose to international fame while she sang her famous "Mast Qalandar" melody here in the late sixties. Women informants who live around the heavily populated area of the shrine reported that during the *'urs* celebrations, which last for more than a week, it is almost impossible to walk in the narrow streets of the city. Sehwan, the historic city built within a large fortress from the time of Alexander the Great, is flooded with large numbers of female musicians who converge on the city to earn a living. The informants reported that most of the women musicians come from the Panjab and the neighborhoods of Sind itself. They perform in every nook and cranny and attract huge audiences.

I found that a favorite melody, sung in the roving-minstrel traditions, is the "Mast Qalandar" *dhun*, a tune reported to be sung all along the Rajasthan, Sind, Baluchistan, and Iran continuum. Reshma sang it in Siraiki at the Lal Shahbaz Qalandar shrine in the sixties with a passion that made her internationally renowned. The melody is dedicated to 'Ali and is sung in all the regional languages along the continuum. Almost every folksinger in the region can sing it because of its simple mnemonics and rhythm. The lyric, although dedicated to 'Ali, is also dedicated to Hazrat Lal Shahbaz Qalandar, a Sufi mystic of Sind. Hazrat Lal Shahbaz is venerated in the lyric as the bestower of children.[55] Reshma's performance uses the standard lyric sung in the popular "Mast Qalandar" folk melody:

Lāl merī pat rakio bhalā	O Lal Qalandar, save my prestige
Jhole Lālan	O thou of the cradle
Sindhṛī dā	O thou of Sind
Sehwan dā	Of Sehwan
Sakhī Shāhbāz Qalandar	Thou bounteous Shahbaz Qalandar
Damā dam mast Qalandar	Thy ecstatic trance is the healing breath
Alī Shāhbāz Qalandar	O 'Ali-Shahbaz Qalandar
Alī dam dam de andar	'Ali's name is the healing breath
Mā̃ vā̃ nū̃ pira bachṛe denā	Thou giver of children to mothers
Behnā̃ nū̃ denā-e vīr bhalā	Thou giver of brothers to sisters
Jhule Lālan	O thou of the cradle
Sindhṛī dā	O thou of Sind
Sehwan dā	Of Sehwan
Sakhī Shahbaz Qalandar	Thou bounteous Shahbaz Qalandar
Alī dam dam de andar	'Ali's name is the healing breath

Performers like Reshma sing the melody in their high-pitched, full-throated voices at the shrine without the support of microphones. They also sing poetic texts that glorify the *karāmāt* (mystical prowess) of Hazrat Lal Shahbaz Qalandar. The Sufi saint is known as a *jalālī pir*, a mystic with intense supernatural energy.

The female roving minstrels are accompanied by small groups of instrumentalists perhaps playing percussion or accordion. But, by and large, they have minimal instruments. They will either play a *yak-tārā* or a *ghaṛā*, an earthen pot used as a drum. Their identity is a ring (*chalā*), which they wear around the middle finger and use to create percussion on a *loṭā* (aluminum pot) or a *ghaṛa*. These minstrels are called *loṭevālī* for playing the *loṭā*, *chalevālī* for playing the *chalā*, or *ghaṛevālī* for playing the *ghaṛā*.[56]

The *loṭevālī* or *chalevālī* are roving gypsy women who move from one shrine to another while their families trade in livestock and peddle inexpensive local textiles and pots and pans. Their audiences are women and men from their own socioeconomic background who participate in the shrine activities at the time of the *ʿurs* and who give them small sums of money during the performance. Women tend to pay less because they are unemployed, while men can be more generous.

I interviewed Reshma, who performs in Pakistan and before large diasporic audiences in the Gulf States, the United Kingdom, Europe, and America. I conducted the interview with her in Urdu, though she sang some melodies for me in Marwari.

A:[57] When you started to sing—did you sing *sufiānā-kalām*?

R: I first started at the Shahbaz Qalandar shrine—

A: Yes—

R: Every year we go to the Shahbaz Qalandar shrine—

A: Yes—

R: I was young at the time when I went there and made a *mannat*—for my brother—and then I went for his *mannat*[58]

A: Yes

R: And I went there for his *mannat*—my brother was arranged to be wedded—every sister wishes that her brother should get married where the tribe wants—that we should get a good match in the tribe—God helped us and my brother got married—where we all wanted him to be married . . .

A: Then you went to Shahbaz Qalandar—to fulfill the *mannat* and you became famous

R: There I sang—

A: Yes—before that what did you do?

R: We were traders—we bought horses—you see, we were traders—we are from Rajasthan—our region, you see, is the desert—our area is Rajputana—Rajasthan is the area we come from—

A: I see—

R: My tribe is Kalyar—we are from Bikaner—we lived in Jaipur—our area touched Jaipur—

A: I see—

R: From there—from there we would bring camels—from the state of Bikaner from Jaipur—from Jodhpur—the camels from there—the camels from that place were famous—they had long necks—meaning to say—their bodies were small—they were beautiful—

A: Yes—

R: Then my mother and father—they would bring the camels to Pakistan and from here they would take cows, buffalo, and horses—race horses—we would then take these horses—my mother and father would take these back to Rajasthan—

A: Was there anyone else in your family who sang?

R: There was no one else—except my grandmother—my father's mother—she was very fond of singing—my father's brother was very fond of singing

A: So—what did you sing?

R: We used to sing our songs from Rajasthan—wedding songs and suchlike—

A: I see—

R: Things like *māṇḍ*—songs of joy like *māṇḍ Banro*—

A: What language do you sing in?

R: This is Marwari—this is the Marwari language of the desert—

A: The famous Shahbaz Qalandar song made you so popular overnight—where did you learn this song?

R: This is a passion—to sing whatever you wish to—whatever words you can put together—

A: Yes—

R: Whatever poetry you can compose—the words have their own meanings—language—words that come from desire—from the heart—from love—and so I sang there—

A: Can you tell me if you sang in Sahiwal—the people there say that you sang in the *jhuggīs* [gypsy tents]—that there was a Nanga—*pir* or *jogī* who prayed for you that made you so famous?

R: We always go to *pirs* and *jogīs*—I still go to them—I believe in all of them—I just went to a *pir*'s shrine—Baba Mushtaq Gilani—his photo is hanging there[59]—we would sometimes live in the *jhuggīs*—whenever night came we would be there—and anyone who belongs to the tribe—got absorbed there—it is not written on anyone's face whether they are tradesmen or gypsies like us—

A: Can you tell me more about yourself?

R: I was born under a *ṭālī* tree—there was no shelter—no *jhuggī*—

A: Yes

R: We were wandering gypsies—wherever markets were—we went—to Sahiwal—Chicawatni—Faisalabad—it was from there that I developed this desire—there people would sing—I would learn that—and sing myself—my tribe's language was Rajasthani—no one understood it—my village was called Malashi and my patron's name is Bheron—and whenever we are in pain or sorrow—we call him—it is the tradition of my tribe—to sing—when we are in pain—day in and day out—we sing the poetry of our patron—Babaji—and this is in Rajasthan—

A: Did other people in the tribe sing like you—like the gypsies?

R: Yes—my people used to sing very well—

A: They sang *sufiānā-kalām*—mystical poetry?

R: They sang excellent mystical poetry—

A: Where did they learn the language of mystical poetry?

R: On our own—they composed their own mystical poetry—

A: Did they not sing the poetry of the Sufi poets—such as the poetry of Shah Latif?

R: Yes—they did—they would go to the Sufi shrine and sing that Sufi's poetry there—then they went to another shrine and sang that Sufi's poetry there—they made their own *kalām* [discourse]—they were themselves the poets and the composers and the singers—

A: Tell me—for someone like you—who is so immersed in the life of the desert—does the desert affect your being—your moods and temperament?

R: It means that whatever our soil is—wherever our ancestors are—their language follows us—the same dialect—the same region—the same deserts—the same simplicity—that is our identity—there is no deceit or pretension there—just like the desert—the people are like that—and it pervades our total being—we cannot live without that—

A: Yes—do other women sing at the shrines there—around the deserts?

R: Several—

A: Do they come to the shrines in Sind to sing mystical poetry?

R: They come and they sing with me—

A: Is it that this is more of a tradition in the Sind—in the Rajasthan area that women will sing at the Sufi shrines?

R: Yes—this is so at the shrines—not so much in Rajasthan—but it is at the Shahbaz Qalandar shrine—and it is at this shrine that I sing—

A: And are other women there, too?

R: Yes—there are other women—women who are looking for a livelihood—they join in the singing of *sufiānā-kalām*—and this happens every year—I go there every year—

A: You go there every year?

R: I go even now—I just returned from there—

A: Yes—

R: The Sufi Shahbaz Qalandar calls for me at least three or four times—I go there and sing for him—I sing for my master—he listens to my songs—

Sikander Baloch and Naseer Mirza at the Hyderabad radio station confirmed Reshma's input thus:

M:[60] These were gypsy women who only sang at the Shahbaz Qalandar shrine—certainly, that is the only place in the Sind now where the *loṭevālī*s come—to sing there—there is no such tradition at Sacchal Sarmast—I am forty-three years old—I have been associated with Radio Pakistan for the last twenty years—we have covered all the *melā*s at the shrines—I have not seen such a tradition at Bhit Shah—not at Sacchal Sarmast—not at Rikhail Shah—or any of the Sufi *dargāh*s [shrines] in the Sind—no *loṭevālī* passes by these shrines—except at Qalandar Lal Shahbaz—another woman who made a name there is Zeena Bai[61]—she used to come here to sing—

A: Is she related to Reshma—or are they from the same family?

M: This is a tradition—Zeena Bai is connected to this tradition—this is a Rajasthani *gharānā* [musical lineage]—Zeena Bai's—that is, the *loṭevālī*—they come to the Shahbaz Qalandar shrine with a *loṭa*—and sing there—and make a livelihood on a rupee, two rupee—the alms they get there—God had given her a great voice—but a great *guvya* [musician]—Ustad Muhammad Khan who belonged to Hyderabad[62]—was greatly impressed with her voice—she created a great spiritual bond with him—she adopted him as her mentor—she chose to live with him—she became his pupil—she learnt classical music under his patronage—he belonged to the line of Ustad Amir Khan Indorewale—there are two *gharānā*s in Hyderabad—the Indore *gharānā* and the Gawalior *gharānā*—Zeena Bai is a product of this century—she was born in this century—and she died in this century—she died around the partition—another person to whom she was spiritually inclined was—Shah of Ranipur—she said that because of his special prayer for her—there was so much *sūr* [melody] in her voice[63]—the lineage of the *pirs* of Ranipur continues even today—she mainly sings his texts—his *kalām*—but at the same time she also sang a lot Shah Latif—she was an *Ahl-e Taśhih* or a Shiʿi—she has also sung about the tragedy of Kerbala and about Imam Hussain in a *pūr soz* (affective, emotional voice)—she sang it with rhythm and had it recorded with a lot of emotion in her voice—she earned a great name for herself because of her *ustād* [mentor]—she is buried in the Hyderabad graveyard where all the great musicians of the city are buried—you see, it is not just that she was associated with a great *ustād*—she had that link with Rajasthan—he too was associated with Rajasthan—it was called the *Maṛichā gharānā*—she too was associated with it—the women who wear those large skirts—they would wear the *colī* [short top]—women who wore that attire—

B: That is the culture—the Rajasthani culture—that is Gujrati—that is Rajasthan—

M: People who knew her—those who saw her until the end—she always wore that dress—

A: You mean the *ghāgrā*?

M: She used to sing in that great *maidānī* voice—in those days—there were no loudspeakers—people report that—in a litter—where the litter is—she would ride a camel—and sing—the range of her voice would resonate—around half a mile—this is a tradition—it is an *ustād gharānā*—whose sons and grandsons are all alive—this is something not very old—she died around Pakistan—say, somewhere around 1946, 1947—

A: This means that there are other *loṭevālīs*, too?

M: Yes—but only a few become great musicians—come to the limelight—producer Saleem Gilani discovered Reshma—and Ustad Muhammad Khan discovered Zeena Bai—that tradition has died when we would go to the *melās*—to hunt for talent—now educated women are there in the field—

Baloch and Mirza informed me of several other dimensions in the research. When I asked them about the *maidānī* voices, they said that this was the poetic content and the dialects in the female musicians' speech.[64] They said that Mai Bhagi, who is also known as Sehra ki Rani or the Rani of Thar, sang in the *maidānī* voices that are the dialects of the Thar region in Sind. The languages used to sing mystical poetry in the Thar region are Dhatki, Kacchi, Marwari, and Sindhi. Zeena Bai, in the roving-minstrel tradition, also used the *maidānī* dialects. With their extensive experience of communicating with women musicians through the radio, I asked both Baloch and Mirza about the female voices in Sufi poetry, and this is how they responded:

B: Why the musicians use the female *alāp* [narrative]—is because there is a beauty in her voice—there is a *niāz-mandī* [humility]—there is a *hilm*—and there is a modesty—when mystical poetry is sung in these voices—it creates the soul of the context—like when we pray—we beg—we sing His *sanā* [praise]—so that is what the female voices do to the context—that is why there is this school of thought in Sindhi Sufi poetry—the *sūng*[65]—in which the lover sings to win back the estranged beloved—this is called *manānā*—it is within these contexts and voices that the musicians build in the ecstasy—
M: The *sūng*—the *manānā*—is done on the *caprị* [castanets]—this is the tradition of Shah Inayat of Jhokevale—but we do not find this in Shah Latif's poetry—his moods are more mellow—
B: Shah's poetry is kind of melancholic—that is why the *faqīr*s at his shrine wear black—it is the same with his followers—his *faqīr*s sing his poetry like females—creating the female voices—his poetry is sung throughout the night at his shrine—there are *maqām*s in his poetry when certain sections are sung at particular times of the night—his poetry is sung on the *tambūrā* [stringed instrument]—it is sung in rhythm—only very sensitive people can listen to his poetry with understanding—people who can enjoy it—they are the people who understand the soul of the poetry—about his *sūrmī*s [heroines]—and they are the people who can get ecstatic about his poetry—

Baloch further reiterated,

B: The words [*bol*] are put in the woman's voice for artistic purposes and then—when the woman sings it herself, it brings out the color—the elegance—whenever women musicians have sung mystical poetry it has been very popular—such as Sushila Mehtani—Bali—Zeena Bai or Mai Bhagi—when women understand the content—understand the soul [*rūh*] of the poetry—and sing it—musicians like Abida Parvin—Mai Bhagi—Taj Mastani—Rubina Qureshi—the listeners enjoy the performances—the performances become very popular—

Some of the women, like Zeena Bai, who sang as roving minstrels at the Lal Shahbaz Qalandar shrine, evolved into trained classical and semiclassical musicians in Hyderabad. Taj Mastani affirmed that she belongs to Sehwan Sharif where the Lal Shahbaz Qalandar shrine is located, but she moved to

1.9 Manganhar musician: Mai Bhagi. Courtesy Institute of Sindhology, Sind University, Jamshoro.

Hyderabad to learn the music arts. Now she sings folk and mystic poetry in concert within the country and abroad among diasporic Pakistani speech communities. She is additionally engaged by large landowners for private events such as weddings and births.

Although the "Mast Qalandar" melody is a favorite among female musicians who sing at the Lal Shahbaz Qalandar shrine, it is also linked with the *dhammāl* (the Qalandari dance performed at the Lal Shahbaz Qalandar shrine in Sehwan every evening). The *dhammāl* that the *qalandar*s or the *faqīr*s perform at the shrine is similar to the dance of the whirling dervishes at Maulana Jalaluddin Rumi's shrine in Konya. This dance creates an ecstasy in which the mind focuses on the name of the Creator and the whole body moves in devotion. In this dance the soul, mind, and body are said to func-

1.10 Manganhar musician: Begam Faqiriani. Courtesy Institute of Sindhology, Sind University, Jamshoro.

tion in deep contemplation of God's name. The state of ecstasy is induced with the rhythmic beat of the *naubats* (drums). Hazrat Lal Shahbaz Qalandar is reported to have said of the *dhammāl:*[66]

For the sake of the love of the friend
I dance over fire
Sometimes I roll in the dust
And sometimes I dance on the thorns
I have become notorious in your love
I beseech you to come to me
I am not afraid of this disrepute
To dance in every bazaar

Both men and women participate in the *dhammāl.* Women perform the dance in a certain section of the courtyard. Many times, families will bring women who are emotionally disturbed to participate in the *dhammāl,* which devotees claim has healing powers. In Baluchistan, such healing ceremonies are called *guāṭi.* The family of the unwell woman will negotiate with the "Sufi" certain terms that will be fulfilled when the woman gets well, such as a vow that there will be a ceremony and the woman's husband or family will buy her an expensive gift, perhaps in gold, if she recovers from her illness.[67] I discovered that one can buy cassettes of healing music for emotionally disturbed persons in the bazaar outside the shrine.

I have only touched the periphery of the female roving traditions, and the

1.11 Jeevni Bai. Courtesy Institute of Sindhology, Sind University, Jamshoro.

1.12 Singing theosophical themes: Sushila Mehtani. Courtesy Institute of Sindhology, Sind University, Jamshoro.

field needs to be further researched. The findings at two major shrines in Sind, that is, Shah Abdul Latif at Bhit Shah and Hazrat Lal Shahbaz Qalandar at Sehwan Sharif, point toward significant female input in Sufi rituals.

LANDOWNERS' HOUSEHOLDS: PATRONS OF FEMALE MUSICIANS OF SUFI LORE

In my search for female minstrels who sing Sufi poetry, I did fieldwork in 1999 among the Sidi and Mohana fisherwomen in Karachi Mori in Sind, Pakistan. The research was among a community that lies about twelve miles from Jamshoro, where Sind University is located. Sidis were initially brought as slaves from Africa to work in the subcontinent of Pakistan and India.

Although they are now free, some of them are attached to the feudal households in the Sind province of Pakistan. Their native language is Sindhi, but they can communicate in Urdu, the national language of Pakistan. They are followers of Islam and pay tribute to their black Sufi saints, Bava Gor, his brother Bava Habash, and a sister, Mai Misra, who in turn trace descent from Bilal, a black follower of Muhammad the Prophet (d. 632 AD).

I was able to observe the speech community through my professional contact with Qalandar Shah, who is the Syed mentor of this community.[68] He is additionally a senior faculty member in English at the University of Sind at Jamshoro. I spoke with the Sidi female musicians Karima and Kubra in Urdu, and sometimes they responded in the same language.[69] Generally, they

1.13 Patronized by a landowner: Hinda Bai, later known as Bali. Courtesy Institute of Sindhology, Sind University, Jamshoro.

1.14 Abida Parvin and female musicians of Sufi poetry. Courtesy Institute of Sindhology, Sind University, Jamshoro.

spoke in Sindhi, and Qalandar Shah interpreted the dialogue for me in Urdu or English. The text of the interview with Qalandar Shah and Kubra is translated into English. Although Kubra is a musician, she is shy to admit her skill as a singer, due to negative community attitudes toward female performers. Her reluctance is accentuated by the fact that her husband holds a position as an "official," a clerk in the Sind University administration. Since her husband holds a visible government position, her identity as a musician is not viewed favorably in the community.

Q:[70] So—I was telling you that the Africans—the Africans are present in the Sind in large numbers—because of the slave trade—they were brought here in large numbers—and then—with the abolition of slavery[71]—here too they were set free—
A: When did they come here?
Q: They had been coming continuously—through the ages[72]
A: Is there no record of them?
Q: Yes—in the history books—in the archives—they came from

Zanzibar—Habash and places—they are also in India along the coastal belts—the interesting thing is that they are called Sidis—

A: Yes

Q: Sidis—which is linguistically derived from Syedi—Cid—the word is there in Spanish and French—Cid—

A: Yes

Q: Syedi—very interesting anthropologically—because although they were slaves they were called "our Syedi"or "my lord"—

A: Interesting observations—good fieldwork—

Q: Their allegiances have been to the ruling families—

A: Yes

Q: Although now they are employed—in various professions that include work with government departments—such as Sind University—they carry on with their singing—

A: Yes

Q: They have their African drum—it stands vertical—they call it the *mugarman*—Do you all have it?

K: No—but our relatives have it—

Q: The beat is African—the dance is African—they dance around it—both women and men dance around it—for them it is extremely sacred—this is their link with an African past—they keep it in different places to sing—do you sing?

K: No—I don't sing—I am ashamed to sing[73]

Q: Her other sister sings—they are not like the Manganhars—the traditional caste musicians that people invite to perform at rituals—but the Sidis are also invited to sing at celebrations such as births and weddings—they have a humor that people like—they sing and their audiences reward them well—

K: We sing in Sindhi—not in Urdu—

A: You go to weddings—do you sing?

K: I don't sing—my sister sings—my sister-in-law that is my husband's sister sings—my husband's sister-in-law who is his brother's wife sings—they all sing—my husband will not let me sing—he says it does not look nice[74]

Q: You see—her husband is a clerk in the university[75]

K: But at weddings we sing—my sister—

Q: Do you sing at the *ziarāt* [shrines]? They have a big congregation in Karachi at Manghopir—in April—Manghopir is the *pir* of the crocodiles[76]—they have a large conference and Sidis from all over come there—they get a big press coverage—Have you been there?

K: No, that is in Karachi—we sing at weddings—songs that are called *sehrās*—in Sindhi—we sing for ceremonials—for the *aulīyā* [Sufi saints]—

Qalandar Shah gave her a prompt, saying he remembered that, as a child when he went to a Sidi shrine, they sang something like "sal-āl -e,"[77] to which Kubra responded very spontaneously with the Arabic chant:[78]

Allāh ho - Nabī : : O: :O[79]	God ho - Prophet : : O : :O
Allāh ho - Nabī :: O : : O	God ho - Prophet : : O: : O
Allāh ho - ho Nabi : : O: O	God ho - ho Prophet : : O: O
O Nabī : : āl :e: e-	O Prophet : : thy family : e : e-
Ho yal :: āl : e : yal:: āl : e	Ho thy family : : family : e : thy family : : family : e
Allāh ho ::: ho:: Nabī ::O: O	God ho ::: ho: : Prophet : :O: O
Nabī yā :: le :: ya :lā :le::	Prophet ho :: thy :: family : thy : family
Ho : yā :: le::	Ho : thy : : family : :
Hey : : sal āl e-	Hey : : blessings on thee and thy progeny e-
Māmā Gor sal vāle le[80]	Blessings on thee Uncle Gor and thy progeny[81]
Māmā Gor sal vāle	Blessings on thee Uncle Gor and thy progeny
Māmā Gor sal vāle	Blessings on thee Uncle Gor and thy progeny
Sal āle : : Nabī yā le	Blessings on thy family : : O Prophet and thy progeny

After my conversation with Kubra, Qalandar Shah's wife and daughters served me a delicious lunch, fish cooked in curry, a traditional Sindhi lunch eaten with rice and flatbread. The village women spent another hour tuning the *ḍholak* (double-sided drum). That in itself was a performance.[82]

Later Kubra's sister Karima arrived. She was the family's musician and gave me further information about the shrines at which she sang, as well as her performances in the landowners' households and community festivals. She said they sing the "Mama Gor" composition at their *pir*'s *melā* after midnight.[83] Later, when I asked her if they sang at other shrines, she affirmed that they mostly sing at their *pir*'s annual *melā*, which is on the sixteenth day after the Muslim festival of Eid ul Azha, when the faithful offer a sacrificial animal. Their *pir* (spiritual mentor) is Qutb Din Darya, whose shrine is called Tando Jahana and is in the Civil Lines at Hyderabad. The women musicians Karima and Kubra also explained that the Sidis have a huge *melā* of another *pir* at Manghopir in Karachi.[84] Qalandar Shah had talked about the annual festival at this shrine in his interview.

I researched the reference to Mama Gor in the poetry of the Sidi musicians

1.15 Sidi and Mohana fisherwomen sing of Sufi mystics, Karachi Mori, Sind.

from Karachi Mori. The first reference to Bava Gor is as an Abyssinian saint whose grave was visited by Sultan Ahmed, a Habshi aristocrat, in 1452.[85] Then there is the oral account of the legend that relates to the travels of Bava Gor to India by "Abdulkader," whose words were attended with respect: "Hazrat Bava Gor Rehmat ullah-elah was a Habshi, and Hazrat Bilal's follower.[86] He was an Abyssinian lord named Sidi Mubarak Nobi, who went on a pilgrimage to the holy city of Mecca. The place pleased him and he remained in the service of the venerable Sallah-ul-Salam.[87] In those times a demonness lived in Hindustan, who through the power of her magic kept a butter lamp burning whose light could be seen all the way to Arabia. Her name was Makhan Devi (Butter Goddess). It was her habit to kill men daily, eat them, and from their blood make a *tilak* (mark) on her forehead. All the elders gathered in Arabia around the venerable Sallah-ul-Salam and said, 'Venerable one, if you give us the command, we will go and kill the demonness.'[88] One day he called Sidi Mubarak Nobi and ordered him to go to Hindustan to break the magic of the goddess and to light the lamp of Islam. Sidi Mubarak

1.16 Sidi musician's *kefīat:* Karachi Mori, Sind

Nobi gathered a great army made entirely of Sidi people. They departed and reached Baghdad, where he became a disciple of Ahmed Kabir Rifa'i and received the *khilafat* (permission to represent) and his name, 'Bava Gor,' from his master. Then Bava Gor departed with his army. They came to Karachi, where they rested. In Karachi there is also a memorial shrine, and everywhere that Bava Gor stopped on his journey a shrine was created and each time one of the Sidis from his army remained in the place."[89]

Bava Gor created a community for the Sidi in the subcontinent, and his sister Mai Misra and brother Bava Habash are said to have followed him. Although I did not find any reference to roving minstrels among the Sidis in Karachi Mori, I recently made some connections to roving mendicants among the Sidis in Ratanpur and Rajpipla in Gujrat of India.[90] I also made some connections to the linguistics of "Māmā Gor" in Kubra's chant. Mama

Gor, who is originally called Bava Gor, is a major Sidi Abyssinian saint in Gujrat, where there is a big shrine dedicated to him, his brother Bava Habash, and their sister Mai Misra in Ratanpur. Supposedly until forty to fifty years ago all the Sidis living near the shrine lived as *faqīrs* and religious mendicants. Some even lived in jungles among tigers. There seems to be a connection between escaped slaves and *faqīrs*. Rajpipla princes invited Sidis occasionally to dance in exchange for token annual donations to the shrine. At harvest and the end of Ramazan they received *jakat* in the form of produce and handicrafts from members in peasant and craft communities in nearby villages.[91] The shrine originated at the time of the king of Rajpipla, who came from Rajasthan in the twelfth century. Basu does not offer any historical discussion on the origins of the shrine, but her interviews with Sidi elders refer to their memories of the past relationship with the raja, whom they visited and for whom they sang. He would send Bhils to their village to deliver grains, oil, and food stocks.[92] An eighty-year-old woman told Basu,

> In the days of the raja we had *ijjat* (honor). He would send Bhils to Ratanpur with big containers of oil, ghee, rice, flour. Nobody was hungry. And all the Sidi houses had rights (*copadio*). Sometimes I went with my sister, with my *Dada* (father's father). He wore a big turban and played a *malunga.* We went for days at a time from village to village. People said, "come, come" and invited us. We ate and drank, sometimes three or four days in one village, sometimes we went further. We received rice and *jovar* from farmers, dishes from potters, oil from the oil-pressers and sometimes also old clothes the people gave us. So we had no difficulties. But now things are much more difficult.[93]

Basu reports similar accounts from other elders of memories of travels from place to place, singing and dancing for rice, oil, produce, and handicrafts.[94] There are also references to the *dhammāl* (the ecstatic dance at an *'urs*) lasting for seven nights, in the manner of the *dhammāl* at the Lal Shahbaz Qalandar shrine.[95] There are references to *mast faqīrs* (intoxicated mendicants) in Basu's research, and more needs to be investigated to establish links between the Sidi minstrels in South Gujrat and their related communities in Sind in Pakistan.

For these reasons, I found use of the terms *Māmā Gor, Allāh ho,* and *Nabī O* as referents in Kubra the Sidi musician's lyrics interesting.[96] The lyric signifies a definite Sidi identity that I have represented in the preceding paragraph. The terms link the Sidi to an Abyssinian past through

Allah → Muhammad the Nabi → Hazrat Bilal → Bava Gor
Allah ← Muhammad the Nabi ← Hazrat Bilal ← Bava Gor ←

The hierarchical referents in the song start with Allah or God, linked through his prophet (*Nabi*) Muhammad and further linked through Bilal and Mama Gor. Most Sidis are convinced that a special *bakhśīś* (gift) has been bestowed upon them by their ancestor Bilal.[97] The signification in the song is communicated through the words, the melody, and the musician's movements of her hands as she sings. The musician herself is a part of the signifying process. The words are used as performative acts to ritualize the event: the initiatory devotional ceremony at a Sidi shrine that pays homage to the prophet Muhammad through Bilal and Bava Gor.[98] The Arabic phrase "sal-vāle" or "sal-āl-e" is a ritual chant to bless the prophet Muhammad and his progeny, and through articulating her speech thus the performer blesses herself. She does the same through the performative act of blessing Bava Gor/ Mama Gor: she actually blesses herself. There are several referents in her speech: Bava Gor and his family (his brother Habash and Mai Misra), the prophet Muhammad and his family (his wives and children discussed here), and the musician and her own family, although the reference to her is only implied.

The signification to Muhammad's family in Kubra's song is a complex one. First, it signifies prayers in the scriptures that send blessings on Muhammad's family, his children, and his several wives. Furthermore, it is a reference to his daughter Fatima, her husband ʿAli (who was also the Prophet's cousin), and their sons Hassan and Hussain. In the internecine conflicts after the Prophet's death, his grandson Hassan was poisoned and Hussain was killed with his sons in the Battle of Kerbala. Kerbala is a trope in Islamic discourse that marks the distinction between Shiʿi Islam and Sunni Islam. Followers of Hussain are the Shiʿi, but in South Asian Islam there is veneration for Kerbala and Hussain's family among both the Shiʿi and the Sunni Muslims. Thus, in Kubra's lyric the trope of Kerbala is used without an overt referent except through blessing Muhammad's family, which she articulates as "yal-āi-e."

When I visited Karachi Mori, the community of more than a hundred women and their children created a rural concert (*melā*) in Qalandar Shah's large village home. His wife, daughters, and sons hosted me. They served me a sumptuous lunch of curried fish with rice and flatbread. After that, the Sidi women musicians and their neighbors, the Mohana fisherwomen, created a performance for me in which they sang texts dedicated to the prophet Muhammad and his family, to the local Sufi saints of Sind, and to the events of Kerbala. The context was almost ritualistic as the Sidi women musicians sang a variety of songs on the *ḍholak* (double-sided drum) in the open courtyard of the house. They created the contexts for whatever discourse I requested. These ranged from mystical songs to the lament poetry of *marsiyā* or *nohā* in the Shiʿi traditions sung during the Muharram rituals.[99] However, since the context was a joyful one, their main focus was on songs that are ceremonial, such as those sung at births and weddings. Sufi poetry that pays tribute to the prophet Muhammad and his family was sung.

Karima, the key Sidi musician, led the singers. Her sister Kubra and some women from the Mohana fishing community supported the singing. Karima entertained all of us as though we were participating in a wedding. She joked with Qalandar Shah's son Kutb and teased him about his forthcoming wedding.[100]

As stated earlier, during my research on the female Sidi musicians in the Sind in Pakistan, I made connections to their related Sidi community in the coastal Gujrat province of India. This happened through the "Māmā Gor" chant that Kubra sang for me.

Bava Gor's sister Mai Misra is mentioned earlier. Her shrine, too, is with her brothers in Ratanpur Gujrat. She is reported to have joined her brothers to fight the female demonness—the Butter Goddess called Makhan Devi.[101] Mai Misra's shrine in Gujrat has become known for healing female infertility, as her brother Bava Habash's shrine is renowned for healing male infertility. Whereas female devotees who are infertile are fed Mai Misra's *kichri*, the male devotees who are infertile are given "Bava Habash's milk" full of hot spices.[102] Infertile female devotees eat the *kichri* and sing *jikar* (devotional songs) at the shrine, such as,[103]

On the Mother's mountain
We have lots of fun
Kinky hair, kinky hair

When we are all at Mai Saheb's
We lots of fun have after eating *kichri*
Kinky hair, kinky hair

We dance *dhammāl* and have fun[104]
Kinky hair

When we
Are all at Bava Habash's place
We dance *dhammāl*
Kinky

At Bava Gor's place
We dance *dhammāl*
Kinky . . .

In connection with the performance of devotional lyrics sung to Mai Misra at her shrine in Gujrat, Basu reports that slaveholders often enjoyed watching comic dances performed by the Sidis.[105] These dances were called *goma* dance, a term most likely extracted from the Swahili *ngoma*. These dances got fused with the local *dhammāl* (ecstasy dance). The devotees at Mai Misra's shrine talk about it and perform it, as do female devotees at similar Sidi shrines. The Sidi female musicians in Karachi Mori performed it for me, and Karima wriggled her body for the bridegroom and her audience as an initiation rite for the forthcoming wedding.

Performance that includes cultural criteria such as verbal, musical, and body language becomes a mark of identity and sometimes an initiation rite, such as Karima wriggling her body for the groom-to-be. Whereas Kubra only sang the "sal-vāl-e" lyric for me, her sister Karima did much more, for example, using comic laughter that involved verbal play combined with body language. The context is a mutually achieved interaction between performers and their audiences. A largely female context, only males such as Qalandar Shah and his son Kutb can enter the intimate veiled (*pardā*) world of women. These men were part of the intimate inner circle because they were heads of the family units. (Kutb was the man in charge of the family in Karachi Mori while his father was living at the university some miles away.)

Such performances are segregated so that women can create a context of their own. They can be themselves without being stared or gazed at by men who do not belong to the inner circle. Although the performance in Karachi Mori was specially organized for me, it was also an opportunity for Qalandar Shah to visit his family.

There is evidence of roving minstrels in the Sind-Rajasthan area. Among them are the *jogī* snake charmers and flute players.[106] However, there is another community that may be linked with the roving minstrels. These are the Manganhar, who are distinct from the Sidi. Alan Faqir belonged to them, and he is reported to have sung on the buses and trains between Rohri and Sehwan Sharif in his youth. He also sang at the *dargah*s (shrines) in the Sind.[107] He confirmed his roving-minstrel lineage in his interview with me.

In Sind there can be no ritual without the Manganhar, be it a birth, a wedding, or a death. They are the designated community musicians, and each community has its own Manganhars. "Manganhar" originated from the words *mangan*, which means "to beg," and *hār*, which means "a garland of flowers." Thus, according to an informant at the institute of Sindhology at Sind University, a manganhar is one who begs for flowers. In the roving-minstrel traditions, alms were given to the minstrels in return for their musical services.[108]

I interviewed Alan Faqir, who claimed to be a *faqīr* of the Bhit Shah shrine. He explained the tradition thus:[109]

F: The Syeds—when they have weddings they invite us to sing—we play the *śādmānā*—when the Syeds come—we play the *haswārī* when a *pir* comes—or if we see a *murshid* come—you see, our family is from this—when we have a wedding—when there is a wedding—we sing—if a son is born—we sing—they come to us and say, "*Faqīr*—play the drums—sing the songs of prayer—*du'ā*—*śādmānā*—*haswārī*—*olang*—or the *candar*—they have invited so many people—the musician who plays the drums is the Manganhar—a manganhar means someone who begs—in India they are called manganiārī—the woman musician too is called a mangiārī—or a mangtī—in those days the money was very little—lots of grain—we used to get paid in grain—lots of it there was—one sack—four sacks—this was more than enough for a poor household—we used to get invited to the Syed households—they would invite us and say, "*Faqīr*, do the *du'ā* [the prayer] for us"—if there was a dispute they would come to the *faqīr* and say, "*Faqīr*, do a *du'ā* [a prayer], that I may be reconciled with my brother"—you see the *vaḍerās* [landowners] have disputes with each other . . . who will tie the horse? Then they come to the *faqīr* and say, "*Faqīr*—I am your slave—*faqīr*—I am your *faqīr*—help me—reconcile me with my brother"—you see, we lessen our life spans with our deeds—

A: Can you tell me more about your women?

F: The women in our families are called *mangtī*—*faqīriānī*—our family is called *faqīr bādshāh*—we beg—*faqīr sāī*—*faqīr sāhib*—this is our family title—the women are *mangtīs*—the women sing *gīts* or *gīc*—they sing *du'ā* [prayer]—He then sang a song and continued:

F: The women sing the *sehrā*—they sing the *lāon* [wedding songs]—They get the *murād*—the female musician gets it—the male musician gets it—we sing songs like "Allah has given you a groom—like the moon—and there will be much prosperity—or Allah has given you a bride like the ruby—and may you grow and prosper—"

. . . .

A: Do women in your setups sing now?

F: The woman would not sing—unless her circumstances forced

> her—if her husband was alive, she stayed at home—but if he was not there then she had to do the man's work—naturally she had to sing—they had to decorate the drums . . . they had to sing the *sehrās* for the weddings—they had to sing the *gīts* or the *gīc*—they had to sing the *du'ā*—they had to sing the *lāon* for the bride and the groom—they would sing the *'arifānā-kalām* of Shah Latif—some songs do not have a poet—you sing songs for the love of God—you sing "*Allāh hū—Allāh hū*" and finish off with "and so says Shah Latif—O Latif, I say your *sanā* [praise]"—my grandmother sang—her name was Mai Hajra—the children's maternal grandmother sang—her name was Mai Bhand[110]

My interview with the musician in 1999 was indeed timely because less than a year later he passed away. It was an unusual interview because he talked informally about the women who sang in his family. Musicians like him are extremely reluctant to discuss the subject because of the shame associated with being caste musicians, especially where women were involved. It is a matter of socioeconomic caste. The musicians perhaps had little choice in the past except to become caste musicians, since social structures discouraged individual enterprise. Today, caste musicians want their children to get educated and be employed in the government service, which promises a stable job and an income, together with social prestige. They further want their children to become professionals such as doctors, engineers, MBAs, or educators. They no longer wish to be associated with the stigma of only being musicians.[111] Alan Faqir's daughter, who was present during our interview, studied liberal arts in a college. Another musician, Syed Zufiqar Ali, is a faculty member at the University of Sind, Jamshoro. He is the son of the renowned musician Ustad Niaz Hussain Khan, who belongs to the Gawalior *gharānā* (lineage). Ali provided me with valuable contacts during my fieldwork in Sind and, although he has a stable faculty position in the university, he pursues the musical trade on the side, working for the radio and television and giving public concerts. Ali claims that his father, Ustad Niaz Hussain Khan, is one of the musicians who composed for Abida Parvin, the renowned female singer of Sufi poetry in Siraiki, Sindhi, and Panjabi. He further asserts that his father composed for female singers of Sufi poetry in the Sind such as Zarina Baluch, Parivash Bhutto, and Shazia Khushk.

Presently, the many communities that were once involved in the roving-minstrel tradition are undergoing transformation due to the newly emerging socioeconomic structures. Although many kinds of communities are involved in the roving-minstrel traditions—the Manganhars, the Sidis, snakecharming *jogīs*, flute players, potters, and many more who lived on the margins of the society—their lifestyles are changing fast.[112]

Over the last quarter of a century the practices have changed. Musicians are now paid in cash rather than agricultural produce. Instead of singing from village to village, these communities "rove" in a different way. The more resourceful among them have become more visible through connections to radio, television, and various arts councils. Clients such as wealthy landlords or individuals in the cities contact them at their urban locations for various festivals. Abida Parvin, for instance, lives in Islamabad and not in her hometown of Hyderabad, because Islamabad is the capital and she can negotiate business from there. Her clients are the foreign diplomats in the city and state and private agencies. Through these contacts she gets invited to perform at concerts and can make a comfortable living. Education among the younger members of the musicians' community has now made it socially more acceptable for them to sing for the multimedia. Baloch and Mirza at Radio Pakistan in Hyderabad affirmed that they no longer have to go to *melās* at the Sufi shrines to hunt for talent. Many educated female and male performers come themselves to the radio and television for auditions and are contracted to sing. In the last ten years, multinational companies like Pepsi have hired young female and male singers for promotional purposes. These musicians, who are mostly professionals such as doctors and engineers, sing for television, and Pepsi sponsors the programs. Furthermore, they sing at public concerts within the country and internationally. Pop groups such as Ali Hyder and ensembles who sing Bulle Shah's poetry with electronic instruments sing substantial Sufi poetry. Female singers like Taj Mastani may be discovered through the radio, instead of at Sufi shrines, as were Reshma or Zeena Bai. I recently heard Hadiqa Kiani, a young, upcoming female performer, sing a lyric in which she uses a metaphor from the Sohni-Mahival myth, which is a favorite form of representation for the Panjabi Sufi poets.[113] The *bol* (words) of the lyric in Panjabi are:

Kanḍe lag jā̃ gī kaccā ghaṛa ban ke	I shall come ashore as the earthen pot[114]
Mē̃ avā̃ gī havā ban ke	Like the breeze I shall come

She sings a folk melody that appears to be drawn from the roving-minstrel tradition as there is the jingle of bells (*talyoon*) in the background that is indicative of the mendicant traditions. The *jogīs* (mendicants) also tied another form of bell called a *ghungrū* to the *yak-tarā* (one-string instrument) that they carried.

A number of musicians whose elders were associated with the roving-minstrel culture were absorbed into government employment because it gives them a stable income and social prestige. However, they keep their base in the parent community in the form of a family home to which they will always return. Only one or two members of the family follow the musician trade.

When I went with Qalandar Shah, my informant, to do fieldwork in Massu Bhurgri, a stronghold of Manganhar musicians seventy miles from Jamshoro, the key woman singer was away. Qalandar Shah had sent word to the village about his coming with me, but the musician had already gone for the last week to a big *vaḍerā* (landlord) wedding. There is perhaps no need for them to travel from village to village and collect alms in the form of produce. Also, the *vaḍerā*s prefer to pay in cash rather than in agricultural commodities. Alan Faqir stated this in his interview. The *vaḍerā*s want to be in the cities for better education for their children, better health care, and more freedom and a quality of life different from the rural setups. With the changing lifestyles of the *vaḍerā*s themselves, there is also a change in their attitude toward patronizing community musicians such as the roving minstrels. The younger generation of landlords no longer lives in the villages. They live in large urban centers like Karachi, Lahore, or Islamabad, or they study in the academies of the West, from where they return to join the country's political forces. The land thus becomes a base from which political identity and votes come.

The younger musicians feel that their elders were perhaps menials of the landowning communities. They say that now education gives them more options. I have seen communities of workers, such as musicians, village barbers, and potters who had a variety of other roles in the landowning structures, disperse within the last twenty-five years.[115] This is because of socioeconomic changes and industrialization and most of all because of awareness among the peasant communities.

Male members of the immediate family of the Manganhars are employed in government services such as the police, education departments, or accounting services. The universities employ them because they are part of the community from surrounding rural and urban neighborhoods. Some of them hold influential positions with the federal government in Islamabad. This the musicians call a *pucci naukri* (a permanent job) that gives them higher social status.[116] Many of my informants in and contacts with these communities were individuals who worked at Sind University. Follow-up research on the mendicant traditions and their transformations is bound to produce interesting results. However, practitioners will allow a glimpse into the community only if the right channels of trust are established for the individuals in the services to "keep face" in social structures that are still very close and tightly knit. Shame (*izzat*) is a concern for men, and they are silent about their womenfolk's singing.[117]

The male musicians are reluctant for a number of reasons to admit that their women sing. It reflects poorly on their own image as breadwinners, for example. Middle-class or bourgeois respectability is a significant factor. Additionally, within the bourgeoisie it reflects poorly on the men's public image when their women are involved in a stigmatized trade such as singing at community rituals. This is evident in Kubra's words when she admits that she is ashamed to sing because her husband will not let her do it. Her husband has a visible public position at Sind University. Thus, if she sings for money as a professional musician, the couple's trades will not blend socially—the husband has a respectable official position whereas the wife is a low-paid musician.[118] The community attitudes in relation to women singing are also linked with women's veiling (*pardā*). Women must not be seen in public, especially by unrelated men. Then, to sing is even more damaging socially for the position of their male relatives who struggle to change socioeconomic class and break out of the old community bonds of servitude to landowners.

The emphasis in South Asian communities is very much on an acceptable, public image of the individual in the social context. Thus, some Manganhar or Sidi musicians who once belonged to the roving-minstrel traditions now struggle to change social class and may hesitate to claim their socioeconomic background as musicians.

CHAPTER 2

Ethnographies of Communication

EMOTION, SONG, MUSIC, AND ECSTASY

In this chapter I describe performances of Sufi poetry sung to music in sociolinguistic terms, looking at both *qawwālī* and *sufiānā-kalām*. Briefly, these are contexts where devotional poetry is sung to music. The speech events may take place in a Sufi shrine, on the outskirts of a shrine during *ʿurs* celebrations, or in a concert setting. The participants of the events are the musicians, who are the *speakers*, and their audiences, who are the *listeners*. Therefore, the discussion here may be perceived in terms of speaking as a cultural system.[1]

The number of musicians in a *qawwālī* concert can range from one to twenty or even more depending on the resources of the group leader. The larger groups are led by one or two *qawwāl*s who sit either in the center, as do the Sabri Brothers, or on the right-hand side, as Nusrat Fateh Ali Khan did. The key musicians, such as those who play the harmonium, sit in the front row, while those who clap and sing the chorus sit in the back row. The group leader is called the *mohri*, which means the "leading chess figure."[2] The leader orchestrates the performance. The other musicians give their input on the cues that they get from the *mohri*. As the group sings, an organized system of turn-taking in speech takes place among the musicians. Turn by turn the musicians "take the floor." Thus, verbal interaction occurs among the *qawwāl* group in addition to their interaction with the audiences.[3]

In the shrine setting of the *ʿurs* at the Nizamuddin Auliya shrine in Delhi, the *qawwālī* performance is guided by a shaikh or his spiritual representative, and the audience is exclusively male, primarily the associates of the *pirzade* or the *sajjādā-nashīn* and his Sufi associates.[4] Under the guidance of the shaikh the performance follows a ritualistic order, and the discourse that the *qawwāls* sing is sacrosanct. During that period, even if the performance is for the grassroots devotees, it is guided by a shaikh and the poetry pays homage to that particular Sufi and his spiritual lineage, including Hazrat 'Ali, the fourth caliph of Islam, from whom the Chishtiyya trace descent. In the Chishtiyya Sufi shrines in Pakistan, such as Hazrat Data Ganj Bakhsh Hujwiri in Lahore and Baba Fariduddin Ganj-e Shakar at Pakpattan Sharif, the same ritual in *qawwālī* discourse is followed. Since this is an exclusively male domain, women's presence at such performances is rare.

Since *qawwālī* in the subcontinent is associated with the Chishtiyya order (*silsilā*) of Sufis, an invocation is always made to 'Ali, the fourth caliph of Islam, from whom the Chishtiyya trace descent. Thus, the ritualistic *qawwālī* performance is always initiated with a *qaul* or saying of the prophet Muhammad, "Mun kunto Maulā fā Alī-un Maulā," in Arabic. During an *'urs* performance at the Chishtiyya shrines the poetry is focused on 'Ali, on the saint buried at that particular shrine, and on his spiritual lineage. Also, the poetry in the shrine setting during the time of the *'urs* is based on sacred texts that the Sufis used themselves. The *qawwāls* frequently use Arabic texts from the Quran and Persian mystic poetry from great Sufi masters such as Amir Khusrau and Rumi in their narratives in order to establish the authenticity of their performances. In short, during an *'urs* performance the *qawwāls* follow a ritualistic order of discourse.[5]

Outside the *'urs* context, and particularly in shrines not associated with the Chishtiyya, the *qawwālī* performance may not necessarily follow a strict ritualistic pattern, as will be seen in the description of the *qawwālī* performance that I recorded at the Bulle Shah shrine in Kasur. Shrine performances and *qawwālī* routines may differ from shrine to shrine.

Qawwālī performances in concert are a product of the twentieth century, a feature of postcolonial politics when large Muslim populations from South Asia moved to the West, particularly to the United Kingdom, France, and Germany, in search of better economic prospects. Later, they moved to the countries of the Middle East for the same reasons. In Pakistan itself, after the partition of 1947, *qawwālī* was promoted in concert and through the media. This was perhaps through the efforts of the postcolonial state-sponsored ministries of culture and the various art councils to create an Islamic identity for the country. Therefore, although it retains much of the traditional character of the shrine in terms of Sufi poetry, style of singing, and instrumentation, the concert is somewhat different. Its audiences are urban elites. In concert, *qawwālī* evolved as an aesthetic musical form, albeit generated through the singing of devotional Sufi poetry.

Within Pakistan, it is the urban middle classes that patronized *qawwālī*, for they can pay to go to the performances. In international settings, *qawwālī* audiences are either affluent expatriates who are connoisseurs of the performances but who are not necessarily Muslims, such as the Sikhs, or western audiences who have an interest in the esoteric elements of Islamic mysticism. Furthermore, *speakers* of the indigenous languages of the subcontinent patronize the events in which the *qawwāls* sing in Hindi, Urdu, and Panjabi and in which they often use the dialects of the Braj regions of central and north India. *Qawwālī* discourse in concert thus has become more diverse. Musicians sing the *qaul* "Mun kunto Maulā fā Alī-un Maulā," which has a devotional intent together with an aesthetic goal. In concert, *qawwāl* musicians sing a variety of texts especially in Panjabi that appear secular. Musicians, as exemplified by Nusrat Fateh Ali Khan during his lifetime, create playful environments through the mystic poetry that they sing, using feminine voices of female lovers like Sohni and Hir for their *listeners* in the United Kingdom. The Sabri Brothers brought in syncretic references to female mystics like Mira Bai, a Rajput princess, for their Indian expatriate listeners at a concert performance in the United Kingdom. This eclectic form of poetry would not be permitted inside the shrine settings of the Chishtiyya or other orders. On the other hand, the concerts create linguistic and musical diversity for *qawwālī* due to the diversity of the *listeners* or the consumers of the speech events, especially in international settings.

The same is true of *sufiānā-kalām*, especially when Abida Parvin sings it with improvisations. A *sufiānā-kalām* performance can also be held in a shrine during the *ʿurs* celebrations of a Sufi saint or poet, on Thursday evenings, or on a daily basis. This form of mystical poetry is usually sung in the vernacular and is a feature of the shrines in Sind, especially those of Hazrat Lal Shahbaz Qalandar and Shah Abdul Latif at Bhit. *Sufiānā-kalām* is additionally sung in concert within Pakistan and in international settings. Female input in this form of performance is significant as is evident from my interview with Reshma and Abida Parvin in the previous chapter. Performers sing the *sufiānā-kalām* in a monologue, and there is no turn-taking as in *qawwālī*. If the musicians sing in a group it is in the choir form where they do not take turns speaking. Moreover, in *sufiānā-kalām* the musicians do not use handclaps and the vibrant percussion of drums that mark the identity of *qawwālī*.

In this chapter I analyze three speech events to distinguish between *qawwālī* and *sufiānā-kalām*, two that look at *qawwālī* compositions and one that investigates a concert in Islamabad. Since *qawwālī* is a male genre I will investigate two contexts by male *qawwāls* and their ensembles, Nusrat

Fateh Ali Khan in the United Kingdom and Muhammad Bakhsh at the Bulle Shah shrine in Kasur.[6] Kasur is seventy miles from Lahore. I did fieldwork at the Bulle Shah shrine, where I recorded a performance and interviewed the *qawwāls* of the shrine. In the male musicians' *qawwālī,* I discovered that many times they sang in female voices. They did it to express the disciple's submission to the spiritual mentor, *represented* as the female.

For the *sufiānā-kalām* I will use a concert performance of Abida Parvin in Islamabad in 1985 where I was a participant in the event. As previously stated, she is a female musician who sings in several Pakistani languages, including Sindhi, Siraiki, Panjabi, and Urdu.

Qawwālī and *sufiānā-kalām* are both musical genres connected to the singing of Sufi mystical poetry in Pakistan and India. The tradition evolved around the thirteenth century AD. *Qawwālī* is embedded in the structures of classical music using elitist Perso-Arabic linguistic forms found in Hindi and Urdu poetry or poetry in vernacular languages such as Panjabi. *Sufiānā-Kalām* is mystical poetry sung in the vernacular languages of the subcontinent such as Hindi, Gujrati, Sindhi, Siraiki, and Panjabi and the other regional varieties. Musicians who perform *sufiānā-kalām* rely on the folk melodies in the environments around them such as the Sufi shrines, the *melās*, and now of course the cassette culture. They even use film melodies.[7]

The *qawwālī* or *sufiānā-kalām* concert is characterized by the intimate communication between performers and audience. In such a concert, space is created so that the audience has free access to the performers, especially during moments of emotional bonding between "addressers" and "receivers."[8] This is especially true of the smaller, more intimate performances called *mehfils*. The performers know their patrons closely and respond to verbal and nonverbal cues from them that condition the structure of the performance. Unlike the strict structure of a western concert that is linear, the concept of time in *qawwālī* and *sufiānā-kalām* concerts is cyclical; there are moments when time is suspended and performers and their audiences are caught in a timelessness. Depending on the audience's response, the performers may sing a particular text for an extensive period of time with all kinds of improvisations and verbal manipulations. The aesthetics of the performance is the quality of timelessness. The quality of Hindustani music is its cyclic movement, somewhat like jazz. The performers can play around a *tāl* (a beat) and continue to improvise around that *tāl,* which may engage their audience at a particular moment. They embellish a particular section of the performance by repeating a verse or a couplet with a particular melody. Thus, within the same time period, they can sing different verses to the same tune and continue their linguistic play with melodic repetition in a cyclical frame, which may create an ecstatic state. Such patterns may be described as statuesque.[9] Thus, one can see that even the linguistic phenomena here are spread over time and space, with music becoming an added variable.[10] In short, between performers and audiences the boundaries of time and space fade away the more both become involved in verbal play. Most performances continue well into the night beyond the allocated time.

Both *qawwālī* and *sufiānā-kalām* are invested with emotions that the musicians generate through music and Sufi poetry in the vernaculars that their *listeners* understand. Although at times their *listeners* are nonliterate, they are conversant with the content through the oral media around them, such as the festivals at the Sufi shrines. Sometimes, they absorb the poetry in community gatherings when members of a speech community get together. Here, the performers demonstrate their competence, through linguistic and musical resources, to the speech communities who participate in the events. The musicians are the speakers who bring their linguistic wealth of poetry, folklore, myth, syntax, and semantics that they build into verbal play with music to mediate ecstatic spiritual experiences for their *listeners*. In the events where the speech communities get together, a "universe of discourse" is created.[11] In this universe, Sufi poetry with its many complex and intricate tropes is sung to music.

In such gatherings, the researcher who looks for communication in a cultural system of speaking does so through the linguistic variables in the musicians' speech, the themes that they sing from Sufi poetry, and most of all the response that their discourse generates among the *listeners*. In other words, the significance lies in what is verbalized and how it is verbalized.[12] An example of such a universe of discourse is Nusrat Fateh Ali Khan's *qawwālī* "Je tū akhīā̃ de sāmne nahī rehṇā" (If thou wilt not nurture my eyes, O Beloved) that he sang before his Panjabi-speaking audiences in the United Kingdom.[13] A large number among his audiences were Sikhs whose first language is Panjabi. The musician and his ensemble sang a text that they initiated with couplets from Baba Farid Ganj-e Shakar's Panjabi poetry. Although Baba Farid (1173–1265 AD) was a Muslim Sufi saint who wrote devotional poetry in Panjabi, his texts are revered among the Sikhs because he influenced the founder of their own religion, Baba Guru Nanak (b. 1469). Some of Baba Farid's poetry is preserved in the sacred texts of Sikhism.

Thus, Nusrat Fateh Ali Khan's linguistic resources in the particular performance under discussion were devotional poetry that was sacred for most of his *listeners*, Sikhs and Muslims alike. His individual competence lay in his narrative skills in the Panjabi dialects that his musicians matched with an appropriate *qawwālī tāl* (beat). He used a lot of *takrār* (linguistic repetition) together with body language, humor, and eye contact with his *listeners* that made them ecstatic. When Nusrat Fateh Ali Khan and his ensemble initiated the *qawwālī* with the following verses from Baba Farid's poetry, his listeners were overcome with rapture and began to shower him and his ensemble with *nazrānā* in pound sterling notes. It was also the melody that captured his *listeners*.

8[14]	B	Sir devī te vafā na mangī-ehī pīr Farīd dā dāse
9	C	Sir devī te vafā---
10	C	Sir devī te vafā na mangī-ehī pīr Farīd dā dase
11	A	Palak palak pardesī-ā̃ kāran--merī akhīā̃ ne savāṇ lāe
12	B	Palak palak pardesī-ā̃ kāran--merī akhīā̃ ne savāṇ lāe
13	A	Allah jāne--
14	A	Allah jāne--
15	A	Allah jāne--
16	B	Kyā̃ derā gyā --tang sāl ga-e nahī āe
17	A	Yār Farīd ābād thī vaṇ o jhokā̃-rab phir vīrān basāe
08	B	Give thy head, expect not loyalty in return, O, this is Farid, the Saint's wisdom[15]
09	C	Give thy head, expect not loyalty . . . .
10	C	Give thy head, expect no loyalty in return --Oh, this is Farid, the Saint's wisdom
11	A	For the one who went--have my eyes shed a monsoon of tears
12	B	For the one who went have my eyes shed a monsoon of tears
13	A	O, God alone knows--
14	A	O, God alone knows--
15	A	O, God alone knows--
16	B	Time has gone by--the return never happened
17	A	O lover Farid, alive were those habitations once--may God bring the wilderness to life again!

The audience danced in ecstasy before the musicians. This is what I mean when I say that at times a performance like this one can be perceived in terms of the interplay between linguistic and musical resources on the one hand, and the performers' individual competence, on the other.[16]

I had to transliterate the *qawwālī* carefully to discover what was mystical about the content and what made the Panjabi-speaking Sikh audiences in the performance so ecstatic. To an untrained ear it would seem like a flirtatious love poem. However, when I transliterated the opening verses of the *qawwālī* where the musicians invoke the spirit of Farid—"Yār Farīd ābād thī vaṇ o jhokā̃-rab phir vīrān basāɛ" (O lover Farid, alive were those habitations once—may God bring the wilderness to life again!)—I understood the mystical trope of the *qawwālī.* The trope was in "Yār Farīd" (line 17 of transliteration), the invocation to Baba Farid. This very poetry had influenced Guru Nanak, the founder of their own faith. Thus, he is a revered Sufi among the Sikhs as well as among his Muslim devotees. Nusrat Fateh Ali Khan was a competent musician and linguist who was ingrained in the traditions of Panjabi Sufi poetry that he acquired through his own *qawwāl* lineage of the Panjab.[17] He was himself a devotee of the Sufi saint and performed at his shrine in Pakpattan Sharif.[18] Hence, he selected verses that would evoke an emotional response from his affluent Panjabi-speaking audiences in the United Kingdom, that is, the Sikhs and the expatriate Pakistani and Indian *listeners.*

In a section of the same *qawwālī* that follows, Nusrat Fateh Ali Khan injected immense sensitivity, humor, and intimacy through poetry, linguistic structures, and music to sing for more than two hours, improvising to the ecstatic responses of his audiences. He sang about a beloved and made allusions to the veil. Had it not been for the very sacred frame at the beginning, when his ensemble invoked Baba Farid, a researcher might have taken the performance for a secular love song where a lover seeks a beloved and serenades her. The latter seems to play hide-and-seek, an episode that Nusrat Fateh Ali Khan articulates with competence through his own verbal play.

18 B Je tū akhīā̃ de sāmṇe nahī rehṇā
19 B Ve bibā sāḍā dil moṛ de
20 A Kar beṭhī sajnā bharosā tere pīār te-roṛ beṭhī dil mẽ --[19]
21 A E-roṛ beṭhī---dil tere itebār te
18 B If thou wilt not nurture my eyes, O Beloved,
19 B Then, O Beloved, return my heart!
20 A Thy love did I trust, O Beloved, my heart I risked --
21 A My heart I made hostage, in thee I put my trust

When I interviewed Nusrat Fateh Ali Khan in 1992, I specifically asked him about this clandestine, flirtatious style of singing *qawwālī* in England before expatriate Pakistani and Sikh audiences that made them ecstatic. Khan smiled quietly and took some time to say that such a state is attained after much *riazat* (practice) in singing mystical texts.

In such performances the "extralinguistic entities" obviously exceed the bounds of poetics and of linguistics in general.[20] By this I mean an exploration of how the environment in the performance is created. For the performers it means swaying their bodies and making eye contact with their audience during the concert. The musicians' body movements, together with the rhythm of the music and language, can create a *kefīat* (mystical delight) among the *listeners.*[21]

A typical performance, whether at a shrine or in a concert, is a jointly achieved collaborative action between musicians and their audiences. The singers will sit in a group with their musical ensemble, facing their audiences. Sometimes, the gatherings are exclusively for men, but in the popular culture of today, whether at the shrine or in the concert, it is usually a mixed group, except during an *'urs* such as at Data Ganj Bakhsh in Lahore, when the shrine establishment segregates the women's sections. Women may be hidden from men's view by a curtain, and in some shrines they sit behind a curtain set up between them and the musicians.

Today, when devotees go to a Sufi shrine, they do so because of their reverence for and belief in the spiritual powers of that Sufi. They believe in the mystic's capability to have performed *karāmāt* (miracles) in his lifetime. The devotees continue to attach the same spiritual powers to the mystic's shrine and the mystic's ability to provide spiritual and emotional relief even after death.[22] Listening to *qawwālī* repertoire or samāʿ and *sufiānā-kalām* for devotional purposes forms part of the rituals that devotees undertake during a *hazrī* or *salām* at the shrine. The *qawwāls* share the same worldview whether they are men or women. They look upon themselves as devotees of the Sufi saint or poet. Lahori supports his claim when he uses the very term "*hazrī*" in connection with *qawwāls* who sang at the Sufi shrines in Lahore before the partition of 1947 and after it.[23] He mentions notable musicians such as Ustad Bare Ghulam Ali, Ustad Chote Ghulam Ali, Niaz Hussain Shami, Fateh Ali Mubarik, and Dina Qawwal, who performed *hazrī* in terms of singing mystical texts at the *'urs* of Data Ganj Bakhsh in Lahore. He also mentions women musicians who performed *hazrī* at the Sufi shrines in Lahore, especially at the time of the *'urs.*

The musicians believe that they reinforce their own spiritual connection with the mystic through the medium of language and music, especially if they sing his poetry.[24] If they sing at a shrine, they consider themselves the *murids* (disciples) of the Sufi, and they believe that their performance is a *nazar* (gift) to the spirit of the Sufi who is buried there. They take upon themselves the role of mediators. As such, they assume the aesthetic ability to enable their audience to make a spiritual connection with their *pir* or *murshid,* who is the Sufi. As competent musicians, they know that they have to transmit the spiritual experience to their audience.[25] They have to become the conduit between the mundane and that world of ecstasy, that esoteric world of the mystic. How do they do it? They create this ecstatic world

2.1 "Women's Entry Prohibited Inside the Shrine"

through the magic of their language and music. The more accomplished the performer the better she can accomplish this. It does not matter whether it is the shrine or the concert, today's singer of Sufi discourse has learned that charismatic art, that fine intersection of language and music, brings about the esoteric state for the ordinary person in the popular culture. I speak here of performers like Ustad Nusrat Fateh Ali Khan, Abida Parvin, and the Sabri Brothers and, to some extent, the unknown, undiscovered performers who sing at the shrines or in small rural communities in social contexts. Performance distribution via electronic media (videos, CD-ROMs, audiocassettes, "dish,") to large expatriate speech communities in the Middle East, Japan, and the West, especially in the United Kingdom, has considerably enhanced the quality and the creativity of the performances.

The performers mediate spirituality through inducing a state that they call *kefīat*. They do this all within the context of a performance. They will use their linguistic resources of poetry, myth, syntax, semantics, and tonal and speech patterns together with music to create the *samā*ʿ. They will improvise linguistic constructions at every stage, and they will create rhythmic melodies with drums and other musical instruments to bring about the *kefīat* in the *samā*ʿ. At the grassroots level, *samā*ʿ is also understood as a context or environment, and the aim of every competent performer of Sufi music and discourse is to create the *samā*ʿ.

Devotional attendance at a Sufi shrine is called *hazrī-denā* in native terms, which means paying a ritual visit. Other native terms for presenting oneself at a Sufi shrine are *salām-karnā* or doing a *ziārat* of the saint, achieved through the rituals that are performed there such as listening to *qawwālī* or

2.2 Female devotion

2.3 Forms of devotion

kalām and performing prayer (*fāteḥā*).[26] During the *'urs* or on Thursday evenings, or at any time of the day or night, devotees flock to the Sufi shrines, to communicate with the mystics spiritually. The communication brings relief to their emotional and personal concerns.

Faqīrs (devotees who wear orange robes) perform the ritual *dhammāl* (dance) every evening at the Hazrat Lal Shahbaz Qalandar shrine in Sehwan Sharif. The large drums (*naubats*), which are played for the *dhammāl*, can be seen lying in the large courtyard of the shrine during the day. Informants at Radio Pakistan in Hyderabad compare the *dhammāl* of the *faqīrs* at this shrine with that of the whirling dervishes of Maulana Rumi in Konya. The passionate whirling dance of the *faqīrs* in a circle is said to express the immense *jalāl* (energy) of Hazrat Lal Shahbaz Qalandar. His devotees believe that many prayers are answered at the shrine and many wishes granted. Reshma, one of the leading female singers of *sufiānā-kalām* in the subcontinent, sang the popular melody

Lāj merī pat rakio bhalā	O, keep my prestige[27]
Jhule Lālan,	O Lalan, protector of the cradle,
Sindhṛi dā,	O thou of Sind,
Sehwan dā,	O thou of Sehwan,
Sak͟hi Shahbaz Qalandar	Benevolent Shahbaz Qalandar

at the shrine in Siraiki, when she was discovered by the media. This was during an *'urs* of the mystic in the sixties. Her linguistic resource was a folk melody that honored Hazrat Lal Shahbaz Qalandar's *jalāl* or spiritual powers as a bestower of children. When I interviewed Reshma, she claimed that she had met with immense success because she offered her musical and linguistic talents to sing of the benevolence of this Sufi mystic. She believes that Hazrat Lal Shahbaz Qalandar has blessed her.

Almost all the performers that I have interviewed for this study believe

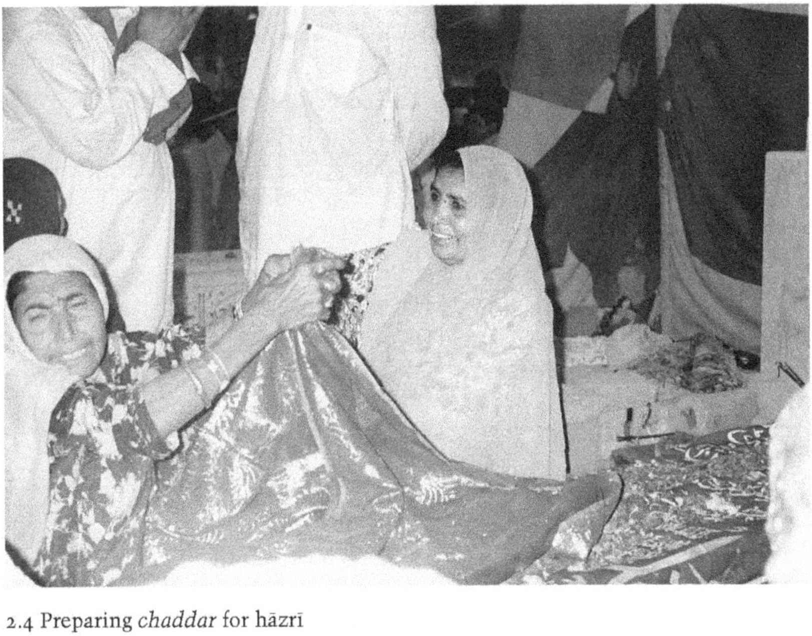

2.4 Preparing *chaddar* for hāzrī

2.5 Melā Chirāgā *'Urs* at Shah Hussain, Shalimar Gardens, Lahore

that they are divinely blessed by their *murshids* (spiritual mentors) for the devotion with which they sing. Female informants in the city of Sehwan Sharif confirmed that many female performers come from the Panjab during the *'urs* of Hazrat Lal Shahbaz Qalandar and sing at the shrine with the utmost devotion. Their audiences are men as well as women. My female informants did not have much information about women singers performing at other times of the year. However, professionals at Radio Pakistan in Hyderabad reported that women musicians come to the shrine only at the time of the *'urs* celebrations.

The Sidi, Mohana, and Manganhar women associated with feudal households in the Sind said that they sing devotional Sufi poetry at their mentor's shrine only on special occasions, such as his *'urs* or a religious event. These shrines are not far from where they live, perhaps within thirty to forty miles. These musicians said that they only perform before female audiences in their *murshid's* shrine and that their female patrons pay them well. They said that they sing some of the same devotional discourse in social contexts among women, such as at birth or a wedding. However, I confirmed at the *'urs* of Shah Hussain in Lahore that women sing before large male and female audiences and that there is no gender discrimination among the audiences. This strengthens the claim of my female informants at Sehwan Sharif that women performers sing before both female and male audiences. This is perhaps due to economic factors: male audiences are bound to reward better, since the males are wage earners and most women are not.

Hazrat Lal Shahbaz Qalandar's shrine is reputed for the *jalālī* or intense supernatural energy of the Sufi. Shah Abdul Latif, Bulle Shah, and Shah Hussain's shrines are said to be of the *jamālī* or aesthetic mystics. The latter Sufis were poets who wrote narratives that could be sung to music. In fact, some were musicians themselves. Shah Latif wrote Sufi poetry in Sindhi, and his best known work is his *Risālo*. Even today, his *faqīr*s sing his traditional poetry at the shrine, in the melodies that he composed. They sing his poetry in the falsetto, imitating a woman's voice. The ritual of singing Shah's poetry to his melodies has been performed every evening since the shrine has been there. The *qawwāl*s at the Bulle Shah shrine in Kasur claim to do the same, that is, sing his poetry to his melodies. They further claim that their family has sung there for the last three hundred years. They assert that they are the guardians of Bulle Shah's oral poetry, some of which has not yet found its way into the written texts.

Musicians like to sing about the *murid-murshid* or teacher-disciple relationship in their performances. The *murid* becomes the lover and the *murshid* the beloved. The former is represented as the submissive female. The metaphor becomes more complex with the infusion of bridal imagery into the relationship. The beloved becomes the bride or sometimes the bridegroom wearing a veil. Musicians sing devotional songs to this bride or to the groom asking them to lift the veil.[28] I discuss the veil in reporting the fieldwork at the Bulle Shah shrine.

The veil in Sufi poetry is intimately related to *kaśf*, or the doctrine of lifting the veil, that is, the Divine Being revealing itself to the lover. Many a song in the discourse of musicians of Sufi poetry revolves around this theme. The prophet Muhammad's ascension to heaven and his meeting with his beloved is embedded in images of the veil. The event is also called the *mi'rāj*. *Qawwālī* and *sufiānā-kalām* singers display their aesthetic skills to sing of the diverse allusions to the veil—the *kaśf* or the unveiling of the beloved. One such *qawwālī* is Ustad Nusrat Fateh Ali Khan's Hir narrative that he sings in concert in the United Kingdom.[29]

37	B	Nī mẽ jānā jogī de nāl
38	A	E-jogī-jogī matvālā[30]
39	A&B	E jogī- jogī matvālā
40	A	Hath vic "Il-Allah" dī mālā

41	A&B	Hath vic "Il Allah" di mālā
42	A	Nām hai ūs dā Kamlīvālā
43	A&B	Nī mẽ jānā jogī de nāl
	B	//Jogī de nāl
37	B	O, with the *jogī* will I go
38	A	O, this *jogī*-- intoxicated *jogī*
39	A&B	O, this *jogī*-intoxicated *jogī*
40	A	"God is one" in his prayer, says he
41	A&B	"God is one" in his prayer, says he
42	A	"The One with the Shroud" is his name
43	A&B	O, with the *jogī* will I go

The performer sings the Hir-Ranjha narrative in Panjabi. In Nusrat Fateh Ali Khan's narrative, Hir wants to go away with Ranjha, wearing rings in her ears, and a *tilak* (mark) on her forehead. Somewhere at the end, the narrative becomes fused with the "Kamlīvālā," which is a reference to the prophet Muhammad, who is known as the Kamlīvālā in the popular Islamic tradition. The belief is that the prophet Muhammad received his revelations while covered by a shroud (*kamlī*), hence the term that means "One with the Shroud," the "Kamlīvālā." Here, in the text of the song, Hir's beloved Ranjha acquires a spirituality that blends with the shroud. Sometimes, the reference can even be to the Divine Being or perhaps a spiritual mentor—the *murshid* whose *representation* is a major preoccupation in Sufi poetry.

This *qawwālī* was sung in the same performance that I discussed earlier and in which there are allusions to the veil, where Nusrat Fateh Ali Khan created a flirtatious discourse with the beloved through the metaphor of the veil.

MALE AND FEMALE PERFORMERS: LINGUISTIC RESOURCES

When I met Nusrat Fateh Ali Khan and asked him about his immensely intimate use of the Panjabi poetic and linguistic structures, he said the following:

> A:[31] Well, it is all about the female voice—it is all about the *nī*—that feminine gender in which you sing—a large number of your narratives are sung in the feminine gender—there is that pervasive—that persistent female voice—
>
> K: What do you think of it yourself?
>
> A: Really—I am not sure—that is why I come here to solicit your

views—all I know is that text after text that you sing—narrative after narrative is sung in that fascinating female voice—I am indeed curious—all this business about Hir—

K: The Sufi poets—in the tradition of Sufi mystical poetry—these mystic poets—when they speak they do it in the female voice—they present themselves as the female—for them their beloved—their mentor—their shaikh—is the male—whereas their own voice is that of the female—their own discourse is that of the female—

A: Yes—

K: They court the beloved in the female voice, they woo the beloved—themselves speaking in the female voice—you can read the entire *sufiānā-kalām*—the entire Sufi *kalām*—that entire discourse is in the female voice—

A: Yes—indeed—

K: You can see this in Amir Khusrau's texts that are in Hindi—the old Panjabi mystical texts—then when you read Baba Farid—Bulle Shah—

A: Yes—

K: In Bulle Shah's mystical poetry—

A: Yes—

K: The narratives are all in the female voice—

A: Yes—

K: There is an elegance in it—there is an elegance—a humility in the female voice—which is lacking in the male voice—all these aesthetics—it is altogether something very different—all these aesthetics—

A: Yes—

K: They have spoken in the female voice—they found it very appropriate—to communicate in the female voice—they found their spirit—their soul—the essence of what they wanted to say in the female voice—

The musician further affirmed,

K: In *sufiānā-kalām*—in *'arifānā-kalām*—these things last—whoever sings mystical texts—sings Sufi songs—leaves an impact—an impact for centuries to come—it leaves an impact—it leaves an impact on posterity—

A: Before this—do you know of any woman who sang Sufi songs—songs that have left an impact on posterity?

K: I think I do not know of any other woman except Abida Parvin—

A: Yes—

K: Probably women have sung Sufi songs—off and on—on different occasions—but I don't know of any such women—probably these women never ever came into the limelight—were never ever acknowledged for their Sufi narratives—

A: Yes—indeed—so, it seems that Abida Parvin has done something new—now about these Sufi mystics—like Bulle Shah was a poet—Shah Hussain—

K: I'll tell you something—something about Bulle Shah—when his shaikh—his mentor got annoyed with him—got weary of him—his *pir*—he went away to spend twelve years among the dancing girls—he adopted the dancing girl's identity—that female's voice—her identity—and returned to dance—dance like the dancing girl—before the mentor—to woo him—to win him back—

A: Like the dancing girl—like the woman?

K: Like the woman!

When musicians sing they invoke the spirit of a particular Sufi in a frame of reverence at the very outset of a performance. As mentioned, I have transliterated Sufi songs from Abida Parvin's and Ustad Nusrat Fateh Ali Khan's performances, where they called upon the spirits of Sufi poets like Baba Farid, Khawaja Ghulam Farid, Sultan Bahu, or Bulle Shah to validate their singing of a particular text.

They sang the text but with a lot of improvisation built into it, according to the context. Much depended on their listeners and the speech communities. Thus, I have discovered that performers like Nusrat Fateh Ali Khan and Abida Parvin, who sang in the vernaculars, had a much wider repertoire compared with performers who could only use the limited texts of the North Indian style of *qawwālī* in Urdu or Hindi. Performers who sang in the indigenous languages had more linguistic resources to draw from, such as the texts of the Sufi poets of their areas, the folklore, and nature, such as references to birds, seasons, and the landscape. As such they had a much wider linguistic and poetic base. Sometimes, they combined the original poem of a Sufi poet with other fragments that they had either created themselves or a songwriter had built into the text for them. They would even take verses from the poetry of different Sufi poets and use them as adjacent texts, improvising the discourse, according to the cues they received from the audience. I noticed this in Abida Parvin's concert in Islamabad where, in one performance, she combined fragments from the poetry of Shah Abdul Latif, Sultan Bahu, and Bulle Shah, thus blending Sindhi, Siraiki, and Panjabi with some

2.6 Singing in female voices: Ustad Nusrat Fateh Ali Khan

Urdu prose discourse to talk to her audience. She mixed four linguistic codes with elements of speech, song, and music to create the state of *kefiāt* (mystical delight) in the performance.

I attended Abida Parvin's concert at the Open University in Islamabad where she sang for three hours in the summer heat of August. The university sponsored her performance. The audience was mainly faculty from the university, students, and bureaucrats from the federal government who work in

Islamabad. The audience was invited, and the context of performance was a postcolonial one. Islamabad is the capital and therefore its population consists of officials linked with the federal government, and the foreign embassies and their support staff. Since the Open University is a state-sponsored institution, the concert was held for the benefit of senior government officials and faculty at the university. Invitations to such concerts are among the perks that go with being part of the official Islamabad bureaucracy. This practice has a colonial heritage. Since I am faculty at the university I too was invited to the concert.

I have worked on the video footage of this performance for several years in order to transcribe Abida Parvin's speech and to study her interaction with her listeners. Almost all the narratives were related to the quest for a Sufi mentor. In fact, she even referred to the metalanguage of the heat and the humidity in the auditorium as a context of energy for the seekers to find the *murshid*, the beloved. She entertained her audience with humorous comments about the heat and monsoon humidity. She caused them to roar with laughter when she said that perhaps in the heat of the auditorium on that August evening some among her audience might find their *murshid*. That evening this woman performer sang in a fiery mood and blasted the orthodox government of the time in the presence of its official bureaucracy by using the frames of Sufi poetry. She was the solo singer of this concert of *sufiānā-kalām*, and she had an ensemble of five musicians, who played the harmonium or accordian, the *tabla* or drum, and the sitar and tambura, stringed instruments used in classical Pakistani and Indian music. Her *shɛhnāīvālā* played like a bagpiper in the ensemble for only two melodies. Her narratives were from the poetry of the Sufi poets in the various Pakistani languages. The order of the narratives that she sang is listed here.

1 Shah Abdul Latif of Bhit	Invocation	Sindhi
2 Khawaja Ghulam Farid		Siraiki
3 Hakim Nasser		Urdu
4 Shah Latif		Siraiki
5 Sultan Bahu		Panjabi and Siraiki
6 Khawaja Ghulam Farid		Siraiki
7 Shah Hussain		Panjabi
8 Sultan Bahu, Shah Latif, and Bulle Shah		Siraiki, Sindhi, Panjabi, and Urdu
9 Shah Latif-Muhmal Rano		Sindhi
10 Folk melody: Lāj Merī		Siraiki
11 Folk melody: Jamālo		Sindhi

In her narratives she ridiculed the so-called "knowledgeable ones" or the caretakers of faith. She compared them to animals, to cattle, to fish, and to frogs. She sang the following text from Sultan Bahu in Siraiki, which she later blended with Shah Abdul Latif's poetry in Sindhi and that of Bulle Shah in Panjabi.[32]

A[33]	01	Ilm paṛhe-e aśrāf na-a thīnḍā
A	02	Ilm paṛhe-e-e aśhrā-āf na-a thīnḍā-ā
A	03	Jeṛhā mundhū̃ zāt kamīnā hū-ū-ū-ū
A	04	Pītal dā soṇā-ā mū-ū-l nā theve-e
A	05	Pītal dā soṇā mūl nā theve-e
A	06	Tuṛe caṛe-as lāl nagīnā h-ū-ū
A	07	Shūm tū̃ sakha kadhā-a na theve-e
A	08	T-ūṛe hovan lākh khazīnā hū-u
A	09	Alī binā-ā imān nahī Bāhū-ū-ū
A	10	Toṛe dafan vic Medīnā hū-ū
A	11	O-lā mi-ā̃ O lā mī-ā̃-O- lā mi-ā̃ Ho lā-ā
A	12	Je rab mildā nāteā̃ tote-ā̃
A	13	Je-e rab-b Je-ā-ā-ā-ā-ā-ā
A	14	Je rab mildā nāteā̃ toteā̃ te rab mildā ḍaḍūā̃ machī-ā̃ nū-ū
A	15	Āj vese sab logū̃ ko pasīnā āyā hūā hai śaid kisī ko mil jāɛ
B		/th /th /th /th [audience claps]
A	16	Je rab mildā-ā nāteā̃ toteā̃ te rab mildā ḍaḍūā̃ machi-ā̃ nū
A	17	Je rab mildā jhangal phirī-ā̃ te rab mildā gāī-ā̃ vachī-ā̃ nū-ū
A	18	Ve mī-ā̃ Bulle-ā rab unhā̃ nū mildā ate dilī-ā̃ sacī-ā̃ achī-ā̃ nū
A	01	One does not become noble from reading books
A	02	One does not become noble from reading books
A	03	And if thou art also by nature mean-O hu[34]
A	04	Thou cannot buy gold for the price of copper
A	05	Thou cannot buy gold for the price of copper
A	06	Even if it is studded with rubies and jewels-O hu
A	07	The miser will never become generous
A	08	Even if he is showered with treasures
A	09	Without 'Ali there is no faith-O Bahu
A	10	For i-t is buried far in Medina hu[35]
A	11	O God, O God, O God
A	12	If God could be found by being washed and cleaned—
A	13	If God . . .
A	14	If God could be found by being washed and cleaned, then the fish and frogs would have found him.

A 15 Everyone in this auditorium is sweating today, perhaps someone will find Him.[36]

A 16 If God could be found by being washed and cleaned, then the fish and frogs would have found Him.

A 17 If God could be found by roaming the jungles, then the cows and calves would have found Him.

A 18 O gentle Bulle, God is found only by those who are true and noble of heart

In the text of the song, for instance in line fifteen, is Abida Parvin's metalanguage of the heat in the auditorium. In lines four to eight she uses simile to describe a miser, and the miser in turn is the so-called scholar who is mean by nature, in her speech. This is expressed in the first three lines of the narrative. Her linguistic sources in this entire section of the narrative are the local proverbs and folk beliefs. Further on, in this very narrative, she derives her speech from Sultan Bahu to talk about the "caretakers of the faith," comparing them with the genuine believer.

A 96 Paṛh paṛh ilm hazār kitābā̃
A 97 Paṛh paṛh ilm hazār kitābā̃- ālim hoe sāre hū
A 98 Ik harf iśq dā na paṛh jāṇan
A 99 Bhulan phiran bicāre hū
B /th /th /th /th [audience claps][37]
A 100 Ik harf ʿiśq dā na paṛh jānan
A 101 Bhulan phiran bicāre hū-ū
A 102 Lakh nigāh je ālim vekhe kise kandhī na caṛhī hū
A 103 Hik nigāh je ʿaśiq vekhe lakh hazārā̃ tare hū
B /th /th [audience claps]
A 104 Ho lā mī-ā̃-Vo lā mī-ā̃
A 96 They read books and think they are scholars
A 97 They read books and think they are scholars
A 98 They can't read a word of love
A 99 The poor souls are lost
A 100 They can't read a word of love
A 101 The poor souls are lost
A 102 Thousands of scholars have we seen but none ever carried them on their shoulders
A 103 But when we see even a single lover, he appears like a myriad stars
A 104 O God, O God

Toward the end of this performance, she speaks to her audience in Urdu in prose narrative and tells them the story of Bulle Shah and his mentor, Shah Inayat.

A 105 Bulle Shāh ke murśid Ināyat Shāh vo śahr-- Uch śahr ke rehne vāle thɛ
A 106 Aur Bulle Shāh rehne vāle the Kasūr ke---
A 107 Uch śahr ko aur Kasūr ko is tarhā biyān kīā hai peś kartī hū̃
A 105 Bulle Shah's mentor Inayat Shah, he--he belonged to Uch city
A 106 And Bulle Shah belonged to Kasur----
A 107 Uch city and Kasur are described as I present it for you here

Abida Parvin brings in the themes of gender, class, and caste, which were issues in Bulle Shah's relationship with his spiritual mentor, Shah Inayat. I shall discuss it in the context of the Bulle Shah shrine. She sings thus in Panjabi:

A 108 Tusā̃ uce tusā̃ dī zāt ucī
A 109 Tusā̃-ā̃ uce tusā̃dī zāt uci tusā̃ Uch śahr de rehaṇ vāle-e
A 110 Asā̃ Kasūrī sāḍī zāt Kasūrī asā̃ śahr Kasūr de rehaṇ vāle
A 111 O lā mī-ā̃ - Vo lā mī-ā̃
A 112 Cal ve Bulle-ā cal authe calī-e jithe sāre ane
A 113 Cal ve Bulle-ā cal authe calī-e jithe sāre ane-e
A 114 Nā koī sāḍī zāt pechāne nā koī sānū mane-e
A 115 Ā-ā-ā-ā
A 116 Bulle nac ke yār manāyā-e
A 117 Ho Bulle nac ke yār manāyā-e
A 118 Sarā dil dā kūfr gunvāyā-e
A 119 Ho Būlle nac ke yār manāyā-e
A 120 Sarā dil dā kūfr gunvāyā-e
A 108 Thou art great and thy caste is great
A 109 Thou art great and thy caste is great—Thou art an inhabitant of Uch city
[Uch literally means high/great]
A 110 I am a Kasuri and my caste is Kasuri and we are inhabitants of Kasur city
A 111 O la mia-O la mia
A 112 O Bulle—let's go where everyone is blind
A 113 O Bulle—let's go where everyone is blind
A 114 Where no one knows our caste and where no one acknowledges us
A 115 A-a-a-a
A 116 Bulle has won his beloved with the dance

A 117 Ho Bulle has won his beloved with the dance
A 118 And he has lost all disbelief of the heart
A 119 Ho Bulle has won his beloved with the dance
A 120 And he has lost all disbelief of the heart

In this narrative Abida Parvin uses the metalanguage of the dance (*nāc*) as a state of ecstasy through which the beloved is won. Earlier I talked of the *dhammāl,* the dance of the *faqīrs* at the Lal Shahbaz Qalandar shrine in Sehwan. Terms such as *dhammāl, nāc,* even *qalandar* are states of ecstasy through which the devotee seeks the *murshid.* The reference could even be to the Divine Being. It is evident, then, that those musicians who sing in concert and at the shrines utilize much metalanguage.

On the basis of the evidence in the performances, it can be said that musicians like Abida Parvin and Nusrat Fateh Ali Khan have used the female voice as myth and narrative in the many Pakistani languages that they know. Their repertoire has been large because they can sing in Urdu, Hindi, Panjabi, and Siraiki as well as the elitist Arabic and Persian texts of the Sufi masters. Abida Parvin has the additional resource of the Sindhi language. Since she is a native speaker of Sindhi, she is able to sing the poetry of Sufi poets like Shah Abdul Latif and Sacchal Sarmast in Sindhi, which her male *qawwāl* counterparts cannot. Abida Parvin therefore has an advantage over her male *qawwāl* counterparts because of her linguistic resources.

QAWWĀLS AT THE BULLE SHAH SHRINE

I now discuss a shrine performance at Bulle Shah in Kasur. The city is about seventy miles from Lahore. I traveled to the shrine with a female friend and her husband, two days before the start of the fasting month of Ramazan. My fellow devotees and I started from Lahore on a beautiful spring afternoon and arrived at the shrine around five o'clock in the evening. When I arrived, the *qawwāls* of the shrine, Muhammad Bakhsh and his paternal uncle Karam Bakhsh, were already singing there. A young man who was said to be a nephew also sang with them. There were two other musicians with them. Their musical instruments were a harmonium (an accordion), a *ḍholak* (a double-sided drum shaped like a barrel), and a pair of tambourines.

Since the shrine is located in the heart of the city, we had to drive the car through extremely narrow streets, encountering large horse-driven carriages (*ṭangās*). The street near the shrine was colorfully decorated with shops that sell all kinds of artifacts such as marigolds, rose petals, candles, and small earthenware lamps called *divās*, which are filled with mustard oil and have a cotton wick in them. They are lit at the shrine. The shops displayed incense sticks, prayer beads, and silver-plated bangles with Quranic verses inscribed on them that devotees take to the shrine, or home as souvenirs. The shops also sell sweets that the devotees buy as *tabarruk, nazar,* or *niāz* (food for distribution in the shrine). Like most shrines, Bulle Shah's tomb is in the center of a brick courtyard covered with a concrete canopy. The crypt is covered with green and red sheets decorated with gold tinsel. The devotees bring these as offerings. There are several small tombs surrounding the main tomb, all within the same compound. Here, the female and male relatives of the Sufi poets are buried. Devotees light candles at these tombs and offer *fātehā* (prayer).

While Muhammad Bakhsh and Karam Bakhsh sang, my companions and I sat close to the ensemble. Male devotees in the shrine made a small circle in front of the musicians and started to dance in rhythm with the music. Later, some *hijṛās* (eunuchs) also joined the group. The *hijṛās* are known as *k͟hāwājāsarā* in the court traditions of the Muslim rulers of the subcontinent, and they held important positions at the court. They were also associated with burial rites such as at the Nizamuddin Auliya shrine.[38] Today in Pakistan and India the *hijṛās* sing and dance at births, especially of male infants, and at circumcisions and weddings.[39] They have their own community networks through which they find out about events and appear with their musicians, *hijṛās* like themselves, to play music while some of them dance. The size of the group may vary from two to any number. The families reward them according to their means. Bulle Shah's was the only shrine where I encountered the *hijṛās*. Most probably they are traditionally linked to the shrine because of Bulle Shah's own life history of having lived among the dancing girls for several years. He is reported to have learned the music arts to win back his beloved *murshid,* Shah Inayat.

The *hijṛas* at Bulle Shah had *ghungrū* tied to their ankles. They danced to the rhythm of the music. Women devotees who until then were performing their rituals of prayer or lighting candles and incense sticks at the poet's shrine or elsewhere joined the assembly to listen to the *qawwāls*. They came and sat with me and my female companion. All together, including the musicians, there were fifty women and men in the shrine.

Complying with my request to sing about the female voices in Sufi poetry, the *qawwāls* sang six different verse compositions that I recorded. All the compositions were in Panjabi, and five were sung as female narratives. The musicians claimed that the five female narratives were Bulle Shah's creations. They said they had inherited them orally from their ancestors who had been *qawwāls* at the shrine for the last three centuries. Only one *qaw-*

2.7 Devotion to the deity: *Hijṛā* at the Bulle Shah shrine, Kasur

wālī was about Muhammad the Prophet; the other five were narratives about different stages of Bulle Shah's spiritual growth as a mystic and his relationship with his spiritual mentor, Shah Inayat. The *qawwāls* sang about Bulle Shah the *murid* (disciple) and Shah Inayat the mentor (*murshid*) through female and male *representations.*

In order to understand the songs we have to take a close look at Bulle Shah's biography. Bulle Shah is said to have lived approximately from 1680 to 1758 AD in Kasur. His original name was Abdullah Shah, and his family were Syeds who had settled in Uch Gilanian, the city of saints in Bahawalpur, where Bulle Shah was born. The family migrated to Kasur when Bulle Shah was six years old. Whereas Bulle Shah was himself a Syed, he chose to become the disciple of Shah Inayat, who did not belong to his socioeconomic caste but is said to have been of *arāī* descent. The *arāī* in the Panjab were gardeners or small cultivators who worked on their own land. There are several legends in the oral lore of the *qawwāls* at the shrine about Bulle Shah defying the mores of his family and community to continue his discipleship of Shah Inayat despite the fact that he was a Syed himself. Many such narratives about Bulle Shah are also reported in the written texts.[40] In this book, the key performers, such as Abida Parvin, Ustad Nusrat Fateh Ali Khan, and the Bulle Shah *qawwāls*, talk about Bulle Shah's relationship with Shah Inayat. They have further used references to this relationship in the poetry of their performances.

The first narrative that the *qawwāls* sang was from Bulle's legendary reconciliation with his mentor, Shah Inayat. The legend of Bulle Shah's relation with his spiritual mentor is that after several years of association Shah Inayat excluded Bulle Shah from his spiritual company. Shah Inayat showed his disapproval of Bulle Shah's poetry, which he considered to be too outspoken against the priestly class. Shah Inayat dissociated himself from Bulle Shah for his outright criticism of issues of gender, class, and caste. Furthermore, he objected to Bulle's ridicule of institutionalized religion. Shah Inayat had to detach himself from his rebellious disciple because he was afraid of the political forces of the time.[41]

2.8 Devotees at a Sufi shrine

Bulle Shah worked hard for several years to win back his *murshid.* He knew that Shah Inayat was fond of music. Therefore, he went and lived among musicians for almost seven years and became their apprentice. After learning the musical arts, he returned to Shah Inayat's company and won him back by playing music and dancing before him. The event of Bulle Shah's winning back Shah Inayat through dance and music is sung in the *qawwālī* and *kalām* traditions. In the first song the *qawwāls* sang they recounted this very event. Bulle Shah portrays himself as a dancing girl who narrates how she won back her beloved through dance. Hence, it is the disciple who is represented as the dancing girl here. The text of the song (*kāfī*) recorded from live speech is as follows:

Menũ tilk lagāvaṇ de	Let me put the mark on the forehead
Kanjrī baṇiā merī zāt nā ghaṭ dī	To become the dancing girl affects not my caste
Te menũ nac ke yār manāvaṇ de	Dance I shall to win my beloved, my mentor
. . . .	. . . .
Menũ yār de zimme lāvaṇ de	Let me make my beloved, my master, responsible for me
Tere ʿiśq nacāyā thyā thyā	Thy love has made me dance
Menũ pīr dī odhi lāvaṇ de	Let me pay the tribute to my master
Ve sāī Bulle-ā te rab jāṇe	O mystic Bulle, only God knows
. . . .	. . . .
Bulle Shah ne pīr dī khātir	Bulle Shah for the sake of his master
Ik nac ke pīr manā-yā-e	Has danced his master back to reconciliation

In the original Panjabi text, the word *nacāyā* is significant because it expresses the act of the dance, which in itself is the metalanguage for ecstasy.

The second *qawwālī* that Muhammad Bakhsh and Karam Bakhsh sang was about a bride who is forced to leave her father's home to go and live with her husband and his family. The metaphor of the journey to the in-laws' home is a preparation for the hereafter, to which every human being is subjected. This, too, represents the disciple-mentor relationship, with the disciple playing the role of the submissive bride. The refrain of the poem that the bride sings to her female friend in Panjabi is this:

Merā bābul kardā dhakā kuṛe	My father forces me, O damsel
Merā bābul kardā dhakā kuṛe	My father forces me, O damsel

The musicians again sing of the implied reference to the veil that covers the bride's face. All the toil, all the suffering is for that final state, that of the *kaśf*, or the unveiling of the beloved, that state of illumination when the disciple meets the mentor.

After this, the *qawwāls* sang a *carkhī-nāma* (spinning-wheel song) for the assembly. Here, the narrative is of a young damsel who spins her trousseau for the forthcoming life in her husband's home. Again, as in the previous song, the hereafter is equated to the in-laws' home. The young damsel is the disciple who must toil diligently to gain the mentor's wisdom. The speech in the song (*kāfī*) is this:

Kar kataṇ val dhiāṇ kuṛe	Heed to thy spinning, O damsel
Kar kataṇ val dhiāṇ kuṛe	Heed to thy spinning, O damsel
. . . .	. . . .
Kar mān nā husn javāṇī dā	Be not arrogant for thy youth, O damsel
Koī dūnīyā jhuṭī fānī dā	This earth is a lie, and will perish, O damsel
Kat le jo kūc katṇā-e	Spin thou, whatever thou needs to spin, O damsel
Nā rehsī nām niśān kuṛe	Alas there will be no name nor sign, O damsel
. . . .	. . . .
Tū sadā nā peke rehṇā-e	Thy shalt not forever be with thy parents, O damsel
Nā pās amṛī de rehṇā-e	Thou shalt not forever be with thy mother, O damsel
O vic vichoṛā sheṇā-e	Alas, there shall be a separation, O damsel
. . . .	. . . .
Tū apnā dāj rachā leh-nī	Decorate thou thy trousseau, O damsel
O Bulle da Sultan kuṛe	He is Bulle's Lord, O damsel
Kar kataṇ val dhiān kuṛe	Heed to thy spinning, O damsel
Kar kataṇ val dhiān kuṛe	Heed to thy spinning, O damsel

The references to the bride and the veil are evident in the poetry of the *qawwāls*, even in the *carkhī-nāma* that they perform for their audiences. Eventually, the damsel will become the bride, or expects to become one.

An interesting *kāfī* that the *qawwāls* sang was about Bulle Shah himself as if he were the bride, and the *qawwāls* were asking him to lift the veil so that they could see the beloved's face. The *qawwāls* sang as though they were the bride's female friends.

O ghungat khol ā-sajnā	Lift thy veil, O Beloved
O ghungat khol ā-sajnā	Lift thy veil, O Beloved
Ghungat cuk le sajnā	Lift thy veil, O Beloved
Ghungat cuk le Bābā Bulle Shah	Lift thy veil, O Baba Bulle Shah
Sakhiā̃ vekhaṇ aīā̃ sajnā--	Thy female friends come to see thee, O Beloved
O ghungat cuk le sajnā	Lift thy veil, O Beloved

Again, the *representation* in this *kāfī* is that of the lover or the disciple. The beloved is the bride and her friends; the disciples ask her to lift the veil from her face. There is a playfulness in the verses, and the beloved or mentor's image assumes multiple identities. Instead of the male, the mentor now becomes the female bride. The *hijṛās* continued to dance with the tempo of the music. Thus, the tropes in the poetry are complex. The Bulle Shah *qawwāls* sang the entire evening, until after the evening prayers, affirming their devotion to the Sufi poet. When I asked Muhammad Bakhsh, the *qawwāl,* why they sang their narratives in the female voice or used the *aurat kī avāz,* he said,

> It is actually not the "female." The voice is that of the spirit. This is the subject of human existence. Life is a spinning, that is why it is the female. If human beings lived the way they are expected to live, all would be fine. We must live in humility. The female, who spins, lives in humility.

When I asked Muhammad Bakhsh about the linguistic and aesthetic sources for their *kalām* (mystic discourse), he answered,

> We use poetic texts from Hazrat Muinuddin Chishti, Baba Ganj Shakar, Data Ganj Bakhsh, Amir Khusrau, and of course we mostly sing Baba Bulle Shah's poetry. We find it easy to memorize Baba Bulle Shah's poetry, while with the others we have to work harder. Sometimes we get poets like Bedam Arsi to write songs for us.

I asked the musicians about their audiences and their goals for singing at the shrine. Muhammad Bakhsh responded thus:

> We sing for the people. We use the mystical poetry of the Sufi saints to talk about the larger meanings of human existence, of living. We are linked to this shrine, we are bound to it, and we sing here out of devo-

> tion to Baba Bulle Shah. The saint will not let us leave this shrine, and even if we do go away to other shrines to sing for the *'urs*, we always return here. Our family has served this shrine for the last three centuries—generation after generation has sung here. We came with Bulle Shah's family from Uch Sharif, and we have learned his poetry from our ancestors, who have always sung here. We sing here twice a day. We sing in the morning from eight to ten, and then throughout the evening.

I sought information about the women in their family. The *qawwāl*s were reluctant to talk. They said,

> Our women have never sung at the shrine. Perhaps, almost a century ago, they would go to the Syed households on special invitation. They would only sing among women. They sang Baba Bulle Shah's poetry for the Syed women.

This claim too was affirmed earlier by the Sidi, Manganhar, and Mohana musicians who sing in the Syed households in the Sind among women audiences only. They sing at the *'urs*, or in social settings such as the *maulud* (the prophet Muhammad's birth anniversary), weddings, and births. Similarly, female singers of Sufi poetry in the Talagang area near Rawalpindi claim to perform only in the feudal households of the Maliks.

On the basis of the various contexts of performance that I have looked at, it can be said that the musicians mediate spiritual experience for their devotees. They are the *speakers*, who apply their linguistic resources of poetry, folklore, myth, syntax, semantics, and all forms of language play accompanied with music. There is the social setting, or what may be called the speech event, that could take place in either a concert hall, a shrine, a folk festival, a household, or a large family setting exclusively for women, as discussed earlier. The musicians establish communication between themselves and their speech communities through language that is emotive for themselves as well as for their listeners. Their goal is to fulfill the emotional and psychological needs of their listeners, which they do through speech and music. They create the communicative channels that I demonstrate with the following model adapted from Jakobson (Fig. 2.9).

In the contexts that are investigated, the performers become the transmitters because they use cultural semantics embedded in a shared meaning between themselves and their audiences, thereby making the process interactional. They add body language in the transmission of the discourse that further enhances the interaction. In Abida Parvin's performance at the

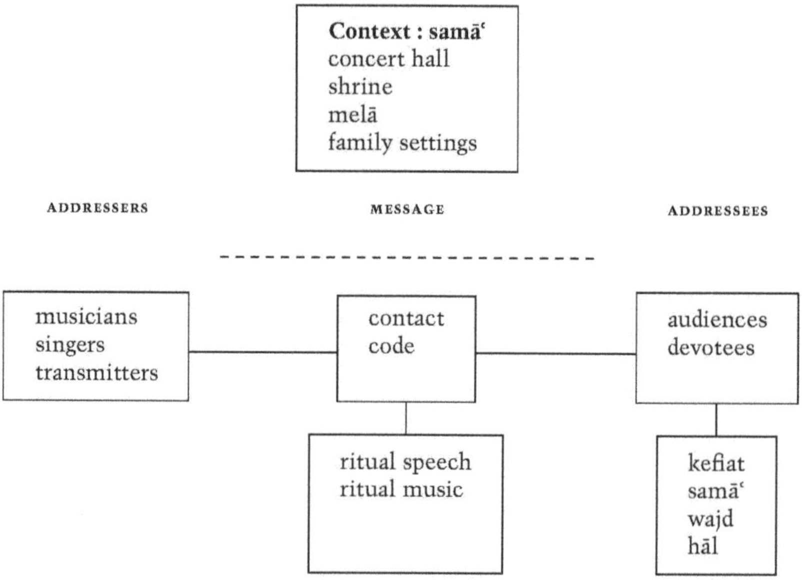

2.9 Performance: The Qawwali-Sufiānā-Kalam communicative model. Adapted from Jakobson, "Closing Statement: Linguistics and Poetics," 351–352.

Open University, the recipients ratify her discourse verbally and through body movement. In Nusrat Fateh Ali Khan's concerts in the United Kingdom, the listeners ratify the poetry and music through body movement and verbal affirmation that lauds the singer's input. The *hijṛās* dance in response to the music at the Bulle Shah shrine. Effectively, all the performances that are investigated show that the event is a communication between musicians and audience.

The performers transmit the experience through linguistic devices that they alter and modify according to the verbal and nonverbal cues they receive from their listeners. The improvisation on certain segments of a text that is largely fixed is closely linked to the interactional processes in the anthropology of performance. The performers continue to sing certain segments of the text for an extensive time period because their audiences are emotionally involved in it. They build the rapport with the singer, who then has to respond affectively to sustain the communicative frame.

Abida Parvin's performance at the Open University illustrates the argument. Since a large number of her listeners were from the Sindhi and Siraiki speech communities, she initiated the performance with a mystical invocation from Shah Abdul Latif's poetry in Sindhi. Later she mixed the linguistic codes. Her performance was successful, because the interaction between the singer and her listeners was intense. She used a variety of texts and codes that she kept changing as she went along. In such a performance, speech production becomes an ad hoc process for the performer, requiring her to draw upon all the linguistic, aesthetic, and emotional resources available to her. The structure of the speech event and its organizing principle are largely created through this interaction, mutually achieved and ratified within a cultural code between performers and recipients.[42]

Sometimes, in a performance like that of the Sabri Brothers in the United Kingdom when they sing the Mira Bai text, the poetry creates a context when some in the audience sink into an ecstatic state and offer large sums of money as *nazarānā*. This pattern occurred in Nusrat Fateh Ali Khan's performance in the United Kingdom when he sang "Je tū akhīā̃ de sāmne nahī̃ rehṇā" (If thou wilt not nurture my eyes, O Beloved). His audience showered him with currency notes in pound sterling. It was a response to the text as well as to the music, especially to the percussion of drums. The audience expressed appreciation of that portion of the performance through the *nazar* or *bel* that they offered him and his ensemble. Also, they fell into an ecstatic state and performed *dhammāl*, which showed their rapture.

Furthermore, the singers use a variety of *styles*. These are mapped in the transliterations in this chapter. It is not uncommon to find metered verses sung to music, and prose narrative in colloquial speech recited without music or sung in duple meter. An example is Abida Parvin's narrative where she tells her audience that she will talk about Bulle Shah and his spiritual mentor, Shah Inayat. The Sabri Brothers speak in prose to their audience in their Mira Bai narrative.

Performers further communicate with their audiences and with each other by playing with the stress and intonational patterns of the language. They manipulate language and create parallelisms in speech and song. An interesting feature is the entire dynamic of turn-taking in speech in the *qawwālī* ensemble. The *qawwāl*s follow a complete organized system of social interaction of "taking the floor," which is mapped out in the transliterations. The musicians know among each other, and through vocal cues, who will take the floor and when. All this is done within a cultural context. I have used the social-interactional approaches to study the speech communication in my work.[43]

The performers further use their linguistic resources for code switching. The major code of a performance can be Panjabi, Siraiki, Sindhi, Pushto, Urdu, or a regional language. Within the major code singers can either start a performance in Arabic or switch to it, because it is the language of the Quran. They will also switch to Persian because it is the language of higher intellectual thought and the code that was used by some Sufi masters such as Jalaluddin Rumi. The use of these prestige codes establishes the authenticity of the discourse for the listeners.

This chapter then describes how *qawwālī* and *sufiānā-kalām* performers interact with their audiences in particular contexts. They draw upon the resources of the Quran and the *hadīth.* They seek inspiration from the lives and the poetry of the Sufis of the subcontinent and the Middle Eastern regions. The diverse resources, including their own linguistic and musical skills, are blended with local folklore, proverbs, and ecology to create an oral culture that is a visible component of the performing arts as well as shrine ritual in Pakistan.

In the last two decades, large expatriate speech communities have given immense patronage to *qawwālī* and *sufiānā-kalām* sung in concert. The musicians recreate it as a performing art, outside the shrine culture, where they still uphold the sanctity of the ritual. And it is precisely in such contexts that some of this study was carried out.

CHAPTER 3

Female Myths in Sufism

HIR, SASSI, AND SOHNI

The complexities of race, gender, class, and caste figure prominently in the narratives of the *qawwāls* and *sufiānā-kalām* performers. Sufi poetry in Pakistan and India was sometimes composed in opposition to the religious establishment and was expressed in subtle ways. It survived through *representation* in myth and the complex tropes of the female voices. Whether or not the Sufi poets were "feminists" cannot be claimed here as the term "feminism" is a fairly recent one. However, the female myths in Sufi poetry certainly represent the voices of marginalized groups and continue to be used as *representative* frames even today. This is evident in Abida Parvin's performance in Islamabad in 1985 that I discuss in this chapter and in my interview with Alan Faqir, a singer of Sufi poetry in the Sind.[1] The female myths in the Sufi poetry of Pakistan and India further give it an aesthetic quality that the musicians have claimed in their interviews with me. They sing the native myths of lovers like Sassi, Hir, Sohni, Mumal, Marvi, and Mira Bai because the myths have become metaphors for the polarities of gender, religious, sociopolitical, and economic hegemony. For instance, Sassi, Hir, and Mira Bai are all upper-class, aristocratic women whose lives end in tragedy, the frame of a classic Greek play. Hir violates her caste conduct to elope with a cowherd, thus bringing shame to her family. Should her society punish her? How is it sung and communicated in the oral Sufi tradition? Why do the musicians sing in the female voices? These are some of the questions that are explored in this chapter.

Sassi's story is also one of "tragically thwarted love." Her voice, too, creates the mythical structures that give the Sufi poets the medium to express their own conflicts and differences with the social values of their time. Sassi becomes the symbol of strength against patriarchy. Her death in the desert is in fact her struggle to seek respite against social injustice. She tries to reclaim her love. In the Sufi lore she becomes a paradigm of moral courage and spiritual triumph.[2] I have not found one standard version of the myth nor specific dates for it as the myths have evolved over the centuries and each Sufi poet creates a context around a loosely structured story that exists in the written or oral sources. According to the myth, Sassi is the daughter of the king of Bhambor in Sind. When she was born, the astrologers predicted that she would bring shame on her family. (A similar prophecy was made about Oedipus when he was born.) Sassi's shocked father consulted with his advisers and they agreed that rather than kill her, they would put her on a raft to float down the river Indus. The raft arrived at a place called Bhambor where a washerman saw it and was surprised to see a living child on it. He brought the girl-child home to his wife, and since they did not have any children of their own, they adopted her and called her Sassi, which means the Moon.[3]

In other versions of the story the chief of Bhambor adopted her himself and when she grew up, he gave her state authority and made her a ruler.

The latter seems a more probable version of the narrative because Sassi is said to have been a powerful ruler. Once, there was a famine in the neighboring state of Kec Mekran, and the people from that territory came to buy corn in her dominion. She allowed them to take the food on the condition that they bring their handsome prince, Punnu, to her. Punnu's father was the chief of the Hot tribe. Sassi held two men from the Kec hostage until they brought Punnu back with them. Punnu came to Sassi with all the pomp and glory that befitted his royal standing. They became married, and he refused to return to his people. His father was so outraged that he sent his brothers to bring him back. Punnu's tribesmen came and stayed in Sassi's palace for several days, pretending to be very cordial with her and her tribe. The tribe held great festivities in honor of Punnu and his tribesmen. At one of these nocturnal banquets, Punnu's brothers drugged Punnu and Sassi, and when they were both incapacitated, they stole Punnu away on a camel. They crossed the desert at great speed, bringing the prince back to Kec Mekran. The following morning when Sassi woke up, Punnu was gone. She ran after him and walked for miles in the desert hoping to find her beloved, but, alas, she never found him and died tired, hungry, and thirsty in the desert. The people built a tomb over her dead body.

When Punnu woke up to find himself among his tribesmen in Kec Mekran, he escaped to go back to Bhambor where he had left Sassi. On the way he saw her tomb. Passersby told him how she had died in the desert. They also told him of her laments for him and all her woes. Punnu wept bitterly at her tomb, until the earth opened for him and he was buried with his beloved.[4]

Such is the myth told in the lands of Sind and Baluchistan. In the oral traditions of the region the legend is sung with all the emotion that manifests Sassi's grief and her distress as she tries to cross the formidable desert to reach her beloved in Kec. Sufi bards have based entire sections of their compositions, such as Shah Abdul Latif's *Risālo*, on the Sassi-Punnu myth. Even the melody in which it is sung in Shah's poetry is called "Sūr Sassi," which means Sassi's melody. In Shah Abdul Latif's poetry, Sassi is the epitome of the lover who seeks the beloved as though the beloved is the Divine Being. Pathana Khan, a renowned male singer of Siraiki mystical poetry, sang in Sassi's inflected voice as she laments for Punnu.[5] The singer invoked the Sufi poet Farid to create the mystical frame or context for his audiences:[6]

01 A U-U-A-A-A-A
02 A Ahkī Guḍ-e--e-dekh-h
03 A Akhī khuś akhī-e-vīl ro-e nā akhiā̃ nāl likhē dā
04 A In-ā akhiā̃ nā-āl jhiṛē de jheṛe-e-e-e
05 A Val akhiā̃ nāl manī-ī dā-ā
06 A E-ye akhī likhē vā-ā-ā-da-ard firāk-ā̃ vāl-e
07 A Val akhiā̃ nā-āl paṛhī dā-ā
08 A Yā-ā-r Farīd in akhiā̃ -kū- kūj nā ākhī ve -in akhiā̃ can likhē dā-ā
09 A O-O- Āp-e bār muhabat cāiūmṛī
. . . .
16 A Sāb dukhā̃-ā̃ sulā̃-ā̃ dī tātā mī -am
17 A *G*am dal(r)d anoha parāt-t mī- am
18 A Bheṛe dukhṛe bār umjhāiūmṛī
. . . .
24 A Sohnā Ho-o t Punal chad Kec gīyā-ā-ā
25 A Sun-n
26 A Sohnā Hot Punal chad Kec gīyā
27 A Gal so-z firāk dā pec pīyā-ā-ā-ā-ā-ā-ā
28 A Sohnā Hot Punal chad Kec gīyā
29 A Gal soz firāk dā pec pīyā
. . . .
56 A Rab avere bar-e sahāiūmṛi-i-i-i-i-i-i-i-i-i
. . . .
60 A Hik vār Farīd-ū yār mil-e

61 A Seru panḍ-ḍ hī jaldā bār tale-e
01 A U-U-A-A-A-A
02 A Look at these eyes—
03 A These happy, joyful eyes–weep not with these eyes–for we write with these very eyes
04 A These eyes that are like fresh-water springs
05 A And we affirm with these very eyes
06 A These eyes testify to the agony of separation
07 A We also read with these eyes
08 A O lover Farid, refrain thyself from reprimanding these eyes; for in them are written the narratives of love
09 A I do carry the burden of lifelong love
. . . .
16 A O Love, thou art the source of all pain
17 A Love, thy sorrows and pangs befall me
18 A O Love, thy agony entangles me for a lifetime
. . . .
24 A My beloved Hot Punal abandoned me and departed to Kec to be with his Hot tribe—
25 A Beauti—
26 A My beloved Hot Punal abandoned me and departed to Kec to be with his Hot tribe—
27 A Around my neck is the mesh of separation
28 A My beloved Punal departed to Kec—O my beloved, thou abandoned me
29 A Around my neck is the mesh of separation
. . . .
56 A Will the Almighty help me to carry this lifelong burden?
. . . .
60 A O Farid, if only once could I meet my beloved
61 A Then would I cast away this consuming fire

In this transliteration the Sufi troubadour casts emotion into the narrative through the use of myth. Sassi's voice gives the poetry an aesthetic dimension that involves the *listener* in an emotional bond with the *speaker*. Essentially, the poet sings of mystic love through Sassi, who carries that "consuming fire" for the beloved within her. There is pain and there is sorrow in that love, because it cannot mature without suffering. Reshma has sung the same myth and describes Sassi's pain:

Mẽ Thal vic hūkā mārā	In the desert do I lament

Hūk in the indigenous ethnopoetic terms is "the pain of the heart when it laments in grief." The test for a competent singer of Sufi poetry is to be able to sing the myth with a passion that moves the listeners to tears. Some of the other metalinguistic words that Reshma uses in this song to describe Sassi's sorrow are "*dohaīā̃*," which means to "cry in agony," and "*kurlānā*," to "squirm in pain." In the Siraiki language, these are the extreme degrees of physical and emotional pain. Performers love to sing the Sassi myth in the regional languages and dialects of Sind, Baluchistan, and the Siraiki-speaking regions. They invoke images of Sassi, who tries to cross the Thal (the desert), where daytime temperatures range from 120 degrees upward in the summer. Reshma refers to Sassi's dry *bulīā̃* (parched lips) as she drags herself in the desert after Punnu. Singers like Reshma use a variety of melodies and styles to sing about Sassi, who eventually dies from unmitigated love.

Some of the other myths that the Sufi bards sing are Umar-Marvi, Mumal-Rano, Sohni-Mahival, and Hir-Ranjha. Shah Abdul Latif's entire *Risālo* is based on these narratives, and he evokes mystical poetry for his tragic heroines to become symbols of otherworldly love. Each one of these romances is sung in its own *sūr*. Thus, there is a "Sūr Sohni" in Latif's poetry to sing about Sohni, "Sūr Mumal-Rano" to sing about Mumal-Rano's tale, and "Sūr Marvi" to narrate Umar-Marvi's story. Shah Abdul Latif created several *sūrs* in this manner, all named after his heroines.[7] Altogether, there are thirty *sūrs* in the *Risālo*, and at least ten are dedicated to female heroines, or *sūrmīs*, as they are called in Shah's poetry. The male equivalent of the *sūrmī* is a *sūrma*, which means a hero; someone who has prowess. Therefore, Shah intends his *sūrmis* to be perceived as women with prowess.

In the Siraiki- and Panjabi-speaking areas, the Sufi bards have further created narratives around the Hir-Ranjha and Sohni-Mahival myths. In the previous chapter I discussed Nusrat Fateh Ali Khan's singing of sections of the Hir-Ranjha myth. I explore the myth further in this chapter through description and narrative.

The Hir-Ranjha myth existed for a long time before Waris Shah (b. 1717 AD) made it famous in the eighteenth century. The myth was probably sung in the folk traditions for several centuries. Bulle Shah, who was a contemporary of Waris Shah, also worked with the Hir-Ranjha myth in Panjabi. The narrative exists in Sindhi, Baluchi, Persian, Urdu, and even in Arabic. It has been further translated into English and French. However, now, whenever a reference is made to the Hir-Ranjha legend, it is mainly to the Waris Shah text.

Waris Shah's text is used for a variety of reasons, the strongest one being his creation of Hir's character. Through her he challenges patriarchy, the

3.1 Hir-Ranjha

clergy, and issues of the socioeconomic caste system. Hir has many arguments with the clergy where she uses the rhetoric of the *Shar'a,* the Islamic legal system based on the Quran and the *hadīth,* to prove its narrow-mindedness and duplicity. In devising Hir's character Waris Shah seems to have banked on the caste inclinations of the Jats, for Hir belonged to the family of the powerful Siyal Jats of Jhang. The Jats of the Panjab are *zamindars* (landowners), known for practicing widow-marriage.[8] Furthermore, it is asserted that Hir was obviously a favorite child and a spoiled one. The Siyal tribe is more than usually considerate toward its women; it is one of the few tribes in the Panjab that allow women to inherit property under customary law.[9]

The Hir-Ranjha myth can be summarized thus: Hir was the beautiful and witty daughter of Cucak Siyal, the powerful Jat chief of Jhang Siyal, which is a vast agricultural territory situated to the southwest of Lahore in Pakistan.[10] In the story, she falls in love with Dhido, who was also known by his tribal name of Ranjha.[11] He was the youngest of the eight sons of Chaudhry Muazzam, also known as Mauju of the Ranjha clan of Jats of Takht Hazara, now Gujrat District of Pakistan. He lost both his parents when he was still very young. His brothers gave him the least fertile part of the ancestral land when they divided the inheritance. They also bribed the religious establishment to support them in this unholy act against their youngest brother.

Since Dhido was unmarried, he depended on his sisters-in-law to cook for him and bring his meals to him in the fields, according to the rural custom. His sisters-in-law did not take care of him, and when he complained they scolded him. In fact, one of them even taunted him and said that, if he was so fussy about being served well, why did he not bring Hir, the famous daughter of the Siyals, to be his bride. Ranjha, therefore, left home to win Hir. He crossed the river Chenab and arrived in the territory of Cucak Siyal, the Jat chief of the region.[12] Here, Ranjha met Hir and they fell in love. Hir brought Ranjha home to her father, who employed him as a cowherd, and because he played the flute skillfully, he soon mastered Cucak's herds.[13]

Hir-Ranjha's romance thrived through clandestine meetings until Kaido, Hir's paternal uncle, a lame man, spied on the lovers. Kaido caused a scandal in the village and even forced Cucak, Hir's father, to descend on the lovers during a rendezvous.[14] Kaido scolded Hir's mother, Maliki, for ignoring the romance, because it was in violation of family honor. He asserted that Ranjha was only a *cāk*, a laborer in the household. Ranjha was expelled. After his departure Cucak's herds of cows and buffalo became unmanageable, for no one could play the flute like Ranjha. Cucak was obliged to ask Ranjha to return, and this time Hir's mother Maliki had to promise Ranjha that he could marry Hir and that she would help the lovers.

The Siyal Jats did not fulfill their promise. Although Ranjha was a Jat like them, Cucak did not think that he had the inheritance that would make him an eligible son-in-law or a powerful ally. Ranjha had further lowered himself by becoming a *kāmā̃*, or a *cāk*, who was considered a menial of the Siyals. In order to maintain their hegemony in the socioeconomic order, the Siyals had to marry their only daughter into a powerful clan like themselves. Cucak's kinsmen counseled Cucak to marry Hir to Saida, the son of the prestigious Khera Jat tribesman of Rangpur, and he agreed to their proposal.

Hir asked Ranjha to elope with her but he refused. As a result, she was married against her will to Saida and sent off to the Kheras against the principles of the *Shari'a*, which stresses that a woman can only be married with her consent. Hir refused to sign the marriage contract. Cucak bribed the clergyman and the two witnesses to fake her consent. She was pushed into the palanquin on pain of death and the Kheras carried her off. On arrival at her in-laws' home, Hir refused to consummate the marriage with Saida Khera. She pretended to be ill and sent a message to Ranjha, asking him to come disguised as a *jogī*.

Hir's sister-in-law Sethi, that is, her so-called husband's sister, helped her meet Ranjha secretly, and when he came she helped the lovers elope. However, they were caught. Hir's family promised to allow them to marry if Ranjha would go back to Takht Hazara, and return with his brothers and *brādārī* (extended family) to marry their daughter. Only then would it be a worthy alliance for the Siyals. While Ranjha was gone, the Siyals poisoned Hir, and he returned to find his beloved being buried. He killed himself at her grave.

Waris Shah composed *Hir* as an epic poem to be sung to music in public contexts. He is said to have recited it with great emotion among his speech communities in the Panjab. Although it is commonly believed that he was a great musician, I have not found any evidence of that in the literature. However, there is now substantial recorded material of Waris Shah's *Hir* available, both on audiocassettes and videos sung in the folk traditions. Many renowned folk artists in the Panjab, such as Reshma, Zahida Parvin, Nazir Begum, Sabiha Khanum, Tufail Niazi, and Iqbal Bahu, have sung it. And indeed there are many spiritual nuances embedded in the narratives of the *Hir* epic, which each singer brings out according to his or her own interpretation of the poetry.

Waris Shah gives the story a spiritual construction. He uses a formulaic initiation for the poem, with an ode to God and to Love, obedience to the prophet Muhammad and to his four companions, and more specifically to Pir Chishti Shakarganj or Baba Farid of Pakpattan. As the poem develops, large sections of the written *Hir* text, from which the singers draw their poetics, bring out the sharp polarities between Hir and the religious establishment. In one of her retorts to the religious establishment, she says:[15]

ʻIśq dā rāh pauṇā	To measure the path of Love
Nahī kam, m-----, q----dā	Is not for the Bigot
Es ʻiśq maidān de kuṭhiā̃ nū	Those who are the caretakers of the laborious path to Love
Rutba Karbobalā deyā̃ gaziā̃ dā	Attain the rank of the warriors of Kerbala
Turt vic dargā manzūr hove	With great speed will be accepted In God's kingdom
Sajdā ʻāśiqā̃ pāk namāziā̃ dā	The humility and prayer of true lovers, true devotees

Rānjhā nāl imān qubuliā mẽ	Faith have I confessed in Ranjha's company
Qisa khatam kar dūr darāziā̃ dā	Create not differences, O Bigot

She further admits, in a song that I have transcribed from Tufail Niazi's *kalām*,[16]

Rānjhan ḍhunḍan mẽ calī	In search of Ranjha do I go
Menū̃ Rānjhan mīlyā nā hī	But Ranjha I cannot find
Rab mīlyā Rānjhā nā mīlyā	God I found, but Ranjha I cannot find
Rab Rānjhā jehe vinā	Even the Divine is not Ranjha
Ve mẽ nahī̃ jāṇā Kheṛiā̃ de nāl	O, with the Kheras I will not go

Nusrat Fateh Ali Khan sang the following *qawwālī* in Hir's voice in which Hir informs her mother that she will not live with the Kheras.[17]

Rānjhe yār val mukh kīvẽ moṛā̃	Ranjha will I not abandon
Mẽ Kheṛiā̃ de o nahī̃ vasṇā̃	With the Kheras will I not live
. . . .	. . . .
Das mãe mukh kīvẽ moṛā̃?	O Mother, can I ever abandon Ranjha?
Phaṭ Kheṛe. . . . phaṭ Kheṛe	Blast the Kheras . . . blast the Kheras
Mẽ te nāl Rānjhe de rehṇā	With Ranjha alone will I exist

Despite her protests, Hir was sent off to the Kheras by force. As she was carried off in a palanquin, she sang her famous lament song, which is traditionally sung at almost every Panjabi wedding at the time of the bride's departure to her husband's home. When a performer sings *Hir*, she uses all the available aesthetic, linguistic, cultural, and emotional resources with the result that even the strongest person is unable to hold back tears. In the terms of the culture itself, the performer's stylistic creation of pain is called *dard*. I quote from a written text:[18]

ḍolī caṛdeā̃ Hir virlāp kitā	As they loaded her into the palanquin,[19] Hir shrieked in lament,
Menū̃ le cale bābulā le cale ve	"They take me away, O my father, they take me away
Menū̃ rakh le babulā	Keep me, O my father
Ghaṭ ḍolī kahar cuk ke	Through treachery, my palanquin, the potters[20] . . . they take me away

Pe dar pe cale ve	They take me away . . . .
. . . .	. . . .
Tere catar chavā̃ bābul rukh vangā̃	Thy shelter was the cool shade of a tree A castle, O Father,
Asī vangā̃ musafirā̃ beh cale ve	Like the traveler we get washed away now, O Father"

In all these sections Hir's abandonment and her loss not only create the romance of the myth but also address patriarchal paradigms of religion, caste, socioeconomic class, and gender, in which the weak are exploited. However, the poets give the narrative a metaphysical and spiritual articulation. Hir is forced into a union against her will to uphold her caste and family honor, for which she dies in the end.

For the Sufi poets there is glory in Hir's death, like Antigone's in a Greek tragedy. In the *Hir* narrative the lovers die, but eventually their struggle, their suffering and pain are a metaphysical triumph. Hir expresses her pain in the many contexts that are investigated. Her beloved assumes a spirituality and sublimity that transcends the divine. Thus, her female voice transforms the earthly plane to reach a transcendental state. This is in keeping with the Sufi principles where *ʿiśq-e majāzī* (personal love) transforms itself into *ʿiśq-e haqīqī* (divine love). In Sufi poetry Hir's voice thus becomes a "frame" or a cultural complex to describe esoteric meanings through the aesthetics of poetry and music.

Within the same traditions, Nusrat Fateh Ali Khan sang another myth, that of Sohni and Mahival. He sang it with his ensemble in a mystical frame in a private *mehfil* in England in 1984. Intimate interactions were seen between performers and the audience, who knew each other closely, and the speech play evolved from that intimacy while the performers sang the Sohni myth in Panjabi.

The background of the Sohni-Mahival story is narrated thus:[21] Once upon a time there was a well-to-do potter called Tulla who lived in the Gujrat district of the Panjab. He had a beautiful daughter called Sohni, which means the beautiful one. He and his wife raised their daughter with great care, so that she blossomed into a mature woman of great beauty and intelligence. In the story, too, is a young aristocrat called Izzat Beg, a rich merchant's son from Bokhara. After many wanderings, Izzat Beg decided to settle in the small village where Sohni lived. Izzat Beg's servant told him about Sohni's beauty, which made him interested in her. He would go to her father's shop on one pretext or another, so that he might see her. Most often he would go there to buy pottery, and so his visits continued, until he spent all his money.

He was forced to work for Tulla, who kept him as a *mahival* (caretaker) of his buffalo. In Sindhi such a person is called a *mehar*.[22]

Now that Mahival worked in Tulla's household, he got to see Sohni quite regularly and their love flourished. Unfortunately, their meetings could not remain secret for long, creating a scandal in the village. Sohni's family threw out Izzat Beg, and Sohni was married against her will to another potter's son, called Dam. Sohni refused to consummate her marriage. Mahival prudently left the village to go and live in another place across the river Chenab. He now grazed other people's cattle but acquired a spirituality through which he became a recognized *faqīr*. Sohni went to the *faqīr* to seek his counsel, for she was still lovelorn. She found that the *faqīr* was none other than her own Mahival.

The lovers renewed their meetings and Mahival crossed the river every night to meet Sohni. He would bring roasted fish that the two ate together. Unfortunately, one night Mahival could not bring the fish for Sohni as he could not catch any. Instead, he cut a piece of flesh from his thigh, roasted it, and brought it to her. He naturally lost a lot of blood and became very weak. When Sohni saw him so pale, she made him confess on pain of death what he had done to himself. Now, she promised to swim across the river herself to meet Mahival. She knew she could do so because, as a potter's daughter, she had learned to swim on a *ghaṛā*, which is a round clay pot. Thus, she would cross the ferocious river every night on a *ghaṛā* to see her beloved, and when she returned, she would hide the *ghaṛā* in a special place. Her family again found out about her secret meetings with Mahival and scolded her for her rashness, but she would not listen.[23]

Finally, her parents discovered where she hid the *ghaṛā* on which she would swim the river to meet Mahival. They removed the baked *ghaṛā*, and instead put a half-baked one in its place, knowing very well that she would drown if she used it. When Sohni took the *ghaṛā* to cross the river that night, she did not realize that it was not the original one. When she was midstream, her *ghaṛā* dissolved and she drowned. Mahival heard her screams and jumped into the water to save her, but the lovers were washed down with the current. Their bodies were found and they were buried together. The entire village mourned their deaths.[24]

This is a favorite tale among Sufi poets, and the musicians among them sing it. They sing of Sohni's loyalty and courage. Sindhi informants claim that this is a true story and that Sohni's tomb is somewhere near Shahdadpur. Others say that she lived in a forest near Hajipur that is fourteen miles from Hyderabad, on the bank of the river Indus. They also claim that there is a forest named Sohni, after her. However, the myth is sung in Sufi poetry in all the regions of the Sind, the Siraiki-speaking area of the Panjab. Ustad Nusrat Fateh Ali Khan and his *qawwāl*s sang it, assuming the *ghaṛā*'s voice; the *ghaṛā* itself became Sohni's intimate female friend and spoke to her:[25]

O dis de kuli sone yār dī[26]	I can see the beloved's abode
O mẽ kī karā̃ kaṇḍā dūr nī aṛī-e?	But alas, what can I do, the anchor is far, my friend.
O ghaṛā kendā	And the *ghaṛā* says,
Mẽ kī karā̃ kaṇḍā dūr nī aṛī-e?	"But alas, what can I do, the anchor is far, my friend.
Eh, kadī na Sohṇī toṛ carhe dī	O Sohni, a love will not blossom
Yār kache dī yārī	That rides not with a ripe friend
Phaṛ palṛā murśid pake dā	Hold on to a guide that is seasoned
Jehṛā tenū̃ pār lā̃ghā-ve	For only will He help you cross the stream
Nī Sohṇī-e	O female Sohni
O mẽ kī karā̃ kaṇḍā dūr nī aṛī-e?	But alas, what can I do, the anchor is far my friend."

In this mystical interpretation of the myth, the *ghaṛā* assumes multiple voices: the role of Sohni's female friend; the mature *murshid* who would help the *murid*, Sohni, cross the stream to the spiritual path; the *ghaṛā* that speaks to Sohni. Sohni drowned because her *ghaṛā* was *kacca* and not mature. Her myth, therefore, became a storytelling device or trope for the singer to talk of the difficulties on the spiritual path, the *iśq-e haqīqī*. Sohni needed a seasoned guide or *ghaṛā* to help her cross the stream. In Nusrat Fateh Ali Khan's narrative, even Mahival responds to Sohni and says,

Ke mẽ 'iśq dī ag vic nī saṛiā?	Have I, too, not been consumed in the same fire, my beloved?

The fire becomes the element that purifies and transforms baser metals into gold. The water is the cleansing element. And so the *ghaṛā* in Sohni's myth becomes a "metaphorical nature of representation," as well as contributing to the aesthetics of the narrative.[27] It becomes a medium that transforms the earthly experiences to the spiritual realm by becoming a kind of *murshid* or mentor. This was communicated effectively in Nusrat Fateh Ali Khan's *qawwālī*.

In Sufi poetry, many narratives are built around the *ghaṛā* or the *ghaṛolī*. Abida Parvin explains the *ghaṛolī* to her audience in one of her concerts, suggesting that it is a container that "receives" the *murshid*'s spiritual bounties.

The Sufi poets made the native myths of Hir, Sassi, and Sohni into complex cultural tropes. The discourse so created and sung to music articulated the concerns of marginalized social groups such as the Sufis themselves, women, minorities, persecuted communities, and the vast majority of the people who were excluded from the power structures supported by the clergy. This was one of the reasons for this verbal art to be a strong component of popular culture in the Pakistan-India subcontinent. Many individuals in the native cultures assert that it was not the conquerors but rather the Sufis who disseminated Islam widely in the subcontinent through their oral traditions and the medium in which they spoke to the people.

MIRA BAI AND LAYLA

In connection with the argument that there is a strong female voice in Sufi ritual, I discuss the Mira Bai myth that the Sabri Brothers sang in concert before an expatriate audience in the United Kingdom.[28] The *qawwālī* was dedicated to Hazrat Khawaja Muinuddin Chishti of Ajmer, and the performers *signified* his *karāmāt* (spiritual powers) with Mira Bai as his devotee.

Mira Bai, the Rajput princess, is herself strongly associated with the creation of mystical texts sung in the Bhakti tradition. Mira Bai was born in Rajasthan around 1498 AD, in a fortress village called Merta, which is forty to fifty miles northeast of Ajmer city. The connection between her and Hazrat Khawaja Muinuddin Chishti appears to be the proximity of her birthplace to Ajmer. A myth has grown up in the area about her devotion to this Sufi saint.

Mira was born as an upper-class Rajput in the House of Rathore.[29] She was orphaned at a young age; her mother died in Mira's childhood and her father died in one of the religious wars. Her paternal grandfather raised her and gave her a spiritual education, which included knowledge of the scriptures. At the age of eighteen she was married to Rana Sangha's son, Bhoj Raj. Her marriage was a great alliance of the Rajputs, as Rana Sangha himself was a powerful Rajput chief of Chitor. Unfortunately, both her husband and her father-in-law died early in her marriage during the religious wars. Mira never had any children from her marriage, and she speaks of herself as a virgin. After her husband's death and that of Rana Sangha, she faced persecution in the House of Chitor. The ruling Rajput family was torn by intrigue. In the course of time Mira, ostracized in the royal household, disappeared among the people, where she is said to have served the poor.

However, Mira's fame rests on her composition of short mystical texts called *bhajans*, kept alive in the oral tradition presumably through the women minstrels or through the *sādhūs* or the mendicants. Others mention a mysterious friend Lalita, a handmaiden, who is said to have fled with Mira from the Mewar palace, when she went into exile.[30] Lalita reportedly shadowed her mistress from town to town, transcribing the songs into a great notebook. Mira's songs have been transmitted in the oral tradition for five hundred years and are not far removed from India's folk songs. There does not seem to be an original manuscript of her poems, except what has been documented from the oral tradition. Perhaps, as some have suggested, where writing has been the prerogative of men, women alone kept Mira's songs alive, passing them across the generations from mouth to mouth.[31] Mira's *bhajan*s together with the female myths that I have investigated here belong to a context with a long tradition:

> There exists in poetry a tradition of outriders or night cadres, of nomads, exiles and rebels of songs. Throughout history, within every literate culture, poets belonging to this lineage have emerged to articulate a brave and defiant opposition to unjust distribution of wealth, religious persecution, oppression of women, and aggressive military exploits. Marauding armies, abusive governments, exploitative churches . . . these come and go across the planet like storm clouds and in their passage cause grievous suffering. Somehow, the poets who sing within this outrider tradition stay with us.[32]

It is interesting that *qawwāl*s in the Islamic mystical traditions should sing about a Rajput princess who was a great mystic herself and the creator of poetry in the popular culture. The Sabri Brothers sing in this woman minstrel's inflected voice that uses the metalanguage of *divānī*, or one who is ecstatic. Mira's devotion to Hazrat Khawaja Muinuddin Chishti is like that of one who is overcome with infatuation. The narrative tells Mira's life story and her journey to Khawaja's shrine. The *qawwāl*s edify for their listeners:

03	A	Mē to dīvānī Khāja ki dīvānī
	B	//Hh-Hh
04	C	D-ī-ī-ī-vānī
05	A	Re-mē dīvānī Khāja kī dīvānī
06	A	Mē to dīvānī Khāja kī dīvānī
	B	//Hh-h
07	C	Ajmer Sharif se tīn sau mīl dūr īk riāsat huā kartī thī
08	C	Jis kā nām hotā thā Mel Karoṛ
09	C	Vahā̃ kī Mahārānī-- Mīrā Bāī--- jo ke Hindū thī
10	C	Lekīn us-e Hazūr Khāja Gharīb Nawāz Rehmat īl Ilhā se

11 C Kitnī aqīdat aur muhabat thī samāt farmāye:
12 C Mīrā Bāī jo thī Mel Karoṛ kī
13 C Rānā Sāngā ke yā uskī śadī hu-ī
14 C Zāhir un to vo-- uskī Māhāranī thī
15 C Re parde parde mẽ Khāja kī dīvānī thī
A //Re parde parde mẽ Khāja kī dīvānī thī
16 A Parde parde mẽ Khāja kī dīvānī thī
17 A Parde parde mẽ Khāja kī dīvāni thi
18 C Tin sau mīl te karke jātī thī vo
19 C Pī ke darśan ko--Ajmer āti thī vo
20 C Us ko ā te hu-e bīs sāl ho gae
21 C Pās rauze ke pahõcī nā is khauf se
22 C Ke huī rā se? Māhārānī pehne hue
23 C Pāõ mẽ sace motī kī pāyal bhī hɛ
24 C Sun ke payāl kī jhankār ho gā gazab
25 C Khāja keh dẽ ge Mīrā tū hɛ be adab
26 A Khāja keh dẽ ge Mīrā tū hai be adab
B //A-h ha
27 C Sun ke pāyal kī jhankār ho ga gazab
28 C Khāja keh dẽ ge Mīrā tū hai be adab
29 C Lekīn zabt ikis vã sāl nā kar sakī
30 C Aur pehlī seṛī par jā kar sadā us ne dī
31 C Kiā sadā us ne dī samāt farmā ye:
32 A ũncī beṛī mere Khāja kī-ī-ī-ī-ī-ī-ī-ī-ī [etc.]
B // ī-ī-ī-ī-ī-ī-ī-ī-ī-ī-ī-ī-ī-ī-ī-ī-ī-ī
33 A ũncī beṛī mere Khāja kī
34 A U suc ho re utaro jāi ure ur-r kahi yo more Khāja-a se[33]
35 A Morī bɛyã pakaṛ le jāe
36 A Ka yo more Khājā se bɛyã pakaṛ le jāe
03 A I am entranced with the love of Khaja
B //Hh-Hh
04 C Entranced
05 A O entranced--I am entranced with the love of Khaja
06 A I am entranced with the love of Khaja
B //Hh-h
07 C There once was a small kingdom that was located three hundred miles from Ajmer Sharif[34]
08 C The name of the kingdom was Mel Karor
09 C Mira Bai who was a Hindu—was a Maharani in that kingdom
10 C For Khwaja Gharib Nawaz had she boundless love[35]

11	C	Her adoration is presented in the following narrative:
12	C	Mira Bai was the queen of Mel Karor
13	C	To Rana Sangha was she wedded—
14	C	Rana Sangha's queen she apparently was
15	C	But secretly did Mira adore the Khaja
	A	//But secretly–did Mira adore the Khaja
16	A	But secretly did Mira adore the Khaja
17	A	But secretly did Mira adore the Khaja
18	C	Travel she would for three hundred miles
19	C	For a mere glimpse of her beloved in Ajmer
20	C	So twenty years went by
21	C	Never did she go near his shrine—
22	C	For fear that a Maharani she was—
23	C	Pearl anklets wore she around her feet
24	C	The jingle of pearls would create suspicion
25	C	And Khaja would say, "Mira, thou art disrespectful"
26	A	Khaja would say, "Mira, thou art disrespectful"
	B	// A-h ha[36]
27	C	The jingle of pearls would create suspicion
28	C	And Khaja would say, "Mira, thou art disrespectful"
29	C	In the twenty-first year Mira was unable to restrain herself
30	C	And she cried out from the temple steps
31	C	What was her cry? It is presented before the audience:
32	A	"O mighty is my Khaja's abode . . ."
	B	// i-i-i-i-i-i-i-i-i-i-i-i-i-i

The *qawwāls* engage their listeners through the exquisite description of Mira Bai's apparel: the fact that she is a Maharani, or a princess, mentioned in formulaic form at the very outset, arouses the listeners' interest (lines 12–32). The laypeople loved to hear such accounts. Her pearl anklets and their jingle as she walked are sensuous images derived from royalty. The performers talk about Mira Bai's ritual, three-hundred-mile journeys to Ajmer for twenty years. She had to conceal her identity as a Rajput princess who could not be expected to become a devotee of a Muslim Sufi saint. Obviously, the description creates the mystery for the audiences of the speech event. These are storytelling devices that create the *samā*ʿ (the environment) for their audiences. I was amused to hear them sing of Mira Bai as Rana Sangha's Maharani when in fact she was his daughter-in-law. But, then, the discussion is about folk beliefs.

The Mira Bai narrative that the Sabri Brothers sing in England breaks religious and cultural barriers. It further mirrors the inherent holistic nature of Sufi poetry. The myth becomes truly cross-cultural, sung for the diaspora in England. For the *qawwāls*, it is most appropriate to sing of a Rajput princess for their affluent patrons who come from the Asian diaspora of the subcontinent. The linguistic codes of Urdu, devotional Hindi, and Rajasthani are suited for their listeners, who hail from a variety of linguistic backgrounds. The Sabri Brothers' singing about Mira Bai is not unusual. Researchers report that from the thirteenth century onward, Hindu mystical songs were recited at *samā*ʿ gatherings. This was because many of the talented musicians were newly converted Muslims. Shaikh Ahmed from Naharwala in Gujrat, who gave expert renditions of Hindawi *ragās*, lived during this century.[37] Akbar, the Mughal emperor, is said to have been a great admirer of Mira Bai, and his court musician, Tansen, is reported to have adapted her poems to his music.[38] The same is true of Hazrat Amir Khusrau's *qawwālī* discourse, which is based on women's *gīt* or Hindawi songs.

The Mira Bai *qawwālī* in England in 1981 is a modernization of the traditional *qawwālī* formulas, updated and recreated for the cosmopolitan, expatriate Asian audiences in England. Can this transformation be viewed as a development of transnational Islam? Perhaps there is a blend of the traditional shrine context with a modern concert setting, where the singers uphold the sanctity of the environment. This is evident from the closing *salām* (hymn) dedicated to the prophet Muhammad, when the *qawwāls* stand up and fold their hands around their waists, as in the prayer ritual, to sing,

Sarkār Medine vāle tum par lākhõ salām	May thou be blessed a thousand times, O Muhammad, Lord of Medina

An interesting feature of the Mira Bai *qawwālī* is that the singers switch codes within indigenous registers, such as Urdu, devotional Hindi, and Rajasthani. Mira Bai's ecstacy is conveyed in a highly melismatic style in devotional Hindi, with the singers stretching out Mira's cry. Tom Solomon, an ethnomusicologist, and I undertook a linguistic and musical analysis of the following section. The Sabri Brothers and their ensemble mime Mira's voice thus:

32	A	ũncī beṛī mere Khājā kī-ī-ī-ī-ī-ī-ī-ī-ī[39]
	B	// ī-ī-ī-ī-ī-ī-ī-ī-ī-ī-ī-ī-ī-ī-ī-ī-ī-ī
33	A	ũncī beṛī mere Khāja kī
34	A	U such ho re utaro jāi ure ur-r kahi yo more Khāja-a se
35	A	Morī bɛyā̃ pakaṛ le jāe[40]

36	A	Kyo more Khāja se bɛyā̃ pakaṛ le jāe
37	A	Kyo more Khāja se bɛyā̃ pakaṛ le jāe
38	A	Kyo more Khāja se bɛyā̃ pakaṛ le jāe
	B	// Khāja se-e
39	A	Kyo more Khāja se bɛyā̃ pakaṛ le jāe
	C	// bɛyā̃ pakaṛ le jāe
40	A	ū̃ncī beṛī mere Khāja kī
41	A	ū̃ncī beṛī mere Khāja kī
	C	// O-O-O
42	A	ū̃ncī beṛī mere Khāja kī
43	A	ū̃ncī beṛī mere Khāja kī
	C	//O-O-O-O-O
44	A	ū̃ncī beṛī mere Khājā kī
	B	// A-A Aa-a-a - a-a-a
45	A	ū̃ncī beṛī mere Khāja kī
	B	//A-a-A-A
46	A	ū̃ncī beṛī mere Khāja kī
	B	//A-A-A-a
47	C	O Khāja- ā-ā--ā- kī --- ū̃ncī mu --dī--ī
48	C	More Khāja -ā-ā
. . . .		
64	C	Mīrā Bāī ke dil se jo niklī sad ā
65	C	Un ko ban kar sahārā khud ānā paṛā
32	A	"O, mighty is my Khaja's abode
	B	// i-i-i-i-i-i [etc.]
33	A	O, mighty is my Khaja's abode
34	A	Thou, descend, O Khaja, from thy mighty abode
35	A	Thou, take me by the arm[41]
36	A	Thou, take me by the arm, O my Khaja
37	A	Thou, take me by the arm, O my Khaja
38	A	Thou, take me by the arm, O my Khaja
	B	// O Khaja
39	A	Thou, take me by the arm, O my Khaja
	C	// thou take me by the arm
40	A	O, mighty is my Khaja's abode
41	A	O, mighty is my Khaja's abode
	C	// O-O-O
42	A	O, mighty is my Khaja's abode
43	A	O, mighty is my Khaja's abode
	C	//O-O-O-O-O

44	A	O, mighty is my Khaja's abode
	B	// A-A Aa-a-a a a-a-a
45	A	O, mighty is my Khaja's abode
	B	// A-a-A-A
46	A	O, mighty is my Khaja's abode
	B	//A-A-A-a
47	C	O Khaja's—mighty abode—
48	C	My Khaja's
. . . .		
64	C	The cry came from Mira's very heart
65	C	And indeed Khaja had to rescue Mira

Lines 34 to 47 were in duple meter and the melody was repetitive; Solomon called it additive. Line 47 was melismatic—Maqbool Ahmed (C) stretched out the vowels as shown in the transliteration. Solomon's explanation was that, musically, the lines from 47 to 63 were in duple meter on percussion. The voices of *qawwāls* B and C were nearly in free meter. According to Solomon, a disjunct relationship occurred between the voices and the drums. Solomon identified line 64 as the beginning of strophe 3, which is the longest strophe in the narrative, with an abrupt return to triple meter. Solomon diagrammed it as shown in Fig. 3.2.

The Sabri Brothers uphold Mira Bai's devotion to a Sufi mystic in their concert in England because of shared spiritual and linguistic perceptions. The Bhakti poems of Mira Bai had common ideological grounds. She sang about the oppression of women, issues of race and caste prejudices, and religious bigotry that were used to intimidate the people. Mira's poetry and that of the Sufi mystics showed alternative paths for seeking relief. This was done through simple, aesthetic, lyrical compositions, framed in folktales familiar to the people. Spiritual and emotional concerns were transmitted in the vernaculars with which the people could identify. All in all, the Sufi approach was a nonthreatening way to bring spirituality to "the folks."

The pattern of Mira Bai's devotion is not unusual, even today. Early in 1999, I photographed non-Muslim Kolhi and Bhil peasant women at Shah Abdul Latif's shrine in Bhit Shah. I was standing in the shrine courtyard when I suddenly saw a train of graceful, colorfully dressed women in their *ghāgrās* (long skirts). They were all clad in flowered veils. They walked toward the shrine exit and hastened to pickups parked by the roadside in which their menfolk waited to drive them back.

Having discussed various regional myths, I will look at another cross-cultural myth that I heard Abida Parvin sing in concert at the Allama Iqbal

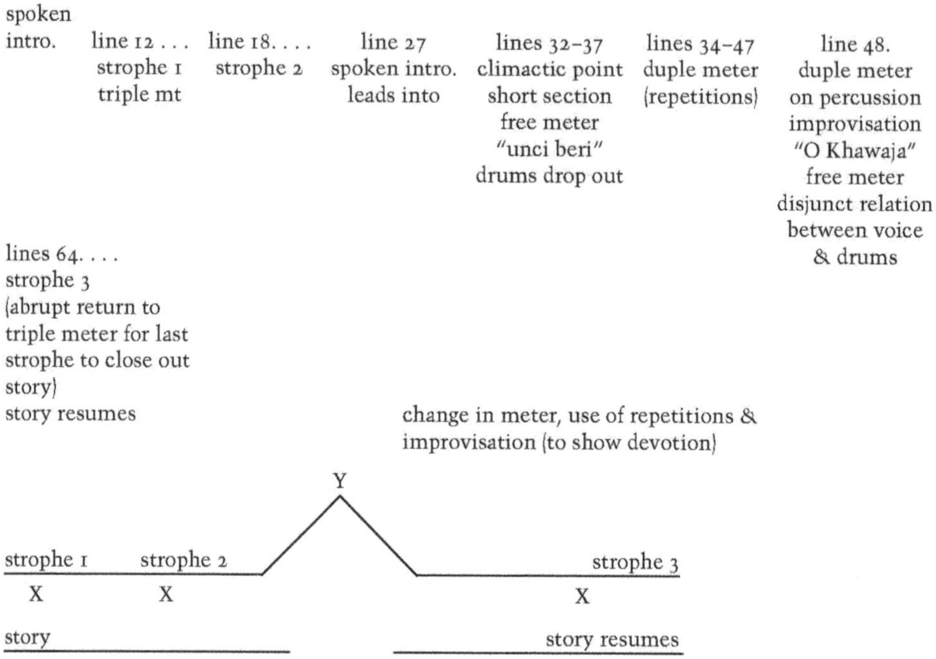
spoken intro.
line 12 . . . strophe 1 triple mt
line 18. . . . strophe 2
line 27 spoken intro. leads into
lines 32–37 climactic point short section free meter "unci beri" drums drop out
lines 34–47 duple meter (repetitions)
line 48. duple meter on percussion improvisation "O Khawaja" free meter disjunct relation between voice & drums
lines 64. . . . strophe 3 (abrupt return to triple meter for last strophe to close out story) story resumes
change in meter, use of repetitions & improvisation (to show devotion)
Y
strophe 1
strophe 2
strophe 3
X
X
X
story
story resumes

3.2 Mira Bai *Qawwālī* model by Tom Solomon: University of Texas at Austin

Open University in Islamabad. She sang the renowned Layla-Majnun story to talk about color and gender. Her intention was to entertain and also to create sociopolitical awareness through myth about the minority provinces or marginalized groups in the country before an august audience of government bureaucrats.

This folktale traveled to the subcontinent from Arabia, although it is also used in the Persian literary traditions: Qays or Majnun was the son of a powerful tribesman of the Banu Amir in Arabia. He was a Syed who claimed descent from the prophet Muhammad. Qays's parents had him late in life, and being the only child he was pampered. He was sent to one of the best teachers in the tribe and did well. While in school, he met Layla, a miracle of creation. She was slender like a cypress tree, and her eyes were like those of a gazelle. She was extremely beautiful, with beautiful dark hair. Her dark black hair won her the name Layla, for does not "Layl" mean "night" in Arabic? And dark as the night was the color of her hair.[42]

Layla and Qays fell in love, and their romance blossomed to such a degree that Qays became obsessed with her. All his friends called him a *majnun*, a madman. The story spread even further, until Layla's family and her tribe were embarrassed. The romance brought shame on them for two reasons: first, because everyone in the community gossiped about their daughter; second, because it was a *majnun* who pursued Layla. Their honor was at stake and thus Layla was withdrawn from school, although she loved Qays. But, for fear of her family and tribe's reputation, she could not express her love.

Majnun went around confessing his love for Layla, and even sent his father to her family to propose marriage, but her family would not relent. Their main objection was that he was a *majnun*. So it went on for several years until Majnun became a poet and wrote the most exquisite love poetry, and his equal could not be found in the whole of Arabia.[43] In his despair for Layla, this poet and lover took to the forests and became a shepherd, with the animals becoming his friends. In the course of time Layla's family married her off against her will to a wealthy tribesman, Ibn Salam. She refused to consummate the marriage. Instead, she and Qays kept exchanging love poems through messengers. Several years went by and Layla's husband died, still hoping that one day he would have her love. Some years after his death, Layla also died. She had grown old pining for Qays. After her death, Qays became even more insane. He spent all his time lamenting at her grave, where his friends found him.[44] Consequently, Majnun became the model of the absolute lover in Arabic poetry and the legend spread to Persia and the Pakistan-India subcontinent, where the Layla-Majnun romance was absorbed into the poetic traditions.

By the time the legend came to the subcontinent, Layla had become "black" and a whole discourse of a dark-complected Layla emerged in the indigenous literatures. Perhaps her dark black hair got transformed into a black Layla. The poetry in this region speaks of a black Layla, whom Majnun loved despite her "color." Abida Parvin sings such a song in her concert at the Open University. She attributes the poetry to the Sufi poet Khawaja Ghulam Farid, who wrote in Siraiki. The voice in the song is that of a woman who laments her separation from her beloved. Sometimes this voice becomes Layla's, at others it becomes Hir's:

A 04 Yār mēḍā pardes gayā O mē kalṛā ves keresā̃-ā̃-ā̃
A 05 Vo lā-
A 06 Hār singhār kū saṭ khatā̃ mē surmā mul na paisā̃
A 07 Tuṭṭī tund cole vālī O mē kapṛe mul na dhosā̃
A 08 Vo la- akhe Ghulām Farīd-ā
A 09 O judhā̃ yār āngaṛ āsī tadā̃ hār singhār keresā̃
A 10 Lokā̃ ākhīyā-ā Majne-e-e tū-ū
A 11 Lokā̃ ākhīyā Majne tū --" O terī Lailā rang dī kāli-" Vo lā

A 12 Majne ɛ javāb ditā: " Tusā̃ akh nahī̃ vekhuṇ vālī-ī-ī
A 13 Cite varq Qurān de-e Qurā-ān de
A 14 Cite varq Qurān de O jehdī sīāhī rang dī kālī- Vo mī-ā̃
A 15 Ākhe Ghulām Farīd-ā O jeh nāl dil aṛ pave O gorī hove yā kālī"
A 16 Mēḍā ʿiśq vī tū̃
A 17 Mēḍā yār vī tū̃ O-O- mēdā iśq vī tū̃- mēdā yār vī tū̃
A 04 My beloved is away in a distant land—my existence will I make black
A 05 O la-
A 06 All adornment do I cast away--never will I put kohl in my eyes
A 07 For clothes have I no desire --never again will I wash my clothes
A 08 O la- says Ghulam Farid
A 09 Only when my beloved returns will I adorn myself again
A 10 To Majnun did the folks say --------
A 11 To Majnun did the folks say, " Thy Laila is dark to look at ----- O la"
A 12 To them did Majnun reply "Thou hast no eye to see!
A 13 "White are the leaves of the Quran---of the Quran
A 14 "White are the leaves of the Quran--black is the ink on them--O God"
A 15 Says Ghulam Farid, "When thou entanglest thyself in love, it matters not whether she be fair or dark"
A 16 Thou art my love
A 17 Thou art my beloved---O-O thou art my love--thou art my beloved

After the female lover has mourned her abandonment, Abida Parvin brings in the reference to Majnun. The poet Ghulam Farid quotes the parable from Majnun, which Abida Parvin sings: When folks asked Majnun about his black Layla, he retorted with an example from the Quran. He questioned them: If the pages from the Quran can be white but the ink be black, then what is so wrong for him to love a woman of color—for isn't it all a matter of the heart—the heart can be entangled with anyone, whether it be a woman of color or one who is fair skinned. In fact, it is the poet Ghulam Farid who asks this question on behalf of Qays or Majnun. In this section there are two themes, one is separation from the beloved or the spiritual mentor and the other is ethnicity. I find it strange that Abida Parvin should sing this narrative at a concert for bureaucrats from the government, talking about issues of ethnicity and gender.

Most of the myths in this chapter are transliterated from concert performances in Pakistan and the United Kingdom. The audiences are urban and highly literate: people of the diaspora in England and the academy and bureaucrats in Pakistan. The singers therefore transmit metaphoric messages through myth and local color, "speaking" to their audience using the multimedia.

To sum up, the Sufi poets who wrote about the tragic deaths of the lovers in their myths did not consider them to be tragic, because they did not interpret them from that standpoint. Their lovers suffer so that they become free of the world and from the matter called the "self" that is tied to the transitory self. For the lovers, death is the opening to the real world, as there can be no fulfillment for them on this earth. This is perhaps a foregone conclusion in Sufi mysticism.[45] Therefore, the musicians sing of the brilliant ever changing metaphors: the *gharā̤* on which Sohni tries to cross the river Chenab; Sassi's struggles through the Thal or the desert; Hir's *jogī* who plays the flute; and Majnun, the ecstatic poet who pines for Layla.

CHAPTER 4

The Female Voice in Sufi Ritual

THE LYRICS

In this chapter I discuss the evolution of the female voice in Sufi poetry as it developed over the centuries, especially in the narratives of the musicians who sing it now. I discuss Amir Khusrau (d. 1325 AD), whose poetry and compositions were sung in United India in the thirteenth and fourteenth centuries and continue to be sung even today.[1] This is true of the poetry of the other Sufi literati who wrote in the subcontinent. How these texts have been adapted to other genres outside *qawwālī* and *sufiānā-kalām* are additionally explored. The changes have come about as the rituals have gradually moved out of the shrine contexts to the more public contexts of the *melā*s or folk festivals and now of course the concert settings, where the musicians use sophisticated electronic media in addition to traditional instrumentation. The multimedia have played a significant role in the changes. The expatriate speech communities outside the subcontinent who patronize the singing of Islamic mystical poetry in western, Middle Eastern, and South Asian settings have further contributed to the changes in the rituals. They have made the contexts eclectic. Their interest has further generated the involvement of other international groups and world music institutions. These factors have modernized the genres that are discussed here.

However, the musicians themselves have largely been responsible for the changes in the rituals. While on the one hand they are involved in the modernization process, on the other hand they uphold the traditions. Whatever improvisations they make are within the linguistic frames that have existed for centuries. Additionally, they have made modulations due to the needs of the speech communities themselves, especially those living in the diaspora. The traditions of singing Sufi poetics grew in the last quarter of the twentieth century, going back and forth between the native cultures and the diaspora. I noticed a trend among musicians to reinforce the singing of the *qaul* and the *girāhs* in concert settings for their expatriate audiences in the same manner that they would do in the shrines.[2] This is pronounced in Abida Parvin's *sufiānā-kalām* concerts where she has introduced Amir Khusrau's *qaul* in Arabic. The *qaul* and *girāh* are used in the devotional *qawwālī* contexts of Sufi shrines and have been sung ever since Amir Khusrau's time.[3]

Some analytical and ethnographic work in the field is commendable and facilitated my own research.[4] However, that work is textual or deals with ethnomusical theory such as Qureshi's. The transliteration methodology of this research that looks at the live speech of the musicians' narratives attempts to throw into relief the female voices and the shifts in the rituals. The female voice is further highlighted through interviews with the musicians and other professionals.

I further look at how the different geographical locations in Pakistan and the speech communities within the country contributed to the changes in the rituals. I attempt to explain this through a linguistic map. Additionally, I have devised a model through which I try to integrate the nodes such as linguistics, themes, myths, ecology, and performances to understand the female voices that are discussed in this book (see Fig. 1.5).

There are several explanations underlying the theory of the female voice in the Sufi poetry of the subcontinent. The most basic appears to be the fact that the poetic form of this discourse is rooted in the indigenous linguistic traditions. Generally, it is the woman who professes divine love, particularly in the *dohā* and *gīt* composed in Khari Boli or Hindawi, and which is investigated here in Sufi poetry. *Dohās* and *gīt* are simple poetic constructions in Hindi, generally, with dominant female voices used in devotional contexts. Amir Khusrau, who is said to be one of the earliest exponents of *qawwāli*, used the Khari Boli form of the *dohā* and the *gīt* as lyrics in a number of his melodies where the speaker is a female.[5] Although many of his best *qawwālīs* are composed in the chaste Persian *ghazal* form, he did frequently use Khari Boli and its simple poetic constructions for his native listeners who largely belonged to the grassroots cultures. Even some of his elitist *qawwālī* compositions are sung in Khari Boli and Purbi. He also experimented by mixing the Persian *ghazal* and the Khari Boli *dohā* to compose his popular lyrics, such as "Ze hāl-e miski makun tagāful" (Be not negligent of the state of the dispossessed).

Unfortunately, a large part of Khusrau's written Khari Boli or Hindawi poetry is lost, but I have researched several of his *dohās* and *gīts*, which are sung in the oral traditions. There are dominant female voices in the poetry. I have investigated native scholars, written texts, and multimedia sources in Pakistan and India to explore the female voices in his lyrics. There is enough evidence to support my argument that substantial Sufi poetry in the subcontinent is sung in the female voice. Male musicians use inflection, and by default, the female voices are heard in their syntax and semantics. In fact, during the early stages of the investigation, the discovery of the many dimensions of the female voices was quite unusual and aroused my interest in the present exploration. I have transliterated some lyrics of Amir Khusrau from live recordings on audiocassettes and videos. The melodies are sung as female narratives and form the basis of discussion.

The *dohā* in Hindi poetry is the equivalent of the Persian or Urdu *ghazal*, and for several centuries it has remained a popular form of poetic composition for devotional purposes. The *dohā*, like the Persian or Urdu *ghazal*, conveys an idea or an image in two verses. It has also been described as an old popular Prakrit and Hindi meter in which a couplet is put together where the two verses rhyme.[6] The *dohā* has additionally been used to express eroticism, valor, meditation, the common life, ecology, proverbs, sayings, and maxims in mystical literature. Because of its simplicity this poetic form has also been used to describe spiritual states and experiences using sensual imagery.[7] Furthermore, the poetic form has been the medium of expression in the mendicants' lore or the roving-minstrel traditions. Poets such as Kabir and Nanak used it to write their mystical poetry.[8]

The poet Amir Khusrau found the *dohā* an appropriate form for the lyrics in his *qawwālīs* and other Sufi poetry. His poetry is now sung even outside the *qawwālī* tradition. I have identified the following *dohās* in his compositions from the live-speech events, which musicians have created for the electronic media. Here are some *dohās* that Ustad Ghulam Mustafa Khan has sung. The first two verses (*dohās*) are Amir Khusrau's spontaneous creations on the death of his shaikh and mentor, Hazrat Nizamuddin Auliya, who is also known as Mahbub-e Ilahi or God's Beloved. It is reported that on hearing of his shaikh's death, Amir Khusrau tore his clothes and blackened his face to lament:[9]

Gorī sowe sej par,[10]	The Beloved lies on her couch
Mukh pe ḍāle kes	Black tresses scattered on her face
Cal Khusrau ghar āpne,	Khusrau, let us go home now,
Rɛn bahī sab des	For the darkness shrouds the earth

Ustad Ghulam Mustafa Khan further sings some *dohā*s that Khusrau composed, and which I have translated with assistance from written texts and Hindi informants.[11]

Khusrau rɛn suhāg ki[12]	Khusrau, that night of the nuptial,
Jāgī pī ke sang	Awake remained with the Beloved
Tan mero, man pīo ke,	The body mine, the soul the Beloved's,
Do bhāī ek rang	Two beings, one color
. . . .	
Cakwa cakwi do jane[13]	*Cakwa cakwi* are two beings
In mat mār koī	None ought to persecute them
Eh māre Kartar ke	Almighty's beaten are they
Rɛn bīchohā ho-e	Separated are they in the dark

I have further investigated current oral sources from the multimedia to find that Khusrau adapted songs or *gīt*s that women sang at seasonal festivals, to write lyrics in praise of his shaikh, Hazrat Nizamuddin Auliya. Like the *dohā*, a *gīt* is a simple poetic construction used to compose a song or a hymn.[14] Here is a *qawwālī* composition called "Rang" (Color), which Shankar Shambu Qawwal has sung in the original melody that Amir Khusrau composed and which I have complemented with a written source.[15] Shahabi and Kakorvi discuss the lyric as a *gīt*. Both the *speaker* and the *addressee* are women; the daughter is the *speaker*, expressing her ecstasy. The Festival of Colors is also the Indian festive event associated with *Holi*, in which individuals in a community play with each other and sprinkle liquid colors for fun, thus soiling their partners' clothes. The *Rang* in *qawwālī* is a constituent of the composition and marks a celebration: In this context it is a celebration of the speaker's union with the spiritual mentor, the *murshid*.[16] I break up the lines here in the Hindi text to identify the gender markers, which are underlined for the reader:

Aj rang hɛ e mā̃	Today is the *rang*, O mother
Rang harī	Green is the color[17]
Mere Mehbūb ke ghar	In my Beloved's abode
Rang hɛ rī	Is the "color," O mother
Mohe pīr pāy-o, Nizāmuddin Aulīyā	I a beloved mentor, Nizamuddin Auliya, have found
Des bides mē̃	Many a country and foreign soil
Dhūṇḍi phirī hū̃	Have I searched
Torā rang mohe bhāyo	Thy color do I fancy

Rē--Nijāmuddin Aulīyā[18]	O Nizamuddin Auliya,
Aiso rang mẽ aur nahī̃	Such color have I not
Dekhī	Seen
Sakhī-rī[19]	O my female friend

The underlying play here, with emphasis on color, is also a celestial one. The color and the celebration also suggest the prophet Muhammad's *mi'rāj* (ascension to heaven). The *mī'rāj* is a favorite *qawwālī* theme in which the musicians invoke bridal imagery.

Amir Khusrau's narrator in the discourse is a daughter who speaks to her mother about the festivity in her mentor's abode. The ritual play in the poetics and the invocation of color imagery fits in with the native social and devotional contexts of the weddings, the shrines, the festivals, and ritual celebrations. In fact, in the semantics the mother becomes the conduit of the speaker's ecstasy for the beloved, that is, *Mahbub-e Ilahi* (God's Beloved). The ecstasy is expressed through color symbolism. Thus, the entire mystical rhapsody is transmitted in the female voices where the daughter is the *speaker* and the mother is the *listener*. In this section of the melody, the following phrases convey the gender:

Rang hɛ-rī	"*hɛ*" is the verb to be, the fact that there is a celebration of the Rang festival; "*rī*" is the female gender marker, a term of address that establishes intimacy.
Dhūṇḍi phīrī hū̃	*Dhūṇḍna* is a verb meaning "to search or look for"; "*ḍi*," the suffix, gender marker; *phirnā* is a verb meaning "to roam"; "*ī*," the suffix, is the gender marker.
Dekhī	*Dekhnā* is a verb meaning "to see"; "*ī*," the suffix, is the gender marker.
Sakhī-rī	*Sakhī* is an intimate female friend; "*rī*," the suffix, establishes intimacy.

All these are distinct syntactic constructions for the female. The marker "*rī*" establishes the intimacy of the relationship, very much like Nusrat Fateh Ali Khan's "*nī*" in his Panjabi *qawwālī*s in which the speakers are females.

Amir Khusrau created many of his compositions using *bol* (verses) related to the seasonal festivals and wedding rituals that are also used as Sufi songs according to context.[20] He even named his *rāgās* (melodic musical scales) after the seasons or the events, for example, there are compositions called "Rāg Bahar" (Spring melody), "Rāg Holi Khamāch" (Holi melody), "Rāg Basant" (Basant melody), "Rāg Sarang" (Music melody), the "Rang" (Color), and many more.[21] The *qaul* and the *tarānā* are said to be the induction of the Perso-Arabic elements into South Asian music that lead to *qawwālī*.[22] Here there is no female narrator as in the "Rang."

Another melody, which I have transcribed from a video created by Pakistan Television, is called "Bābul" and is sung as a *ṭhumrī*.[23] The lyric and melody are both associated with Hazrat Amir Khusrau, and the video was produced during the centennial celebrations for the poet in Pakistan. The Pakistani speech communities, especially those who migrated to Pakistan during the 1947 partition from North India, identify with the poetic, linguistic, and musical traditions of North India and do much to preserve them. The "Bābul" is a wedding tune that the bride's friends sing at the time of her departure from her father's home. The bride's lament is reported to have been originally sung in the rural districts of Avadh during weddings, with an emotion that brought even the strongest listeners to tears. *Allāvālah*s (people close to God) read spiritual meanings in the lament and wept.[24] This is quite similar to the *Hir* that is sung in the Panjabi traditions and which also brings the listeners to tears. There are esoteric meanings embedded in the composition as the bride's departure from her *bābul* (father's home). It is considered to be the departure from an earthly, transitory life to a transcendental home, which is equated with the home of the in-laws. The ritualistic sending away of the bride in the traditional contexts in the subcontinent is similar to the funeral despite the preceding festivities to celebrate it as an auspicious event:

Kāhe ko bīyāhī bides sun bābul mere	Why hast thou married me in a foreign soil, listen, O my father?
Bhāīõ ko dene mahal do mahal-e	To my brothers thou gave palaces,
	And many, too
Mujh ko dīā pardes	To me thou gave the foreign soil
Re sun bābul mere	Listen, O my father
Ham tore bābul āngānā kī cīṛīyā̃	I am, O father, like the little birds in thy courtyard,
Rɛn base uṛ jāẽ	When night falls, they fly away
Re sun bābul mere	Listen, O my father
Ham tore bābul belay kī kalīyā̃	I am, O father, like the little buds in thy Arabian jasmine
Ghar ghar māngī jāẽ	Every home seeks them
Re sun bābul mere	Listen, O my father
Kāhe ko bīyāhī bides sun bābul mere	Why hast thou married me in a foreign soil, listen, O my father?
. . . .	. . . .

Tāq bharī mẽ nī guṛiā̃ jo choṛī	A mantle full of dolls that I left
To choṛā sahelīõ kā sāth	Left all my female friends
Re sun bābul mere	Listen, O my father
Dole kā pardā uṭhā kar jo dekhā	Lifted I the cover from my palanquin, To see,
To āyā parāyā pardes	The arrival in another's foreign soil
Re sun bābul mere	Listen, O my father
Ye dekh Khusrau yũ mukh bole	Having seen this, Khusrau says,
Jam jam raho suhāg re	"May thou always be blessed in matrimony"
Sun bābul mere	Listen, O my father
. . . .	. . . .

I find the aesthetic construction and the sociolinguistic context of this melody extremely moving, especially the words of its female narrator.

The song where the child-bride calls herself the bird in her father's courtyard or the bud in his Arabian jasmine recurs often in the poetry written in the vernacular languages. These were familiar metaphors for the audiences. The mantle full of dolls that the child-bride leaves behind or the cover that she lifts from the palanquin, to find herself in the strange, unknown home of her in-laws, are powerful but familiar social symbols. They are what T. S. Eliot calls "a cultural node." These were the contexts that poets like Amir Khusrau, Mira Bai, and others in the Sufi and Bhakti traditions addressed through female metaphors and female poetic conventions. Today, they are projected through dramas and documentaries produced for television that highlight gender, class, and socioeconomic caste issues within the fold of patriarchal paradigms.[25]

When the Sufi bards communicated with their listeners, they had to speak in an idiom the audience could understand. Naturally, the speech had to be in the indigenous canons related to women's linguistic and poetic traditions and their rituals. Amir Khusrau was as adept at mixing linguistic codes and literary traditions as he was at creating musical innovations and improvisations in which he used the indigenous resources. In present times, Ustad Nusrat Fateh Ali Khan and Pandit Ravi Shankar created something quite similar through mixing their own native linguistic and musical resources with world music. As a vocalist, Nusrat Fateh Ali Khan generated one of the largest *qawwālī* repertoires in the Pakistani languages, especially in Panjabi, with dominant female voices.[26]

For the Sufi poets women were the major participants or consumers of shrine activity and speech events where Sufi discourse was disseminated. Thus, the linguistic medium and metaphor had to be in voices that were meaningful to women and their networks. I also maintain here that these songs are not just articulated within restricted shrine speech events, they are chanted on all occasions when members of a speech community come together in social contexts, be they celebrations or death rituals.[27] The style of articulation may be adjusted according to the context.

Another composition I have looked at to study the female voice in Sufi discourse is Amir Khusrau's famous "Ze hāl-e miski," which is a novel experiment in the Persian and Hindi *ghazal* form where half the verse is in Persian and the other half in Hindi. Interestingly, my present transcription is based on a duet that Mukesh, a renowned male singer of *ghazal*, and Sudha Malhotra, a female singer, both from the Indian film world, have sung. They take turns singing the verses in Persian and Hindi to create a fascinating context of code switching. In this text the references are to women. The discourse is between two females who talk about love. In the composition Amir Khusrau metaphorically celebrates his own *ʿiśq* (love) for his spiritual mentor, Shaikh Nizamuddin Auliya. Khusrau, the poet, becomes the female who speaks of the intensity of love. I break up the original verse into lines so that the reader can follow the linguistic code. The first line, which is half the verse, is in Persian. In Amir Khusrau's original lyric half the verse is in Persian and the other half in Hindi or Khari Boli, which is a masterpiece of linguistic and poetic creativity. The translation brings out the context and is a poetic representation, not a literal translation:[28]

P[29]	Ze hāl-e miski makun taghaful	Do not be negligent of the dispossessed
H[30]	Dar āie nainā banā-e batiā̃	When thou weavest tales with thine eyes
P[31]	Ke tāb-e hirjra nā dāram-e ja	O love, I can no longer bear the separation
H[32]	Nā leho kāhe lagā-e-chati-ā̃?	Why dost thou not hold me to thy bosom?

From here on, the female singer continues the lyric in Khari Boli or Hindi.

Sakhī pīyā ko jo mẽ nā dekhū̃	O my female friend, if I do not see my beloved
To kaise kāṭū̃ and herī ratiā̃?	How can I endure these dark nights?
Nā nīnd nainā	There is no sleep in the eyes
Na ang chainā	There is no peace for the body
Nā āp ā-vẽ	Neither do you, my Beloved, come!
Nā bhejẽ patīā̃	Nor do you send me letters

"Sakhī" is a favorite word in Khusrau's mystical poetry, which is also sung in *qawwālī*. Women use it in an intimate context to address each other, especially in the *gīt*. I have mentioned the *gīt* earlier as a form that Khusrau used to compose Hindi poetry. *"Pīyā"* in the first line of the preceding section is "the Beloved," a favorite noun/word in Hindi love poetry. There are other such linguistic, aesthetic, and syntactic devices that are used to invoke the female voices in the musicians' narratives.

For instance, the female voice can be seen in this section from a modern-day *qawwālī* that Abdul Rahim Faridi and Abdul Ali Faridi sing.[33] The lyric is transcribed from a concert performance in the United Kingdom, and the linguistic codes are Khari Boli or Hindi mixed with some Panjabi for the musicians' multicultural audiences in the diaspora. The speaker in the lyric is a female, who supplicates Hazrat Muinuddin Chishti of Ajmer, although the vocalists are by default male musicians. The gender markers in the lyric are underlined.

Māngat māngat same guzrīo	A lifetime have I begged
Pehan ke gale kafanī	Wearing a shroud around my neck
Mẽ dar pe jāũ gī	I shall go to thy doorstep
Khwājā kī joganīā	Khwaja's *jogan* [female disciple]
Mẽ ban jāũ gī	I shall become
. . . . .	. . . . .
Sakhī more Khwājā se kahīo:	O female friend, tell my Khwaja,
"Dekhā do jo kuch	"Show whatever
uṭhā ke ghũnghaṭīa"	Lift thy veil"

The qawwals then go on to sing the following short section in Panjabi:

Ā-Ā- Ā-----Ā ---O-O-O-O- Ā	A-A- A -----A ---O-O-O-O- A
Mere Jānīā---A jā- O--O -O	O my Beloved---O come-O--O-O
Mẽ terīā̃ O soṇiā	I am thine, O Beloved
O-O-hā̃--hā̃	O-O-O yes, O yes

And so the musicians continue to sing while they switch codes from Khari Boli to Panjabi. In this lyric, even in the dynamics of code switching, the female voice is retained, which confirms the hypothesis that cross culturally the female voice is dominant in Sufi poetry.

This lyric would have been sung in the same gender, linguistic codes, and style in Amir Khusrau's time in the thirteenth and fourteenth centuries, although perhaps the musical instruments would have been somewhat different. Modern-day *qawwāl* parties use electronic devices in addition to the traditional instruments. The Faridi *qawwāls'* narrative is sung in the established North Indian style of music. The gender construction of the *kafanīā* (shroud) and the *ghungaṭīā* (veil) in the musicians' narrative is interesting, for both are male nouns for objects. Additionally, the vocalists use the genderized form of the noun *jogan*, which already signifies a female mendicant, derived from the male form, the *jogī*. They add the "*īā*" to *jogan* and make it *joganīā*. Such devices convey *ījz* (humility) and further create intimacy in the performance through the forms of address.[34] The *ghungaṭ* invokes bridal imagery (kaśf), which is the lifting of the veil in Sufi poetry and indeed a favorite erotic image with the Sufi poets.

THE FEMALE NARRATORS

In the Sufi poetry sung in the oral traditions in the Siraiki belt around the Multan, Bahawalpur, Mianwali, and northern Sind areas, the female voices are again prominent. A large number of Abida Parvin's lyrics are derived from resources such as the *kāfīs* (short verses for expressing mystical thoughts). The *kāfī* is a lyrical composition meant to be sung with music, its subject is mystical, and its central theme is repeated in the refrain to create the *samāʿ* (the context). It uses folk motifs from the environment to emphasize the mentor-disciple relationship. Furthermore, the earthly metaphors (*ʿiśq-e majāzī*) communicate *ʿiśq-e haqīqī* (spiritual union with God). Shaikh Farid, also known as Baba Farid (1173–1262 AD), is said to be the creator of the *kāfī* form in which the human soul is treated as a female and contextualized in the imagery of the medieval institution of marriage.[35]

The *kāfīs* that are investigated here are the creation of the Siraiki Sufi poet Khawaja Ghulam Farid. The female narrator in the *kāfīs* mourns her separation from her beloved, who has gone to a distant land:[36]

Mẽ tă tekŭ mintă kardī [37]	I beg thee, O beloved
Sāval asā nŭ bhāl	O beloved, cast thy good fortune on us

In another *kāfī* the female lover is described in bridal imagery such as the following:[38]

Musāg malīndā gūzar gayā ḍehn sārā [39]	The entire day have I spent to polish my teeth
Singhār karīndā guzar gayā ḍehn sārā	The entire day have I spent to adorn myself

Kajlā pāyām surkhī lāyam	Kohl I put on my eyes, my lips I color
Kītam yār vasārā	The beloved I recall
Kāng ūḍenḍe ūmar vihāntī	A lifetime have I spent to shoo away the crow[40]
Ayā nā yār pīyārā	But thou, my beloved, never came

Khawaja Farid additionally uses Hir's voice for that ultimate spiritual union or *'iśq-e haqīqī* through the imagery of *'iśq-e majāzī* (earthly love), as in these lines:[41]

Haṭan mē Rānjhaṇ hoī	With Ranjha have I become one
Rehā farq nā koī	Between us is there no separation

These *kāfis* are somewhat similar to the images of the suffering and pining female in Bhakti poetry where the theme of separation is called *virāhā* and its narrator the *virāhīnī*.[42] The feelings of separation expressed through the female narrator belong to the indigenous poetic traditions in the vernacular languages. The woman professes divine love. The *sufiānā-kalām* singers, like Abida Parvin, Reshma, and Surraiya Multanikar, sing in the *virāhīnī* voices. Furthermore, *virāhīnī* poetry is also sung in the Sindhi devotional contexts, such as the *mauluds* that celebrate the Prophet's birth. In these songs the devotee is a young bride or bride-to-be who awaits her bridegroom, who is equated with the prophet Muhammad. All kinds of bridal imagery, such as the wedding ceremonies of the *mehndi* (henna), is expressed in the lyrics. Interestingly, such poetry equates the concept of the *virāhā* with the Sufi concept of *'iśq*, the burning, consuming longing of the soul for union with God.[43] Amir Khusrau also adapted these voices in his discourse.

Some native critics claim that the use of the female narrator in the Sufi poetry of North India could partially be an influence from the Persian poetic genre called the *cāmā*.[44] Like the Hindawi *gīt*, it is said to be a popular poetic form suitable for adaptation to music and was used in rural Persia for women's songs. The *cāmā* is a poem or a song in Persian not exceeding seventeen couplets.[45] Thus, the lyrics that are studied so far appear to belong to a variety of indigenous, hybrid, oral poetic traditions.

Another poetic convention which is linked with the female voice is that of *rekhtī*, one of the major poetic genres in the Deccani literature of South India. *Rekhtī* is a subgenre of Urdu poetry written in the *ghazal* form in which the narrator is a woman and where the narrative idiom, too, is said to be that of women: "*aurtõ kī bolī.*" *Rekhtī* is set in gendered opposition to *rekhta* (by which standard Urdu *ghazal* poetry is known) and seems to have become equated with any poetry having a female narrator, regardless of poetic diction.[46] The presence of the female narrator in the Deccani poetry has made it noncanonical in the mainstream Urdu literature. The descriptive expression found in the canonical North Indian literatures to discuss such poetry, "*aurat kī taraf se jazbāt kā izhār karnā,*" means expression of passions or emotions from the woman's side.[47] Petievich further uses Platt's definition of *rekhtī*, which is derived "(from *rekhtah*), s.f. Hindustani verse, written in the language of women and expressing the sentiments, etc. peculiar to them," to argue that generally poetic conventions of canonical Perso-Arabic literatures have marginalized creations where the narrator is the female, thus confirming my hypothesis that the female voice is predominant in the grassroots, indigenous *sufiānā-kalām* traditions and sometimes the *qawwālī* discourse in indigenous contexts.

It appears then that since Sufi poetry in general uses the *rekhtī*, the *dohā*, the *kāfī*, or the *vāī* for its narratives, as in Shah Abdul Latif's poetry, there is generally a female narrator in the discourse. The poetry is in the female narratives such as Sassi or Marvi's voice. Due to the presence of the female narrator, poetry like the *rekhtī* is considered a subgenre in the canonical poetic traditions of North India. The canonical literatures of the other vernacular languages have to be investigated for samples, and the female voices of Sufi poetry have to be situated within those canons for evaluation. However, since this poetry was meant to be sung for ordinary people who were barely literate, there was no point in using the canonical Perso-Arabic forms in the assemblies where it was sung. For the same reasons then it can be said that the Sufi poets used women's speech, as in the *cakkī-nāmā* and the *carkhi-nāmā*, where the narrator is the woman who sings at the grinding or spinning wheel. Jairazbhoy, in his fieldwork among the folk performers of Rajasthan, observed that, although such discourse was addressed to the male listeners, there were also female participants and listeners in the assemblies who were hidden from view "or were behind the *cilman* or the screen."[48] The poetry was directed to them as well. The Sufi created spiritual semantics that they sang or recited for their indigenous audiences.

Irrespective, Nusrat Fateh Ali Khan's use of adaptive strategies to bring the grassroots *sufiānā-kalām* traditions within the folds of *qawwālī* through feminine myths is a major contribution in the fusion of linguistic and musical traditions. He was able to integrate his repertoire effectively within the fold of world music. This may very well be a part of his training with his *qawwāl* lineage and may need to be explored further by listening to the repertoire of his father, Ustad Fateh Ali Khan, or those of his uncles Ustad Mubarik Ali Khan and Ustad Salamat Ali Khan. All the musicians trained him through the classical-music traditions of the subcontinent. In my personal interview with Nusrat Fateh Ali Khan, he said that he commissioned Bari Nizami, Ahmed Nadeem Qasmi, and other national poets to write his lyrics. His songwriters recreated the traditional, indigenous myths and texts for him.

I did find that the Bulle Shah *qawwāls* sing the Sufi poet's Panjabi poetry in the Panjabi *ang* (style), where they create the female myths in their lyrics. The female myths are generally sung in the *sufiānā-kalām* of the vernacular languages with minimal musical instruments, the most basic being the *yaktārā*. However, one may claim that due to the large Panjabi speech communities within the country and in the diaspora, musicians like Nusrat Fateh Ali Khan and Mehr Ali and Sher Ali can be identified with the Panjabi ang of *qawwālī* performance. This is in contrast to the North Indian style of the Sabri Brothers, who sing in Urdu. The differences lie mainly in the linguistic resources.

Another input on the female narrator in Sufi discourse is that both Sufi Islam and the Bhakti movement were revolts against the established clerical orders. The established orders took upon themselves the interpretation of the faith, creating power structures for the ruling classes. Economic hegemony could only be sustained through religious, social, and cultural structures upheld by clerics and patriarchs. "Shame" and "honor" in this context became associated with control of women's sensibilities. I cite the improvised Sufi poetry that Abida Parvin used in her 1985 performance in Islamabad: There are references from Shah Abdul Latif's poetry and Khawaja Ghulam Farid's texts. The musician certainly used frames from Sufi poetry to chastise the religious establishment and to speak for marginalized groups.

The clerics, especially the Brahmins, tried to annihilate the female energy cults and replace them with the dominant male cults. But this was prevented by the countermovements having their roots in the masses.[49] Among such countermovements were the devotional discourses of the Sufis and the Bhakti.

MOTHERS AND DAUGHTERS

In the Sufi discourse of the subcontinent, the visibility of female power is expressed through the female narrators, the female myths, and the intergender and intragender relationships, especially between mothers and daughters. The myths are brought out in the oral lore, such as in this *kāfī* from Shah Hussain, the Panjabi Sufi poet. Pathana Khan sings the narrative in Siraiki:

Mā̃ ɛ nī mē̃ kenū̃ ākhā̃?	O my mother, to whom shall I tell?
Dard vichauṇ dā hāl?	To whom narrate the agony of my separation?

In several texts, which are explored here, the Sufi poets seem to follow the Quranic injunctions that advocate reverence for the mother as the creator of life, for example, Sura 4:1, which says,

> And (reverence) the womb
> (That bore you)

Sura 16:78 affirms,

> It is He who brought you forth
> From the wombs
> Of your mothers
> When ye knew nothing; and He
> Gave you hearing and sight
> And intelligence and affection

These concepts are built into the worldview of the speech communities for whom the Sufi poets created their devotional assemblies. Cross culturally, the same theme is found in Shah Abdul Latif's *kapā'ītī* (cotton-spinning songs) in his *Risālo:*[50]

> Not withstanding the spinners
> Carded the strands well
> And spun out very fine yarn
> Accumulated wealth, O mother

This text, like the *cakkī-nāmas* and the *carkhī-nāmas*, uses the spinning of cotton as a spiritual metaphor. The Sufis, especially the Qadiriyya in the cotton-growing areas along the Indus, used *kāpā'ītī* for their poetry.[51]

The intragender relationships appear in the lyric sung by Tufail Niazi, a Panjabi folksinger, when he sings the *Hir*.[52] This is a moving context in the narrative as Hir realizes that she has been poisoned. Ranjha has gone to Takht Hazara to bring his *barat* (wedding party). Hir invokes her lament and begs her mother, Maliki, to perform all the rituals of a Panjabi wedding when Ranjha arrives. She makes Maliki her ally against patriarchy:

Mãɛ nī jad Rānjhāṇ āve	O my mother, when Ranjha returns
Būhe tel cuāvẽ	Dribble thou oil at the doorstep for him[53]
Sārā e pinḍ jitnā vī	The entire village, all of them,
Ode khūn dā verī-e	Are thirsty for his blood
Odī jān dā verī-	They are all after his blood
Magar tū merī mā̃-ē	But thou art my mother
Menū̃ ode nāl piyār-e	Thou knowest I love him
Ik enī gal kar dẽvī	Only do me one little favor
Mā̃-e nī	O my mother,
Jad Rānjhāṇ āve	When Ranjha comes
Te būhe tel cuāvẽ	Dribble thou the oil at the doorstep
Kar ke śagan	Perform thou the rituals
Javā̃yā̃ vāle	Which are done for a son-in-law
Cum sir gal nāl lā̃nvī	Kiss his forehead, hold him to thy heart
Mandṛā bol nā muhõ ākhī	Utter thou no harsh words
Tū mathe vaṭ nā pā̃vī	Let there be no frowns on thy forehead
Pardesī dī bā̃ phaṛ ke	Hold thou the exile's arm
Merī qabar te ān biṭhā̃vī	And bring him to my grave

In the intragender dialogue between Hir and Maliki, Hir says that she will herself tie the ceremonial wreath of flowers around his crown, which is done for a bridegroom.

Kithe dithṛa Rānjhān merā?	Where is my Ranjha lost?
Mẽ pā̃vā̃ sehra	I shall tie the flower wreath around his crown

In the recital, Hir uses the metaphor of the exile both for herself and Ranjha. She becomes an exile when she is forced into the palanquin to go to the strange land of the Kheras, and now Ranjha becomes an exile, coming into Cucak's territory to marry her.

Hir's relationship with her mother, Maliki, is indeed complex: the mother is both the confidant and the mediator between her daughter and patriarchy. At times she supports her daughter. At other times she reprimands Hir's actions and her involvement with Ranjha:[54]

Menū̃ saṛiā lokā̃ diyā̃ taniā̃ ne,	My heart burns to hear the taunts from people
Loī śarm dīmukh tu tudh lāī	Thou hast cast shame to the winds
Mār ḍakare karan gev vaḍ ke tere	They will cut thee into pieces

Cucak bāp te sakā Sultan bhāi	Thy father, Cucak, and thy brother Sultan
Aḍarīe cancal hārīe nī saḍe	Thou wanton, spoilt, playful hussy!
Sarē tū̃ ɛ kī khāk pāi?	What dust thou throwest in our faces?
Cūrī kuṭ ke[55]	Thou poundest bread for dessert
Uṭh ke nit Bele jāē	So that thou can go to the pastures?
Ranjhe de pās jēvē dādiā̃ ne?	To meet that Ranjha, as thou would meet thy paternal granny, aye?

In another instance, Maliki scolds Hir for retorting, in the manner of low-born women. Here, she uses caste distinctions to emphasize Hir's "wantonness."[56]

Karan mā̃ peyā̃ nāl javāb	Answering back even their mothers and fathers
Sā̃vē kuṛiā̃	Only daughters of
Bhaṭ lohārā̃ tarkhāniā̃ nī[57]	Flatterers, blacksmiths, and carpenters do,[58]
Nāl caṛā̃ karan fazūl harkatā̃	Then doing silly things
Kuṛīā̃ dhobanā̃ āte mūciaṇiā̃ nī	Only daughters of washerwomen and shoemakers will do

Although Hir's situation is a tragic one, I found immense humor in both the written and oral sources. Both sections above demonstrate this. Maliki makes fun of Hir when she suspects her motives for leaving the house to go out. She makes fun of Hir's preparations to meet Ranjha as though she were visiting her grandmother. I found it in a *qawwālī* that Nusrat Fateh Ali Khan sang. Hir asks her mother in jest,

Rānjhā khasnī- ē?	Stealest thou Ranjha from me?
Kheṛā dasnī-ē?	Showest thou the Khera to me, aye?

In the instances that are discussed here, it appears that the isomorphisms of gender, class, caste, and religion are formulated in myth that is sung and in which the dominant voices are those of women. In using such myths, the Sufi poets were fully aware that they were creating oral discourse that was meant to be sung in ethnographic contexts for the people. They used verbal art to address social issues in accordance with radical Sufi Islam.

It is interesting to see similar relationships between mothers and daughters in the Persian version of the Layla-Majnun myth written by Ganjavi Nizami, a Persian poet around 584 AH (the second half of the seventh century AD). As Layla lay in bed, quite certain that her death was near, she spoke to her mother thus:[59]

> My mother, oh my dear mother . . . I have suffered so much in secret that now I must talk. Before my soul escapes, the grief in my heart breaks open the seal on my lips. . . . Listen to me mother! When I am dead, dress me like a bride. Make me beautiful. As a salve from my eyes, take dust from Majnun's path. Prepare indigo from his sorrow, sprinkle the rosewater for his tears on my head and veil me in the scent of his grief. I want to be clad in a blood-red garment, for I am a blood-witness like the martyrs. Red is the color of the feast! Is not death my feast? Then cover me in the veil of earth, which I shall never lift again.

Layla continues her lament with her mother and says in grief,

> He will come, my restless wanderer—I know. He will sit at my grave searching for the moon, yet seeing nothing but the veil. . . . Treat him well, comfort him, never look harshly upon him . . . because I have loved him. . . . When he comes, mother, and you see him, give him this message for me! Tell him: "when Layla broke the chain of the world, she went thinking of you lovingly, faithful to the end. . . . ." Tell him that, mother!

One wonders if the Hir dialogue with her mother is directly adapted from the Layla-Majnun myth in Persian. It is quite possible that this is the case, as Sufi poets like Waris Shah and others were well read in Persian and Arabic literatures. And if Waris Shah was using sources such as Ahmed Gujjar's creation of the text, as is claimed, then the poets who created the narrative were quite erudite in Persian and Arabic literary sources.

However, the cross-cultural and cross-linguistic connections of the female narrators are quite interesting. Can it be assumed that these voices are modeled on the fertility cults of the Indus Valley and its neighboring regions? Jairazbhoy and Catlin's recent film of folk performers in Kacch of Indian Gujrat demonstrates that Shah Abdul Latif's poetry of the *Risālo* is sung there in the Sindhi language.[60] The filmed sections show performers singing Shah's Mumal-Rano, a Sindhi-Baluchi myth of lovers in the mystic poetry of the region. In my discussions with a number of researchers it appears that there is the possibility of a continuum of historicized myths and discourse from Rajasthan to Sumeria.[61]

THE POLITICS OF THE FEMALE MYTH

There is evidence of the female power principle in the Sassi myth that originated in Baluchistan and Sind, the area currently referred to as a continuum in ethnomusicology, based on legends and mystical discourse sung in the region. Sassi is said to have been a ruler. Assuming that there were matrilineal structures among the Brahui who live in Baluchistan, the myth expresses the conceptual worldview of a community and the "continued visibility of the power of women as part of the cultural heritage" and therefore as a part of historicized discourse.[62]

When I interviewed Alan Faqir, a musician who sings Sufi poetry in Sindhi, and asked him about the female myths, this is how the discussion evolved between us.[63]

> A: Tell me something—why do you all sing these myths of females like Sassi and Sohni?
> F: The listeners' interests are in these myths—they love to hear these *dastans* [narratives]—they like to hear, "Once upon a time there was a king—" they love to hear stories like—

And he sang:

> F: Marvi is not in the Malir — There is no justice with the amir
> Marvi is not in her homeland — There is no justice even with the chief[64]

Alan Faqir exclaimed, "You see, there is no justice even with the chief—!" He went on to recite:

> F: Punnu is not in the Kec — Sind is not the amir[65]

Alan Faqir asserted in his interview about Sind:

> F: It has been looted—it has been plundered—it has been assaulted—but it goes on—it has not died—it will not die—it has existed for centuries and it shall exist—Sindhri[66] is beaten—and yet Sindhri goes on—it will go on even in its misery—it will not sink—such as when the Mongols came—the Tartars came—the Sassanids came—they all came and went—and yet we sit here—this land stays—God wishes—it will

4.1 Recreating Shah Latif's heroines: Alan Faqir

stay—Sain Latif[67]—even at that time talked of this land—Marvi is the land—Malir is the land—all these women—Marvi—Sassi—Sohni—leave their homes to walk on this soil—sometimes the rivers are dry and they walk on this barren land—who is this Marvi—whose nails are red—and her hands have the red henna on them?—Latif put a message in his legends—whether it is Marvi or Sassi or Sohni—or Leela-Canesar—whether it is Shireen-Farhad—or Rano—he puts them all in his narratives—he does not talk of Hir-Ranjha—of Layla-Majnun—because they have no graves—Shah only wrote of that which could be verified—he was influenced by Rumi—

A: Yes

A: Shah Latif—he is my mentor—he is my *murshid*—he sings the *alap*—*vo-vo-vo*—he is calling out for the love of someone—see—*vo-vo-vo* can be anything—the *vo-vo-vo* can have any number of meanings—

> it can be a woman—I have sung the *vo-vo* or the Shah's *faqīr*s sing it—*vo-vo-vo* is a complete world—the world of ecstasy
>
> . . .

Then, the musician, who was already in a state of *kefīat,* chanted in the interview,

Vo	That
Vo nahī hɛ	That is not it
Allāh hū-hū vo- vo[68]	God is great - that-that
Allāh hū - allāh hū	God is great - God is great
Mujh mẽ tū maujud hɛ	Thou art present in me

4.2 Alan Faqir on *yak-tarā.* Courtesy Institute of Sindhology, Sind University, Jamshoro.

Mẽ azl kā śa'ur hũ	I am the Eternal Light
Ke har nām kā nūr hũ	The Light to every name
Allāh hū	God is great
Jo nā jāne būd hũ	Am the great Eternal Mind
O-O -vo - o-	O-O- that - O
Allah hū	God is great
. . . .	. . . .

Alan Faqir continued his narrative,

> F: Shah's melodies are named after the *dastān* [legends]—in which a particular *sūrmi* [heroine] is mentioned. For instance, he created "Sūr Sassi," "Sūr Marvi," "Sūr Sohni," and so on.

While he sang, I asked the musician who had trained him to sing like that, and he said his *dādi* (paternal grandmother) had taught him to sing, but he also confessed that no one had ever asked him that question.

I have discussed a wide variety of sources, such as the written poetic texts, scholarly critiques, and multimedia sources. The most useful have been the interviews with the musicians. I have devised the model that I call a "node" that helps articulate the intricacy of the female voices in Sufi discourse (see Fig. 1.5). My aim is to follow the complexities of the many female voices and their extensions in the lore of the musicians who are the speakers and the transmitters. Sadly, Alan Faqir died in 2000.

CHAPTER 5

Closing the Circle of the Mystic Journey

WOMEN'S PARTICIPATION

Women's participation in disseminating Islamic principles through the Sufi shrines is common and may be seen in the daily rituals and special events held on Thursday evenings. Their presence as devotees and caretakers is visible during the *ʿurs* (the death anniversary of the Sufi saint). For instance, at the Hazrat Lal Shahbaz Qalandar shrine at Sehwan Sharif, the woman *faqiriānī* or caretaker gives out water to the devotees. In the Islamic tradition giving water to the thirsty is a *savab* (charitable deed). The act of giving water to the thirsty is eulogized in the oral Sufi traditions, especially in relation to the Battle of Kerbala. Hussain, the Prophet's grandson, his children, and family were denied water in desert temperatures for three days. Eventually, Hussain was killed in this battle. The lore of the musicians contains references to this event.[1]

Both male and female musicians sing about the women in the prophet Muhammad's life, such as his mother, Amina, and his wet nurse, Dai Haleema. They sing about the loyalty of his wife Khadija, who was one of the first people to acknowledge his prophecy. In addition, references are made to his wives, and to his daughter Syeda Fatima.[2] Moreover, in the Shiʿi oral narratives references are made to Syeda Fatima and to the Prophet's granddaughter, Syeda Zainab. The latter is said to have assumed the political responsibility of Hussain's family after all the male members died in the Battle of Kerbala except for Imam Zeinul Abedin, who was sick and could not go to the battlefield. I have found several examples in the oral and written sources in the indigenous languages where male musicians use inflected

5.1 Serving devotees: *Murīdiānī* at Hazrat Lal Shahbaz Qalandar, Sehwan Sharif

female voices.[3] The female voices in Sufi poetry emanate from events like the Battle of Kerbala and verses about mothers, such as Mary, mother of Christ.[4]

Among the women who brought Islam to the subcontinent are the Bibi Pak Daman, or the Pure Women. These were six women who, according to tradition, belonged to the prophet Muhammad's family.[5] Their shrines are in Lahore. Supposedly, they were the survivors of the Battle of Kerbala and came eastward to the subcontinent to take refuge. Upon arrival in Lahore, they engaged in missionary activity. Since they were erudite in reading and interpreting the Quran and were conversant with the prophet Muhammad's *hadīth*, they established *zikr* assemblies for the incantation of the Quranic texts. They guided the lives of the laypeople. It is reported that seven hundred male scholars came with the Bibi Pak Daman to Hind, as the land was known then.[6] Thus, the Bibi Pak Daman are said to have held mystical assemblies with male Sufi scholars. They involved the men in disseminating Islam among the lay non-Muslim populations in the Panjab. The women spoke to the male scholars and to their audiences from behind the veil. Pir ʿAli ibn ʿUsman Data Ganj Bakhsh Hujwiri (d. 1071 AD), who was himself a great Sufi mystic, was a devotee of the shrines of the Bibi Pak Daman.[7]

He offered prayers at their shrines and spent considerable time in meditation at the shrines.[8] These shrines reportedly were there long before Data Sahib arrived in Lahore. The Bibi Pak Daman generated an interest in Islamic discourse with their audiences because of their eclectic approach in which mysticism (*tassawaf*) was a component.[9]

Tassawaf grew among the Muslim communities of Arabia and its surrounding areas. Within these communities Sufi poetry emerged from the Quran and its recitation, Arab poetry and its pietistic invocations, prayers composed in praise of God, and the belief in God as a loving God. Such factors promoted Sufism and created a saintly tradition in which the love of God and the Prophet occupied a central position. Ascetic pietism discouraged involvement in worldly affairs; those who were influenced by it included the Prophet's Companion, Abu Dharr al-Ghifārī.[10] The same philosophy influenced early adherents of Sufism such as Rabi'a al-'Adawiyya (b. 717 AD) and Hasan al-Basri. The mystical perception further inspired the poetry of Rabi'a al-'Adawiyya (d. 801 AD) and that of other women mystics in the Islamic traditions, such as the princess Jahan Ara Begam (1614–1681 AD), daughter of the Mughal emperor Shah Jahan.[11]

In addition to mystical poetry, Princess Jahan Ara Begam wrote two scholarly works in Persian, the *Munis 'ul Arwah,* which is a biography of the Sufi saint Hazrat Muinuddin Chishti of Ajmer, and a narrative of the Chishtiyya *silsilā.*[12] Princess Jahan Ara's discourse, *Sahibiyyā,* is an autobiographical account of her spiritual association with Hazrat Mulla Shah Badakhshi, a Qadiriyya Sufi of Kashmir.[13] Princess Jahan Ara's biographies contain descriptions of her performances of rituals at the Sufi shrines of her spiritual guides. They are similar to the rituals described in this book.

The princess states that she read the Quran at Hazrat Muinuddin Chishti's shrine in Ajmer. Princess Jahan Ara Begam confirms that she read the *Yāsīn* and *al-Fātehā* from the Quran several times before entering the shrine.[14] She narrates her spiritual experiences when offering *namāz* (Islamic prayers) in the shrine.[15] From these historical descriptions and from the fieldwork that I have done among women at the Sufi shrines, it is evident that the shrines became devotional spaces for women. Since women were not allowed into the male domains of the mosque, the Sufi shrines became centers for their devotional activities. Here, the women could pray, meditate, and seek emotional support through their female networks and the rituals that took place around them. Thus, both the elitist and lay worlds of women merged in the rituals at the Sufi shrines. Princesses like Jahan Ara Begam found peace and spiritual comfort there as did attendant handmaidens.

Women also frequently visit one of the largest mosques in the Islamic world, the Masjid-e Nabawi in Medina, which has great devotional significance for believers. There is much emotion tied to the pilgrimage at this mosque. The Prophet and his Companions prayed here, and after the Prophet's death he was buried there.[16] Women pray in the Masjid-e Nabawi and offer devotional rituals such as reading the Quran, saying the regular *namaz*, and offering *nawāfil* (optional prayers). Many a *qawwāl* or musician in the Islamic world eulogizes the pilgrimage to this mosque or narrates the dream of touching the lattice of the mosque where the Prophet prayed and is buried. This is a significant image found in both the oral and written Sufi traditions of the Islamic world.

Furthermore, in the lore of the musicians there are references to the Kaaba, which every Muslim desires to visit as a pilgrim.[17] The pilgrimage is called Hajj, and a smaller pilgrimage is called Umra. Almost every musician, male and female, refers to it either directly or as a simile or metaphor. Abida Parvin and other noted female musicians sing about these holy sites in their performances.[18]

Like the mosques, the Sufi *khanqahs* (monasteries) were centers of learning where the faithful were inducted into spiritual discipline. Women such as Princess Jahan Ara Begam were among them.[19] Mulla Shah Badakhshi introduced her to the spiritual practices of the Qadiriyya order. Her brother Dara Shikoh was her intermediary.[20] Therefore, it is not surprising that the *khanqahs* that the Sufis used for schools or centers to educate people, including large numbers of women, became shrines after the death of the Sufi teachers. Devotees created rituals from their teachings and poetry. They found solace in visiting the shrines and interacting with the Sufi's descendants who eventually became the caretakers of their legacy.[21] An entire ritualistic and spiritual world grew around these shrines where women and children went in large numbers to pray, to supplicate, to bring offerings, and to seek relief from emotional, familial, and financial concerns.

Throughout the centuries the Sufi shrines have provided women with security and shelter. Princess Jahan Ara confirms it through her *hāzrī* (attendance) at the Ajmer Sharif shrine of Hazrat Muinuddin Chishti. She says in her *Munis ʿul Arwah*, "My sincerity and love demand that after having come to such a place of sanctity and a corner of safety, I stay here, but I must return to my house."[22] Princess Jahan Ara's feelings of safety at Hazrat Muinuddin Chishti's shrine affirm the emotional strength that some Sufi shrines have given to women.[23] Women's participation has been furthered by women patrons in the Muslim world who have supported the creation of centers for Sufi practices where women can seek refuge in times of difficulty.[24]

In the world of the Sufi shrines women found musicians who would sing

5.2 *Guluband* of Hazrat Lal Shahbaz Qalandar, Sehwan Sharif

the poetic texts that touched their hearts and articulated their pain. Not only is the speech of the musicians religious and devotional, derived from the Quran and the *hadīth,* but it is also aesthetic and fulfills emotional needs of the audiences and of the musicians themselves. This is demonstrated in the interview with the *qawwāls* at the Bulle Shah shrine in Kasur. They claim to sing in the female voice because it expresses humility and submission. I have found references to Hazrat Amir Khusrau and to the *qaul* and *taränā* in Princess Jahan Ara Begam's *Munis 'ul Arwah.*[25] Furthermore, there are accounts of payments to musicians indicating that the princess's devotional activities involved *qawwāl*s and musicians.[26] As stated earlier, Amir Khusrau was one of the early creators of *qawwālī.* He was educated and trained in Sufi practices by his spiritual guide, Hazrat Nizamuddin Auliya (d. 1325 AD), who belonged to the Chishtiyya order; the singing of *qawwālī* is particularly associated with this lineage. Amir Khusrau resided with his *pir* in Delhi, and when his *pir* died in 1325 AD, Khusrau died within the year.[27] Hazrat Nizamuddin Auliya's shrine is in Delhi.

Hazrat Nizamuddin Auliya was an outstanding scholar of the Quran, *Shari'a,* and *hadīth.* Scholars from all over the Muslim world, including those from the Islamic societies of Southeast Asia such as Malaysia and Indonesia, visit his shrine. Additionally, Muslim groups from Australia stay at the shrine, and Islamic conventions are held there. The poetic discourses of Amir Khusrau, Hazrat Nizamuddin Auliya's disciple, are inspired by Islamic sources as are his female voices.

The Quran itself influences the female voices in Sufi poetry sung at the shrines, at the festivals, and in concerts.[28] In terms of their faith (*imān*), men and women are considered equal. This can be seen in the following *suras*:

> For Muslim men and women—
> For believing men and women,
> For devout men and women,
> For true men and women,
> For men and women who are
> Patient and constant, for men
> And women who humble themselves,
> For men and women who give
> In charity, for men and women
> Who fast (and deny themselves),
> For men and women who
> Engage much in Allah's praise
> For them has Allah prepared
> Forgiveness and great reward.

This sura is embedded in references to the Prophet's wives (his *azwaj*). As seen in the following lines, the sura extols the females in the Prophet's family:[29]

> And recite what is[30]
> Rehearsed to you in your
> Homes, of the Signs of Allah

And His Wisdom:
For Allah understands
The finest mysteries and
Is well-acquainted (with them).

The Sufi practices of singing devotional texts may be said to have developed directly from the desire to expound Allah's wisdom through his Prophet. Thus, when musicians present that message, it is for a devotional purpose. Sufism is clearly a legitimate part of the Islamic tradition. Sufi poetry using the female voice is within the same Islamic traditions.

For example, musician Pathana Khan invokes a mother in the Siraiki Sufi poetry to describe the mystic pain of seeking the beloved. He sang:[31]

Mā̃-e nī mẽ kenū̃ akhā̃	O my mother, to whom shall I narrate
Dard vichauṇ dā hāl?	The agony of separation?

These verses are derived from the Quran, and the singer's source is the written text of a Sufi poet. The Sufi poets propagate the mystic messages in accordance with the Quran, and the dominant voices in these messages are those of women. A musician who sings Shah Abdul Latif's *vāī* from the *Risālo* would represent Sassi's voice:[32]

O mother! I have no argument, nor influence or social intercourse,
None whatsoever, with the Baluchis

The source of this emotion and idea is the Quran and its many verses about mothers. Sassi speaks with her mother, but in effect she shows the allegiance required toward a mother in Islam. In Shah Abdul Latif's poetry one of the strongest sources of influence is the Quran. Since large sections of the Quran are quoted in his *Risālo,* musicians in Sind hold Shah's written text in the utmost veneration.

All the musicians whom I interviewed who sing Sufi poetry invoke the Quran, or a Quranic saying, or the *hadīth* to initiate a performance. Alternatively, they may start a performance with a saying from a Sufi poet whose written narratives are derived from Quranic sources or sources from Islamic history. The musicians' oral sources are built within the written traditions of Islamic mysticism. Outstanding performers like Abida Parvin, Nusrat Fateh Ali Khan, the Sabri Brothers, and Mehr Ali and Sher Ali create the female voices in their poetry with complete knowledge and understanding of the Quranic and Islamic sources of their discourse. They are able to sing the narratives with understanding because of their training for several generations in the mystical traditions. They are fully conversant with the written sources and can talk about them with fluency, as I have found in my interviews with them and in the analyses of their performances.

The musicians contextualize their narratives in the Islamic traditions and are able to transmit the poetry with emotion. This is observed throughout the Islamic world. For instance the Sidis in Sind and Kacch claim descent from Hazrat Bilal, a freed African slave of the prophet Muhammad. Hazrat Bilal's *āzān* (call for prayer) is legendary in Islamic communities for its melody. Sidi women render ritual musical services in the households in the Sind, and their voices are heard in films such as *The Musical Instruments of Kacch and Its Neighbors.*[33]

As stated, the Sufis came to the subcontinent to disseminate Islam among laypeople and to educate them. They integrated poetry and music as a methodology, using the indigenous traditions or other grassroots cultures with Islamic discourse. They used simple mnemonics that their devotees enjoyed while they learned them. Additionally, their resources were the multicultural and multireligious contexts in the environments around them.

The Sufi *khanqahs* in the subcontinent were centers of learning where spiritual guides inducted individuals into the *silsilās* (lineages) through intellectual and spiritual training. Rituals such as ablutions, prayer, fasting, and *zikr* were a part of their training. In my interview with Nusrat Fateh Ali Khan, he affirmed that when he taught *qawwālī,* he initiated his pupils into the spiritual rituals of *zikr.* As such, he trained his students to do the *wudu* (the ablutions of cleaning themselves with water) before participating in the *qawwālī* sessions with him.[34]

The Sufi texts and contexts of the subcontinent that are investigated in this book are those that the Sufis used with music to impart education among the laypeople. Foremost among their educational principles were tolerance and acceptance of other religions and cultures. Therefore, it is no wonder that the female myths in their poetry are drawn from cross-cultural sources just as are the forms of their poetry. It is not surprising that non-Muslim women such as the Kolhis and Bhils are devotees at Sufi shrines like that of Shah Abdul Latif in Bhit Shah and that Shah's shrine is known in the region as a *jamālī* (aesthetic) shrine. And, because of the strong presence of the *sūrmis* (tragic heroines) in his poetry, his *faqīrs* sing his poetry in the falsetto that imitates a woman's lament.

Female voices are also predominant in the poetry of Amir Khusrau, and they function on many levels. Sometimes, they are voices that express love between a disciple and the spiritual guide. At other times, they call for social reform of such practices as child marriages. Sometimes, the female voices are used for mere aesthetics. Khusrau's verses are simple, written for his lay audiences as well as for the elitist *qawwālī* discourses. The female voices are created for devotional purposes; the verses are also sung as wedding songs. They can be read as expressions of tolerance influenced by the surrounding cultural domains.

I have mentioned earlier that Sufi poetry was created in the political turmoil of the subcontinent. For instance, in the thirteenth and fourteenth centuries through the following centuries, the region was a place of extreme contrasts. On the one hand, society witnessed the grandeur and splendor of the Muslim aristocracy and the opulent lifestyles of the rajas and maharajas; on the other hand, most of the population was struggling under feudal tutelage. Society was crushed with illiteracy, poverty, disease, caste, and gender apartheid.

The Sufis, through their teachings and through their poetry, provided relief to the people. Their *k͟hanqah*s became places where laypersons found simplifications of the Quranic teachings. The Sufis spoke to the people in metaphors that they could understand, in images that came from the life around them, such as those of spinning, weaving, grinding, and husking. Images in Sufi poetry were drawn from woman's domain, such as that of her work. The *sabr* (perseverance) in the musicians' *cakkī-namā*s and *cark͟hī-namā*s is derived from the story of Job and the story of Jonah, applied through the toiling female.

The female voices in the musicians' narratives are additionally borrowed from the indigenous sources where the woman is empowered with *shakti* (strength). She is the creator and life force. All the sources from which the musicians draw inspiration, including the Quran, glorify the woman.

When I interviewed Surraiya Multanikar, a woman musician who sings the *kāfī*s (mystical verses) in Siraiki about the female myths, she said that she did not believe in any female myths. She said that the female narratives grew around real events in communities among young women, and these events happened a long time ago. Concerning *wajd* (ecstasy), she said that it may not necessarily be induced through music. This is an experience that anyone can attain through *zikr* (spiritual incantation).

Musicians such as Surraiya Multanikar are associated with the powerful landowning Syeds of Multan and Bahawalpur who claim descent from the prophet Muhammad's family. Their training is supported by the Syed households, and these musicians perform in the family shrines of the Syeds. This

5.3 Singing in Siraiki: Surraiya Multanikar

is partly because of the large landholdings where the affluent Syeds support the shrines of their ancestors. They arrange annual rituals such as the Eid and the Muharram ceremonies marking the tragedy of Kerbala.

Eid ul Fitr is celebrated after the fasting month of Ramazan, and the night before Eid ul Fitr is called Cānd Rāt, when the new moon for Eid is seen. On that evening the women in the Syed households decorate their hands with henna. Ritual songs derived from devotional contexts are sung at these events.[35] Several weeks after the Eid ul Fitr Muslims celebrate Eid ul Azha, when the faithful sacrifice an animal such as a sheep or cattle. This event celebrates the Hajj ritual. In Pakistan, poetic texts may be sung at each of these events. These are sung in Muslim households, including those of the Syeds. Female musicians create festivity in the *zanānā* (women's section), narrating events from Islamic history, and they are paid well for their services. In Sind, the Sidis of African descent and the Manganhar musicians render the ceremonial singing of devotional narratives.

INTERNATIONAL SETTINGS

In expatriate settings, the devotional contexts are sustained differently. In the last three decades a large number of professionals and skilled workers from the subcontinent have moved to the West and to the Gulf States. In the United Kingdom, in cities like Birmingham, Manchester, Leeds, Bradford, and Glasgow, they have found employment.[36] Professionals such as doctors, engineers, and businesspeople, they live in London and its suburb of Southall, making it one of the most affluent subdivisions of businesspeople from Pakistan, India, and Bangladesh in the United Kingdom.

Similar communities of professionals have provided the human resources in Paris, Montreal, Toronto, New York, Chicago, Los Angeles, San Francisco, St. Louis, Houston, and other cities. They are ardent patrons of *qawwālī* and *sufiānā-kalām* concerts. The patronage of the affluent Pakistani and Indian audiences, especially the Sikhs, can be seen in the video footage that I obtained in the United Kingdom, from concerts performed in the eighties. The patrons showered the musicians with pound sterling currency notes to express their appreciation.

Similarly, workers from Pakistan, India, and Bangladesh helped to build the cities and highways in Iran, the United Arab Emirates, Qatar, Bahrain, Kuwait, Oman, and Saudi Arabia during the peak of the oil boom in the 1970s and 1980s. They further provided medical, engineering, educational, and social services.

The statistics of these migrant workers who support Sufi rituals in the diaspora are given in this chapter. I have used a wide range of statistical data to illustrate that expatriates from the subcontinent have created a demand for Sufi mystical concerts. It was primarily the interest of these communities that brought the Islamic tradition of singing devotional poetry to music within the fold of world music. They created the demand not only for the concerts but also for spiritual music on CDs and audiocassettes. In the United Kingdom, videocassettes of live *qawwālī* performances further fulfilled the needs of the audiences.[37] Thus, an entire electronic culture developed around Sufi rituals, drawing a large number of western audiences as well.

The 1981 census of Pakistan estimated that 1.7 million Pakistanis had migrated abroad to the United Kingdom and other European countries, Canada, the United States, and the Gulf countries.[38] Indicators for the cities in the United Kingdom in the eighties are given in table 1. During this period numerous *qawwālī* and *sufiānā-kalām* ensembles from the subcontinent came to perform in the West. The statistics of Pakistani migrant groups are given in table 2. The statistics of Indian groups in the Arab world are given in table 3.[39] A sample of the socioeconomic backgrounds of the Gulf States' Bangladeshi immigrants can be gleaned from the statistics in tables 4 and 5. Again, those in the major cities are likely to have been supporters of the speech events I discussed.

One can deduce from the statistics that the number of expatriates has grown throughout the past twenty years. Ritual Sufi poetry sung to music has

TABLE 1. *Population by ethnic group: Great Britain, 1981–1987 (thousands of persons)*

Ethnic Group	1981	1985	1986	1987	Percent of minorities in 1987
Pakistanis	284	406	413	392	15.8
Indians	727	689	784	761	30.6
Bangladeshis	52	99	117	116	4.7

SOURCE: John Salt and Reuben Ford, "The United Kingdom," in *Handbook of International Migration* (London: Greenwood Press, 1990), 333.

TABLE 2. *Pakistani migrant groups in the Gulf countries in the 1980s*

Saudi Arabia[a]	0.608 millions
United Arab Emirates	0.358 millions
Other Middle Eastern countries	0.280 millions
Total Middle East	1.245 millions
All other countries	0.544 millions
Total	3.035 millions

[a]Public performances of *qawwālī* and *sufiānā-kalām* are not held in Saudi Arabia.

SOURCE: M. Fahim Khan, "Pakistan," *Migration of Asian Workers to the Arab World*, ed. Godfrey Gunatilleke (Tokyo: United Nations University, 1986), 111 (recorded from Bureau of Immigration, Government of Pakistan).

enabled the expatriate communities to recreate devotional environments and to provide entertainment. The statistics show that the majority of groups comprise unskilled workers, and they are the ones who come in large numbers to the concerts. These groups also form the lay populations at the Sufi shrines in their own countries. In the twelfth, thirteenth, and fourteenth centuries, communities like these flocked to the assemblies of the Sufis in the subcontinent.

In the United States, the audiences at the Sufi ritual concerts in cities like New York, Chicago, San Francisco, Los Angeles, and Houston belong to higher socioeconomic strata. The Pakistani and South Asian communities in the United States have been patrons of *qawwālī* concerts. The figures in table 6 from the U.S. Census Bureau[40] obtained in 2000 demonstrate the statistics.

It can be seen that, for the last two decades, *qawwālī* and *sufiānā-kalām* musicians from Pakistan and India have fulfilled the devotional needs of their expatriate audiences. They have performed before international audiences and have created contexts from Amir Khusrau's time (d. 1325 AD) using the Prophet's *qaul* (sayings) for *qawwālī*. In the 1980s, Nusrat Fateh Ali Khan's *qawwālī* performances in France initiated the West's interest in the oral cultures of Islamic mysticism. These performances are based on *zikr* texts, which the great Sufi masters have used for centuries.

As the interest of the diaspora communities and western audiences de-

TABLE 3. *Estimates of the Indian migrant population in the Gulf*

Country	*1983*	*1987*
Saudi Arabia	270,000	240,000
Kuwait	115,000	100,000
United Arab Emirates	250,000	225,000
Oman	100,000	184,000
Libya	40,000	25,000
Bahrain	30,000	77,000
Iraq	50,000	35,000
Qatar	40,000	50,000
Others	21,000	21,000
Total	916,000	957,000

SOURCE: Deepak Nayyar, "International Labor Migration from India: A Macro-Economic Analysis," in *To the Gulf and Back,* ed. Rashid Amjad (New Delhi: International Labor Organization, 1989), 101.

TABLE 4. *Occupational distribution of migrants (percentages)*

Engineers	2.2
Doctors	1.2
Other professionals	2.1
Technicians	2.6
Construction workers	50.5
Transport-equipment operators	15.3
Production	6.4
Services	8.0
Fishing and agriculture	3.1
Clerical staff	1.2
Others/skill not known	7.7

SOURCE: S. R. Osmani, "Bangladesh," in *Migration of Asian Workers to the Arab World,* ed. Godfrey Gunatilleke (Tokyo: United Nations University, 1986), 23–27.

TABLE 5. *Volume of Bangladeshi migration and composition by skill category*

Year	Total Number	Category (%)			
		Professional	*Skilled*	*Semiskilled*	*Unskilled*
1976	6,087	9	29	9	53
1977	15,725	11	41	3	45
1978	22,809	15	36	5	44
1979	24,485	14	29	7	50
1980	30,573	6	40	8	46
1981	55,787	7	40	4	49
1982	62,805	6	33	5	56
1983	26,477	4	34	7	55
Total	244,748	9	36	6	50

SOURCE: S. R. Osmani, "Bangladesh," in *Migration of Asian Workers to the Arab World,* ed. Godfrey Gunatilleke (Tokyo: United Nations University, 1986), 23–27.

TABLE 6. *Pakistani, Bangladeshi, and Indian Migrants in the United States*

	Estimate	*Lower Bound*	*Upper Bound*[a]
Asian Indian	1,822,582	1,710,597	1,934,568
Bangladeshi	37,774	25,046	50,502
Pakistani	149,386	121,511	177,261

SOURCE: *Census 2000 Supplementary Survey Summary Tables*

NOTE: Data based on twelve monthly samples during 2000. For information on confidentiality protection, sampling error, nonsampling error, and definitions, see http://factfinder.census.gov/home/en/datanotes/exp.c2ss.html (4 September 2001).

[a]Data are based on a sample and are subject to sampling variability. The degree of uncertainty for an estimate is represented through the use of confidence interval. The confidence interval computed here is a 90 percent confidence interval and can be interpreted roughly as providing 90 percent certainty that the true number falls between the lower and upper bounds.

veloped in the Sufi version of Islam, Nusrat Fateh Ali Khan and the other musicians, such as the Sabri Brothers, Faridi Qawwals, and Mehr Ali and Sher Ali accentuated their performances through using the female voices for devotional purposes. They created ingenuity in their female myths. They sang about the veil, which has innumerable connotations in Islamic culture. They sang about Hir, Sassi, and Sohni. Many of Hir's discourses with the "religious establishment" are about the application of the *Shariʿa*. Sohni's narrative in which she tries to cross the river represents her search for the divine or a spiritual guide. This is also heard in Abida Parvin's performances. By using the female voices the musicians express humility and surrender to a spiritual force.

In the last fifteen years an immense interest in Sufi music has become apparent all over the Muslim world. Recording companies have capitalized on this interest and have built substantial archives of excellent Sufi music on CDs. Through their efforts sacrosanct and secretive Sufi rituals such as those in Iran are now available to listeners.[41] Obviously, the linguistic and musical elements of Sufi mysticism have bewitched diasporic speech communities as well as the wider world audiences. These very linguistic and musical elements must have drawn the laypeople to the Sufi shrines of Pakistan and India in the last several centuries. It is not surprising that the shrines provided the space for speech communities to listen to ritual, devotional poetry that had shared meanings. These contexts represented the shared religious worldview of the participants of the events, especially the women.

When I interviewed Nusrat Fateh Ali Khan, he claimed that it was his goal to make Pakistani youth interested in Islam. Khan aimed his performances toward his young audience. He said that he modernized *qawwālī* so that the youth would find meanings in Sufi poetry. According to him, "Tradition should not be seen as a dead thing. It is the responsibility of musicians to make music for the people of their time." Nusrat Fateh Ali Khan's performances have now influenced young musicians in Pakistan. They use the resources of Sufi poetry such as that of Bulle Shah for their lyrics. The young musicians additionally seek inspiration from the Prophet's life and incidents from the history of Islam. The female voices from these sources are significant in the performances.

In this book I have reported discussions with both female and male musicians of Sufi poetry who have demonstrated their reverence for the narratives that they sing. I have looked at elitist as well as grassroots sources of performance. Much work remains to be done.

Proposals

I propose the following areas for future research:

- Studies of Sufi performance rituals in other Muslim societies.
- Information gathering about Pakistani and Indian *qawwāli* performances in Europe, the Gulf States, the United States, and Canada and compilation of research. This research would reveal many linkages of the

indigenous Sufi musical and linguistic traditions with world music. Such a study would demonstrate how musicians have reinforced traditional *qawwālī* structures from Amir Khusrau's time and recreated old linguistic forms and melodies. A study of Abida Parvin's innovations within *sufiānā-kalām* traditions and her introduction of *qawwālī* elements into it will be groundbreaking research.

- Further investigation of women's participation in Sufi rituals with a focus on the linguistic components and the sources from which they are drawn.
- Research into the written and oral sources of the narratives of Sufi musicians, both females and males, in other Muslim societies.
- Research into the written discourses of scholarly women who have delved into the areas of Islamic mysticism, for example, Princess Jahan Ara Begam in the subcontinent or her researcher, Qamar Jahan Begam.
- A translation of the work of women Islamic mystics into English or any other international language in order to make their work accessible to the world.
- A collection of the poetry and writings of women who have addressed areas of Islamic mysticism. Javed Nurbaksh's *Sufi Women* can be used as a guide to investigate the primary sources about these women.
- Documentation of oral histories about Sufi women from families associated with mystical practices.
- A collection of multimedia materials about female participation in Sufi rituals.
- Documentation of all the available resources including print, multimedia, and oral histories in Sufi rituals. (The Institute of Sindhology in Hyderabad, Sind, is one such source.)
- Transliterations with translations of female voices in Sufi songs from international Islamic contexts.
- Programs in applied linguistics and folklore that will integrate the oral traditions of Sufism. These can be built into gender studies, multicultural studies, language teaching, ethnomusicology, and interdisciplinary areas.[42]

Many Muslim societies, like those in Pakistan, are a gold mine of oral heritage where the female voices are dominant. Related to the female voices are the Graeco-Indic traditions.[43] These socities can return to their own roots and strengthen their heritage through building the traditional creative Islamic sources of the female images. They can use poetry and the creative arts in educational and social programs. There is much that can be done, and women scholars can move these efforts forward. They will have to empower themselves by looking into Islamic sources, both written and oral, for their work. They will have to go into the field and network with scholars, professionals, and grassroots women in Muslim societies. They will need the support of males willing to support women's perspectives. And last but not the least, they will have to rely on their own courage and conviction.

Glossary

abiāt Plural of *bait,* which is an Arab word meaning a couplet of verses. The form is adopted in Panjabi Sufi poetry and signifies a stanza of four lines. Sultan Bahu and Waris Shah use the *bait* form in their poetry, such as the *Abiāt-e Bahu* and Waris Shah's *Hir.*

adab Cultural norms for appropriate conduct; sanctity.

Ahl-e-Taśhīh Followers of Ithna-Ashri Shīʿi Islam.

alāp An introductory *rāg* preparatory to singing.

ʿAli Cousin and son-in-law of the prophet Muhammad; fourth caliph of Islam and "titular head of all Sufi lineages."

Allāh God.

Allāh-hū *Zikr* chant of Sufis.

Allahvālā One who is God fearing.

amir The chief of a clan or tribe.

ang A regional style of music, for instance, the Panjabi *ang* in *qawwāli.*

aqīqā In Islamic societies ritual shaving of an infant's hair within a few days after its birth. An animal such as a goat or sheep is sacrificed.

arāī A caste of landowners in the Panjab.

ʿarif One who is skilled in divine matters.

ʿarifānā-kalām Sufi poetry sung in Pakistan and India in the indigenous languages.

aślok Derived from Sanskrit *ślokā,* which is a devotional or philosophical verse; devotional verse sung to music.

aulīyā Plural for *vali* (friend); a term used for Sufi saints, as in Nizamuddin Auliya of Delhi.

ʿaurat Urdu/Hindi term for a female.

āzān The ritual call for prayer among the Muslims.

azwāj The prophet Muhammad's wives.

bābul Father; also, ritual songs that mourn a bride's departure from her father's home.

bādshāh An emperor.

bait A couplet of verses with mystical or Sufi content; a form also used in folk poetry.

bakhśiś A gift or something given in charity.

Balūchī From the Baluch, a province of western Pakistan; also, the language of Baluchistan.

banī Devotional verses such as those of Guru Nanak; verses of supplication, entreaty, humility, and reverence.

banjārā Generally defined as carriers of grain; in oral culture a reference to roving minstrels.

bārāt The bridegroom's ceremonial procession.

bātin In Sufi literature, words that have covert or hidden meanings.

Bava Gor Abyssinian lord named Sidi Mobarak Nobi; Ahmed Kabir Rifa'i perhaps gave him the title Bava Gor in Baghdad. The first reference to him in India is in AD 1452. He was perhaps a descendant of Hazrat Bilal, an African slave whom the Prophet freed. He established the African Muslim community in the subcontinent known as the Sidi, Sheedi, or Syedi. There is a shrine dedicated to him, his sister Mai Misra, and Bava Habash in Ratanpur, Gujrat.

bāzār A marketplace.

bel Monetary offerings to musicians during a performance.

bhajan Indian devotional poetry sung to music.

Bhakti Devotional movement in India linked with Hinduism, starting from the sixth century onward, that expressed the devotee's emotional attachment to a personal God; Surdas (d. AD 1563), Tulsidas (d. AD 1623), and Mira Bai (b. AD 1498) were linked with the Bhakti, and their poetry was composed in the indigenous Indian languages.

Bhīls Aboriginal landless roving peasants in Sind.

biddat The introduction of novelty or change in religion; schism, heresy, innovation.[1]

bol Words in a lyric.

brādārī An extended-family structure, derived from the term "brother" or "*bradar.*"

Brahaūī A Baluch tribe; also, the culture and language of that tribe.

Brajbhāśā Premodern Hindi and language with an established literary standard.

cāk The Panjabi term for a menial in a household; for example, Ranjha became a *cāk* in the Siyal household.

cakkī-nāmā From the term *cakkī,* which means a grinding wheel; in Sufi poetry the songs that women sang at the grinding wheel; a genre of Sufi poetry in the subcontinent composed in the indigenous languages such as Panjabi and Bijapuri.

cāmā A genre of Persian poetry; a song.

candar A ceremonial Sindhi melody played on auspicious occasions.

Cānd Rāt "Night of the Moon": the evening before the Muslim Eid festival when the moon is seen in anticipation of the event; traditionally, women celebrate it by wearing glass bangles and applying henna to their hands.

Canesar The hero of the Baluchi-Sindhi myth of Leela-Canesar in Shah Abdul Latif's *Risālo*. Leela is the heroine; the lovers were separated through stratagem but were united at the end through death.

capṛī Wooden castanets that are played for rhythm in Sindhi folk music.

carkhī-nāmā From the term *carkhī* which means a spinning wheel; in Sufi poetry the songs that women sang at the spinning wheel; a genre of Sufi poetry in the subcontinent composed in the indigenous languages such as Panjabi and Bijapuri.

cas In Panjabi, the flavor of a language.

challevālī From *challa*, which is a ring; *vali* is the female form in languages of the subcontinent for "one who owns"; female roving minstrel who sings at folk festivals and produces rhythm on a clay or aluminum pot with her *challa* (ring) that she wears on her finger.

child-bride A bride who is a child; a common practice in the subcontinent to marry off females before they reach puberty.

Chishtīyyā A Sufi order of the subcontinent identified with supporting *qawwālī*.

cilman A curtain made of split bamboo that usually hangs on a door.

cimṭā A pair of extended tongs that folk musicians use to create rhythm.

colī A tiny bodice that women wear above a skirt or sari.

conversation analysis The methodology of Sacks, Schegloff, and Jefferson to study live speech; an inductive, empirical study of the interactions in speech, especially turn-taking.

dādā Grandfather; a fond name that Sidis use for the giant *mugarmān* or vertical drum that belongs to the community.

dādī Paternal grandmother.

dard Indigenous term for emotional pain.

dargāh A Sufi shrine built with a courtyard around the tomb of a Sufi saint; also, a court.

dervish (Urdu, **derveś**) A Sufi mystic or religious mendicant.

dhammāl The vigorous ritual dance performed at Sufi shrines in Panjab and Sind.

ḍholak A barrel-shaped drum that can be played on both sides, usually played for folk music.

dhun A tune.

diaspora A dispersion of communities or people who were originally homogeneous.

dīvā A tiny clay lamp whose wick is drenched in mustard oil.

dīvānā A man who is inspired or is in ecstasy.

dīvānī A woman who is inspired or is in ecstasy.

dohā A genre in poetry written in couplet form.

dohāī To lament in emotional pain.

ḍohrā A couplet in Sindhi poetry whose content is secular; it is a term musicians use for Sufi poetry, such as *ḍohrā denā,* which means to sing a *ḍohrā.*

ḍolī A palanquin in which a bride is carried.

du'ā A non-ritual intercessionary prayer.[2]

Eid ul Azha Religious ritual of Muslims at which an animal is sacrificed.

Eid ul Fitr Religious ritual of Muslims after Ramazan.

ethnography of speaking A methodology to study speech communication in a community or group. The terms "ethnography of communication" and "ethnography of speaking" have been applied by sociolinguists to the study of language in relation to the entire range of extralinguistic variables that identify the social basis of communication, the emphasis being on the description of linguistic interaction. The student of such matters is known as an ethnolinguist.[3]

extralinguistic Related to aspects in social contexts that are other than linguistics, such as body language, eye contact, facial expressions, gestures, or tones of voice.[4]

faqīr A male religious mendicant linked with Sufism.

faqīriānī A female religious mendicant linked with Sufism.

al-Fātehā First chapter of the Quran ("The Opening"), which is also recited as a prayer for the dead at Sufi shrines.

fiqr Sufi asceticism.

ghāgrā A long skirt that peasant gypsy and tribal women wear.

ghaṛā (Sindhi, **ghāgar**) A clay pot to store water that can also be played for percussion.

gharānā To belong to a musical or artistic lineage.

ghaṛevālī Female musicians in the subcontinent who play the *ghaṛā;* these are usually roving minstrels.

ghaṛolī A term in Sufi poetry for a vessel that receives *murshid,* or the spiritual master's bounty and wisdom.

g͟hazal A poetic genre in the Arabo-Persian tradition that expresses love.

ghinnāwā A form of traditional oral poetry in Arabic, such as wedding and circumcision songs, that Abu-Lughod has studied among the Aulad 'Ali Bedouin tribes along the Libyan border.[5]

ghungaṭ A veil in Urdu-Hindi poetry (masculine form).

ghungaṭīā A veil in Urdu-Hindi poetry (feminine form).

ghungrū Ankle bells worn by dancers.

ghungrūvālā A musician who plays the *ghungrū* in an ensemble.

gīc Ceremonial songs usually sung by females at births and weddings in the Sind.

Gilani A branch of Syeds who claim descent from the prophet Muhammad.

girāh A knot; a verse inserted in a *qawwālī* text and sung repetitively, with a thematic link to a passage of the song text.[6]

gīt A hymn or song.

goma A dance that the Sidis perform at their shrines.

guāṭī A ritual for making vows at Sufi shrines in Baluchistan.

Gurmukhi A script of the Panjabi language in the non-Arabo-Persian form; it is used in India particularly for the holy texts of Sikhism.

hadīth Traditions or sayings of the prophet Muhammad, usually attributed to his companions or his wives.

Hajj Annual ritual pilgrimage that Muslims make to Mecca and its environs in Arabia; the stone for the structure was laid by Abraham.

harmonium An accordian-like musical instrument with bellows and a keyboard.

Hassan A son of 'Ali, the fourth caliph of Islam, who died from poisoning.

haswārī A ceremonial Sindhi tune usually played with drums and bagpipes; Sindhi musicians claim to play it for the *pir*s and *murshid*s when they appear at festive ceremonies such as a wedding.

hāzrī Ritual attendance at a Sufi shrine.

hāzrī-denā The verb form of *hāzrī*, or ritual attendance at a Sufi shrine.

hijṛā A eunuch, transvestite, or hermaphrodite; in the subcontinent the *hijṛās* are ritual musicians who have a ceremonial role at weddings and births; some dress as females in public and private lives.

Hijri The start of the Islamic year, which commences on the date of the prophet Muhammad's departure from Mecca to Medina on July 16, 622.

hilm Extreme humility or submission.

Hindko A language of the Hazara district of Pakistan.

Hir The androgynous heroine of the Panjabi myth of Hir-Ranjha; Ranjha is the hero and becomes a menial who grazes cattle in Hir's household.

Holī A festival in India in which the participants spray colors on each other.

hūk A deep lament.

Hussain A son of 'Ali, the fourth caliph of Islam. He was martyred in the Battle of Kerbala in 680 AD.

'ijjat *'Izzat*, or honor.

'ijz Submission.

imān Faith.

'iśq Intense spiritual love in the Sufi poetry of the subcontinent.

'iśq-e haqīqī Divine love in Sufi poetry of the subcontinent.

'iśq-e majāzī Personal love in Sufi poetry of the subcontinent.

jakāt Zakat, obligatory charity in Islam.
jalāl Grandeur, power, or majesty.
jalālī Adjective of *jalāl.*
jamāl Beauty.
jamālī Adjective of *jamāl.*
jamālo A folk tune in the Sind; also, a dance.
Jāṭ A tribe of Rajputs who are mostly cultivators.
jazbāt Poetic sentiments.
jhuggī A makeshift tent made by roving tribes; sometimes a *jhuggī* is set up only with branches and odd rags.
jogan A female ascetic.
joganī A female ascetic.
joganīā A female ascetic.
jogī A male ascetic. Shah Abdul Latif uses terms like *jājak, manganhār, atāi, pān, chaṛan, rāgī, baraṭ,* and *rabābī* for the *jogī.*
Kacch Indian territory adjoining Gujrat.
kafan A shroud (masculine form).
kafanīā A shroud (feminine form).
kāfī Sufi devotional poetry in Pakistan and India; also, musical mode for singing *qawwālī* and Sufi poetry.
kajāwā A camel's saddle.
kalām Speech or discourse: a generic term for Sufi mystical poetry in the subcontinent, usually sung as *kāfī.*
kalimāt Plural of *kalam;* a part of speech; speech that is a confession of faith; verses of Sufi mystical poetry that affirm faith.
kāmā A servant or menial (Panjabi).
kamlī The short form of *kambal;* a blanket.
kamlīvālā One with the blanket; a reference to the prophet Muhammad, who is said to have received his revelations while under a blanket.
kapā'tī Cotton-spinners' songs, in Sind.
karāmāt Actions, such as the performance of miracles, attributed to Sufi saints.
kaśf A term in Sufi poetry that means to open or to reveal oneself; usually when the beloved reveals him- or herself to the lover.
kefīat State of spiritual inspiration or mystical delight.
Kerbala A plain on the bank of the river Euphrates in Iraq renowned for the Battle of Kerbala, where Hussain, the son of 'Ali, was martyred in 680 AD.
k͟hānqāh A Sufi monastery.
k͟hāwājāsarā A eunuch, transvestite, or hermaphrodite; they rendered important state services in the courts of the Muslim kings of the subcontinent.
k͟hayāl A classical music genre; also, metaphysical thought in Sufi poetry.
Kheṛās A powerful clan of landowners in the Panjab mentioned in the Hir-

Ranjha myth. Hir was married against her will to Saida Kheṛā. Many of Hir's laments are about being carried away by the Kheṛās against her will.

Kolhis Aboriginal landless roving peasants in the Sind.

kurlānā To be in agony.

lagan To be attached passionately.

lāon A Sindhi nuptial song.

layl Night (Arabic).

Layla A heroine in Nizami Ganjavi's myth of Layla, who is renowned for her dark hair. However, in the subcontinent Layla is notable for her dark complexion.

Leela A heroine in the Baluchi-Sindhi myth of Leela-Canesar. Canesar is the hero. The lovers were separated through stratagem but were united at the end through death.

loṭā A round aluminum receptacle with a curved pipe-like spout to pour water; sometimes used as a percussion instrument by the female roving minstrels in the subcontinent.

loṭevālī A female minstrel who plays the *loṭā.*

mahārāja A stately king.

mahārānī A stately queen.

Mahbub-e Ilahi God's beloved: a name for Hazrat Nizamuddin Auliya of Delhi.

Mahival The hero in the Sohni-Mahival myth of the Panjab.

maidānī The dialects of the Tharparkar district in Sind; also, a full-throated voice to sing in the desert.

majlis A congregation or company of people; a social context.

Majnun The hero in Nizami Ganjavi's Layla-Majnun myth. He loved Layla with a passion. *Majnun* in the Arabic language means one who is crazy or demented.

Maliki Hir's mother in the Panjabi myth of Hir-Ranjha; she is her daughter's ally against the patriarchy.

malir Fertile, green land (Sindhi).

malūngā A braced musical bow that Sidi musicians of African descent use in India for their ritual performances; its use is widespread in Africa.

manānā To conciliate or appease an aggrieved beloved.

mānḍ A folk tune of Rajasthan.

mandir A Hindu temple.

Manganhār Hereditary professional musicians in the Sind and Rajasthan.

mangiārī A female musician in the Sind and Rajasthan.

mangtī A female musician in the Sind and Rajasthan; also, a woman who begs.

mannat To make a vow or to fulfill a vow.

maqām A level or station of spiritual attainment in Sufism in Pakistan and India.

marsiyā An elegy in the Urdu literary tradition.

Marvi The heroine of the Baluchi-Sindhi myth of Omar-Marvi. Omar kidnapped Marvi hoping that he would win her with his riches, but she pined for her people and her village. In the end her people rescued her from Omar. Shah Abdul Latif uses the myth in his *Risālo*.

masjid A mosque.

Masjid-e Nabawi The mosque of the prophet Muhammad in Medina where he prayed and in which he lies buried.

mast In the Sufi context, one who is inspired or in ecstasy.

mast qalandar Intoxicated mendicant; a melody sung to ʿAli, the fourth caliph of Islam.

maulud Celebrations that commemorate the prophet Muhammad's birth; hymns sung in praise of the Prophet during his birth celebrations.

mehfil A social context or gathering.

mehver A vortex or central force.

melā A festival or fiesta.

melā-cirāgā Festival of Lights held annually at the Shalimar Gardens in Lahore, coinciding with the ʿurs (death anniversary) of the Sufi poet Shah Hussain.

melisma A section in a composition sung to one syllable of speech, for example, Mira Bai's melismatic cry in the Sabri Brothers' *qawwālī*.

Mira Bai Upper-class Rajput princess born around 1498 AD. She was a poet and is associated with the Bhakti in India.

miʿrāj The prophet's ascension to heaven, where God is believed to have revealed Himself to His beloved prophet.

mnemonics A strategy or device that assists the memory in oral culture. Usually such a device is linguistic, for example using rhythms and rhymes to remember concepts or ideas.

mohallā A neighborhood in a city.

mugarmān A tall vertical drum played in a standing position with thumping and stroking of both hands; held sacred by the Sidi communities in Sind, Baluchistan, Rajasthan, and Gujrat who use them in their shrines and for rituals; most likely has an African origin in accordance with the origins of the Sidis themselves.

Muhammad Ahmed Mustafa (d. 632 AD), Prophet of Islam. He was born among the Quresh tribe in Arabia and died there.

Muharram Beginning of the Islamic year; also, in parts of the Muslim world a month of mourning for the martyrdom of Hussain at Kerbala.

Mumal The intelligent heroine of Sindhi myth. She married Rano, a vizier or minister of Umarkot, but got separated from her beloved through a misunderstanding. In the end the lovers were united in death.

munājāt Short prayers and invocations that are sung in Sufi poetry.

murād Desire; a vow or the fulfillment of a vow.

murīd A devotee or disciple.

murshid A spiritual guide, master, or mentor.

nabī A prophet; the prophet Muhammad.

nāc Dance.

namāz Required ritual prayers that Muslims offer five times a day.

naubat Large percussion drums that were used to announce important events in medieval India when it was ruled by powerful kings; also used for the *dhammāl,* or ecstasy dance in a shrine like Hazrat Lal Shahbaz Qalandar at Sehwan Sharif in Sind.

nawāfil Optional ritual prayers that Muslims offer.

nazarānā Monetary offerings to musicians during a *qawwālī* performance; a gift that a disciple may offer a teacher or master.

niāz A devotional offering of food.

niāz-mandī Supplication, humility, submission.

ngoma Swahili word for a dance that requires drums.

nohā A poem that laments the tragedy of Kerbala. It is usually chanted at a Shiʿi *majlis.*

olang A *ḍhol* or drum rhythm played at the bridegroom's home in Sind.

pān Betel leaf, chewed in South Asia.

Panjabi Language and culture of the Panjab province of Pakistan and India.

paṛāo A camp or halting place.

pardā A practice among Muslim women to veil themselves.

pardesī A traveler in an unknown land.

pīr A Sufi spiritual teacher or guide.

pīrzāde The descendants of a *pīr.*

pīyā A beloved.

Punnu The hero in the Baluchi-Sindhi myth of Sassi-Punnu.

Pūrbī A Hindi-related dialect of North India.

pūr-soz Music or vocal chant that can induce emotional pain.

Qādirīyyā A *silsilā* (lineage) of Sufis.

qalandar A wandering Sufi dervish or ascetic.

qaul Sayings of the prophet Muhammad sung in *qawwālī;* a famous saying.

qawwālī Sufi devotional poetry sung with music, especially percussion instruments.

Qays Name of Majnun in Nizami Ganjavi's myth about Layla and Majnun.

Qurʿān The holy book of the Muslims revealed to the prophet Muhammad.

rabāb A stringed instrument similar to the violin.

racāoT o give color or to create the context through linguistic means.

rāg A melodic mode or scale in classical music theory; Amir Khusrau is said to have named some of his *rāgs* after the seasons of the year. Thus he created compositions called "Rag Bahar" (Spring melody), "Rag Holi Kamach" (Holi Melody), and "Rag Basant" (Basant melody).

Rāg Basant A *rāg* named after the spring festival of Basant.

ragīnī A *ragīnī* has the feminine character of a *rāg*. "Sur Ramkali" is a *ragīnī*.

rājā A stately prince.

Rajasthan The western province of India, largely a desert with its own nomadic culture.

Rajput A warrior clan of India.

Ramazan The Islamic fasting month.

rang Ritual hymn in *qawwālī* that marks celebration and is sung at the Nizamuddin Auliya shrine in Delhi. It signifies Nizamuddin Auliya coloring his beloved Amir Khusrau in his own spirituality. This is sung after the *qaul*.[7]

Rānjhā The hero in the Panjabi myth of Hir-Ranjha. Hir is the heroine. Ranjha becomes a cowherd in the household of Hir's family; Ranjha is also a tribe name.

Rāno The hero in the Sindhi myth of Mumal-Rano. The heroine is Mumal. The lovers get married but are separated through misunderstanding, only to be united in death.

raqs Ecstatic mystical dance; activity induced from inspiration at a ritual Sufi musical assembly.

rekhtā North Indian poetry written in the Arabo-Persian tradition in which the narrator is a male.

rekhtī South Indian Deccani poetry in which the narrator is a woman.

rīāz To practice the musical forms.

rīāzat To practice the musical forms.

Risālo Shah Abdul Latif's Sufi epic narrative in Sindhi. It is based on thirty *sūrs*; nine of the *sūrs* are named after Shah's female heroines (*sūrmīs*).

rūh The soul or the spirit.

ṣābād Devotional poetry in Hindi usually sung with music.

sabr Patience, fortitude.

sādhū A Hindu mendicant.

ṣādmānā Melody played on ceremonial occasions in Sind.

sajjādā nashīn "The one seated on the prayer carpet"; official successor to a saint's shrine and therefore to the saint himself.[8]

sakhī A female friend; an addressee in the indigenous poetry of the subcontinent.

salām Ceremonial closing of oral Islamic rituals in the form of a prayer.

salām-karnā Ritual attendance at a Sufi shrine; to greet.

samā' A spiritual assembly or context of Sufi poetry and music.

sanā Devotional praise or eulogy.

Sassanides Persian kings ruling from the third to seventeenth centuries AD.

Sassi/Sasui Heroine of the Baluchi-Sindhi myth of Sassi-Punnu. Punnu is the hero. She dies in the desert following her beloved Punnu to Kec-Mekran.

sehrā Flower garlands that brides and bridegrooms wear around the forehead; a genre of wedding songs in the subcontinent.

Shaikh-ṣekh A spiritual guide in Sufism; a leader, a prominent person, and a scholar.

Shalimar Gardens Gardens built by Shah Jehan, the Mughal emperor.

Sharīʿā Islamic jurisprudence.

shɛhnāī Windpipes that are played ceremonially, usually at weddings.

shɛhnāīvālā A musician who plays the *shɛhnāī.*

Sidi Also known as Sheedi or Syedi in Sind and Gujrat; African descendants of Bava Gor, who was a follower of Hazrat Bilal, a slave freed by the prophet Muhammad.

sihārfī Mnemonic poetry known as the Golden Alphabet, known from the ancient Near East and the Old Testament. It was used among the Turkish dervish circles and in Swahili religious verse. The *sihārfī* was used by the Sufis in the subcontinent in vernacular languages such as Pashto, Panjabi, and Sindhi, where each word was charged with a certain meaning, such as the *alif,* which was linked with Allah/God.[9]

silsilā A Sufi lineage of people who trace spiritual descent from a particular order such as the Chishtiyya, Qadiriyya, or Suhrawardiyya in the subcontinent.

Sind The southern province of Pakistan.

Sirāikī The language of the region between the Sind and Panjab, for instance, Bahawalpur.

sitār Stringed instrument used in classical music.

Siyal Clan name of Hir's family; powerful landowners of the Panjab.

Sufi A mystic in the Islamic tradition.

sufiānā-kalām Islamic mystical poetry in Pakistan and India.

suhāg Nuptial.

Suhrawardiyyā A Sufi *silsilā.*

sūng A choir that sings at the Sufi shrines in Sind.

sūr A melody; also, pitch and tone.

Sūr Holī Kamach A *sūr* named after the Holi festival.

Sūr Maruī/Marvi A *sūr* in the *Risālo* based on the Omar-Marui myth; it is a melancholic *sūr.*

sūrmī A heroine; generic term for the heroines in Shah Abdul Latif's poetry; derived from the term *sūrmā* (hero).

Sūr Mumal-Rano A *sūr* in the *Risālo* based on the myth of Mumal-Rano.

Sūr Rām Kalī Early-morning *sūr;* one of the *sūr*s in the *Risālo.*

Sūr Sasui/Sassi A *sūr* in the *Risālo* based on the Sassi-Punnu myth.

Sūr Suhni/Sohni A *sūr* in the *Risālo* based on the Sohni-Mahival myth.

Syed One who claims descent from the prophet Muhammad's family.

tabarruk Ritual food distributed publicly at Muslim ceremonies.

tablā A pair of small kettle drums used in classical music.

takrār Incessant repetition.

tāl Rhythmic cycle which is sometimes complex and revolves around repeating the pattern of the beats; "clap" on stress pulse in *qawwālī*. (Qawwals do not use this term synonymously with *thekā*, as do classical musicians.)[10]

ṭālī A shady indigenous tree in the subcontinent.

tambūr A stringed instrument similar to a mandolin or Turkish guitar.

ṭangā A horse-drawn carriage on two wheels.

tarānā A genre of vocal classical music sometimes used in *qawwālī* where "the text derives from invocations in Persian."[11]

tarz "Traditional, old tune."

tassawaf Sufi mysticism.

tauhīd The Unity of Being.

ṭhumrī A semiclassical song genre in the woman's voice; the singer's virtuosity lies in how she elaborates on the lyrics through melodic, melismatic embellishment and word painting.

tilak A ceremonial mark on the forehead.

Umra Optional ritual pilgrimage to the Kaaba for Muslims, which can be performed at any time of the year.

Urdu Language of the Muslims of the subcontinent, written in the Perso-Arabic script.

ʿurs From the word *ʿurus* (wedding); death anniversary of a Sufi saint.

ustād One who has mastered a skill, such as music.

vaḍerā A feudal landlord in the Sind.

vāī Verses sung in Sindhi poetry for devotional purposes. After a couple of verses there are refrain lines, and the last words of the verses rhyme. The theme of a *vāī* is love or prayer, and its purpose is congregational. As such, a *vāī* is sung as a chorus. It is a characteristic of Shah's poetry in the *Risālo*; Shah's *faqīrs* at his shrine in Bhit Shah are renowned for singing the *vāī* in the falsetto.

virāhā Separation or unfulfilled longing; also called *birāhā*.

virāhīnī Pining female who is separated from her beloved; a genre of love poetry in the indigenous languages of the subcontinent where the female mourns her separation from the lover.

wajd Ecstasy, rapture, or trance induced from mystical arousal.

widow-marriage Traditionally, a Hindu widow committed *satti* by burning herself on her husband's funeral pyre. The practice was discontinued under British rule. Some sections of Indian society, such as the Siyal Jats of the Panjab, permitted a widow to remarry, and she was not forced into *satti*.

Yāsīn Sura Yāsīn, chapter thirty-six of the Quran, is the "heart" of the holy scripture.

zāhir The overt meaning of a word in Sufism.

zanānā Enclosed space exclusively for the use of women (in the subcontinent).

zakāt Alms that Muslims give to the needy according to the Shariʿā.

ziārat The ceremonial "viewing" or attendance at a Sufi shrine where the devotee offers *fāteḥā* (prayer) for the dead saint.

ziarāt Plural for Sufi shrines.

zikr A chant in the Sufi mystical tradition where the devotee repeats God's name and His qualities, such as "Allāh-hū."

Notes

AUTHOR'S NOTE: TRANSLATIONS, TRANSCRIPTIONS, AND CONVERSATION ANALYSIS TRANSCRIPTION NOTATION

1. I refer to them as transliterations. Most descriptions of the conventions are quoted from Jim Schenkein, ed., *Studies in the Organization of Conversational Interaction* (New York: Academic Press, 1978), xi–xvi. However, some conventions are reworked for the audience.

2. Chapter 2.

3. Chapter 3.

4. Kubra, the Sidi musician's chant from chapter 1.

5. Chapter 2.

6. Overlap with the performer's singing.

PREFACE. WOMAN'S PLACE IN SUFISM

1. Gilbert Rouget, *Music and Trance* (Chicago: University of Chicago Press, 1985), 255.

2. It is in North America among the Muslim communities in the diaspora that I participated in mosque rituals among women, where a substantial portion of the mosque is allocated for them to perform prayer rituals and other activities in the same manner as men.

3. Saiyid Athar Abbas Rizvi, *A History of Sufism in India,* vol. 2 (New Delhi: Munshiram Manoharlal Publishers, 1983), 480–81. Rizvi mentions the saintly mothers of Shaikh Abdul Haqq Muhaddis Dehlavi, Khawaja Baqi Bi'llah, and Mian Mir, who played a role in making their sons great Sufis. He also mentions Bibi Jamal Khatun (1639 AD), sister of Mian Mir, who, according to Dara Shikoh, was the Rabi'a of her times.

4. M. Wahid Mirza, *Life and Works of Amir Khusrau* (1934; reprint, Lahore: Panjab University Press, 1962), 17.

5. David Crystal, *Dictionary of Linguistics and Phonetics* (Oxford: Blackwell, 1997), 140. This is a methodology to study speech communication in a community or group. The terms ethnography of communication and ethnography of speaking have been applied by sociolinguists to the study of language in relation to the entire range of extralinguistic variables that identify the social basis of communication, the emphasis being on the description of linguistic interaction. The student of such matters is known as an ethnolinguist.

6. Harvey Sacks, Emanuel Schegloff, and Gail Jefferson, "A Simplest Systematics for the Organization of Turn Taking in Conversation," in *Studies in the Organization of Conversational Interaction*, ed. Jim Schenkein (New York: Academic Press, 1978), 696–735. This is a methodology to study live speech; an inductive, empirical approach to study interactions in speech, especially turn-taking.

7. 'Ali ibn 'Usman Data Ganj Bakhsh Hujwiri (d. 1071 AD).

8. The word *'urs* is derived from *'urus*, which means a wedding. Thus, the *'urs* celebrates the Sufi's union with the deity.

9. Charles Keil and Steven Feld, *Music Grooves* (Chicago: University of Chicago Press, 1994), 238–45; Sharilee M. Johnston, "Poetics of Performance: Narratives, Faith and Disjuncture in Qawwali." (Ph.D. diss., University of Texas, 2000), 271–2; Peter Manual, *Cassette Culture* (Chicago: University of Chicago Press, 1993). The research overlooks the development of *qawwālī* music in international settings.

10. Kanhyalal Hindi, *Tarikh-e Lahore* (1884; reprint, Lahore: Majlis-e Tariqi-e Adab, 1977), 76–77; Mufti Ghulam Sarwar, one of my ancestors, is mentioned together with my paternal grandfather, Mufti Muzaffar Din, in Kanhyalal's history of Lahore. Mufti Ghulam Sarwar is the author of a history of the Panjab, *Tarikh-e Makhazan Panjab* (1887; reprint, Lahore: Maktab-e Nabawwiya, 1987). Mirza (46) affirms that *qawwālī*, or the singing of mystical discourse, was popular in those days among the Sufis. On authority from Firishta he mentions one *qawwāl* named Abdullah, who came to that city from Turkey (Rum) and enlivened the assemblies of Shaikh Bahauddin Zakariya, the father of Shaikh Sadruddin of Multan. Rizvi (311) mentions only one Shaikh Rukunuddin Multani. I have visited the shrine of Rukunuddin several times, adjacent to the shrine of Hazrat Bahauddin Zakariya in Multan.

11. This may be the renowned Hazrat Shams Tabriz (d. 1248) who was the spiritual mentor of Maulana Rum (d. 1273), or another local Sufi by the same name. One of my students did take me to the shrine of one Hazrat Shams Tabrizi in Multan in 1998. Multiple shrines to the same person are not unusual. Sometimes it involves an actual relic, at other times simply a connection via a *silsilā*.

12. M. Wahid Mirza, *Life and Works of Amir Khusrau*, 14, where he quotes from Raverty (vol. 1, 598–9), 14.

13. *Tarikh-e Lahore*, 76–77.

14. See Gail Minault, *Secluded Scholars: Women's Education and Muslim Social Reform in Colonial India* (Delhi: Oxford University Press, 1998); Qamar Jahan Begam, *Princess Jahan Ara Begam: Her Life and Her Works* (Karachi: Library of Congress, CC no. 91-931192, 1991).

15. M. Wahid Mirza, *Life and Works of Amir Khusrau*, 43, 46, and more.

16. Peter Jackson, *The Delhi Sultanate: A Political and Military History* (Cambridge: Cambridge University Press, 1999), 178.

17. The Rourkee College of Engineering was a leading institution created by the British Raj to educate the intelligentsia in the Pakistan-India subcontinent. Sir Syed Ahmed Khan established the Aligarh Muslim University during the British Raj to create an educated Muslim elite who would assist the rulers in running the empire in the subcontinent.

18. A term fondly used among *mohajirs* (refugees) from North India who migrated to Pakistan after the 1947 partition. Baran is the old name for Buland Shehr, thus the name Barni or Burney.

19. Lila Abu-Lughod, *Veiled Sentiments* (Cairo: American University Press, 1986). Abu-Lughod has done fieldwork among the Awlad 'Ali, a Bedouin tribe who live in the Western Desert along the Libyan border. The tribe perform the *ghinnāwā*, a tradition of oral Arab poetry. Soraya Altorki and Camillia Fawzi El-Solh, eds., *Arab Women in the Field: Studying Your Own Society* (Syracuse: Syracuse University Press, 1988) is a collection of articles dealing with fieldwork that native women scholars carried out in their own societies. Kamala Visweswaran's *Fictions of Feminist Ethnography* (Minneapolis: University of Minneapolis, 1994) is based on the author's fieldwork in her own community in Madras and its neighborhoods of Mylapor and T-Nagar. However, none of the research is in Sufi rituals, and their methodologies are different. Frances Trix's *Spiritual Discourses* (Philadelphia: University of Pennsylvania Press, 1993) is a study of the Bektashis of the Albanian Bektashi Tekke. The research was mainly carried out in the United States with one key informant, Baba Rexheb. I use a variety of live speech samples from the extensive fieldwork I did in Pakistan and the data that I collected from archives. I transcribed and translated the speech samples together with my interviews with the musicians, both women and men who sing Sufi poetry. As a native of the culture I bring my own interpretations to the study.

CHAPTER I. HISTORY AND ECONOMY OF WOMEN IN SUFI RITUAL

1. Katherine Ewing, *Arguing Sainthood* (Durham, N.C.: Duke University Press, 1997); Pnina Werbner and Helene Basu, eds., *Embodying Charisma* (London and New York: Routledge, 1998).

2. Regula Qureshi, *Sufi Music of India and Pakistan* (Cambridge: Cambridge University Press, 1986).

3. Annemarie Schimmel, *Mystical Dimensions of Islam* (Chapel Hill: Uni-

versity of North Carolina Press, 1975), *As Through a Veil* (New York: Columbia University Press, 1982), and *My Soul Is a Woman,* trans. Susan Ray (New York: Continuum, 1997).

4. Margaret Smith, *Rabiʿa: The Life and Work of Rabiʿa and Other Women Mystics of Islam* (1928; reprint, Oxford: Oneworld, 1994).

5. Arthur J. Arberry, *An Account of the Mystics of Islam* (London: Allen and Unwin, 1950) and *Sufism* (London: Allen and Unwin, 1969); Ali Asani, "The Bridegroom Prophet in Medieval Sindhi Poetry," in *Studies in South Asian Devotional Literature: Research Papers 1989–91,* ed. F. Mallison and A. Erswistle (New Delhi: Manohar, 1994); Richard Eaton, *The Sufis of Bijapur* (Princeton: Princeton University Press, 1978); Reynold Nicholson, *The Mystics of Islam* (1914; reprint, London: Routledge, 1963); Saiyid Athar Abbas Rizvi, *A History of Sufism in India,* vol. 1 (New Delhi: Munshiram Manoharlal, 1978); Spenser Trimingham, *The Sufi Orders of Islam* (Oxford: Clarendon Press, 1971).

6. Reshma, a renowned singer of Sufi poetry, informed me that she sings at the shrine of Bibi Pak Daman in Lahore whenever the Bibi summons her—it can be at any time, night or day.

7. The faithful in South Asian Islam believe that the souls of those who die visit their tombs on Thursday evenings.

8. *Aqīqā* is a celebration that ritualizes the shaving of an infant's hair along with sacrificing a goat.

9. Charles Keil and Steven Feld, *Music Grooves* (Chicago: University of Chicago Press, 1994), 238–45.

10. The two separate genres of performances of Sufi music are discussed in the material that follows. Briefly, classical *qawwālī* created by Amir Khusrau (d. 1325) starts with the *qaul* of the Prophet in Arabic. *Sufiānā-kalām* is the poetry of the Sufi poets sung in the vernacular languages with minimal instrumentation.

11. Concert at the Marriott Hotel in Islamabad that I attended in 1993. Abida Parvin, *Chants Soufis du Pakistan,* compact disc, Auvidis Distribution, 298492600038.

12. Abida Parvin, ibid.

13. Adapted from Peter Manuel, *Cassette Culture* (Chicago: University of Chicago Press, 1993).

14. Islamic Web website, "Population of Muslims around the World," http://islamicweb.com/begin/population.htm (14 December 2000). Numbers of Muslims as of December 2000 were Afghanistan 22,664,136; Bangladesh 129,194,224; China 133,100,154; India 133,295,077; Indonesia 196,281,020; Malaysia 10,380,704; Pakistan 125,397,390.

15. Annemarie Schimmel, *As Through a Veil,* 16.

16. Ibid., 30.

17. Saiyid Athar Abbas Rizvi, *A History of Sufism in India,* vols. 1 and 2.

18. Margaret Smith, *Rabiʿa: The Life and Work of Rabiʿa and Other Women*

Mystics of Islam; Robert Fernea and Elizabeth Fernea, "Variation in Religious Observance among Islamic Women," in *Scholars, Saints, and Sufis: Muslim Religious Institutions in the Middle East since 1500,* ed. Nikki R. Keddie (Berkeley: University of California Press, 1972), 385–401; Bo Utas, ed., *Women in Islamic Societies* (New York: Olive Branch Press, 1983); Pnina Werbner and Helene Basu, eds., *Embodying Charisma.*

19. Annemarie Schimmel, *Mystical Dimensions of Islam,* 178–86.

20. John Platts, *A Dictionary of Urdu, Classical Hindi, and English* (London: Oxford University Press, 1982), 795.

21. Sometimes there can be more than one singer.

22. Reshma is believed to have been a *loṭevalī* until she was discovered by the radio in the sixties. An interview with the musician is documented in this chapter.

23. Peter Manuel, *Cassette Culture.*

24. Reynold Nicholson, *The Mystics of Islam;* Khusro Hussaini, "Bund Sama," in *Islamic Culture* 44 (1970):77–85; Annemarie Schimmel, *As Through a Veil;* Gilbert Rouget, *Music and Trance* (Chicago: University of Chicago Press, 1985); Regula Qureshi, *Sufi Music of India and Pakistan;* Ali Asani, "Propagating the Message: Popular Sufi Songs and Spiritual Transformation in South Asia," *Bulletin of the Henry Martyn Institute of Islamic Studies* 15, nos. 3–4 (1998):5–15.

25. Regula Qureshi, *Sufi Music of Pakistan and India,* 119. She distinguishes the terms adequately within the "frameworks of spiritual arousal." She identifies trance through degrees of ecstasy, and the terms she uses are *behoshī, wajd,* and *hāl.* Additionally, references to trance, ecstasy, and *wajd* are found in Gilbert Rouget's *Music and Trance,* Annemarie Schimmel's *Mystical Dimensions of Islam,* and Reynold Nicholson's *The Mystics of Islam.*

26. Regula Qureshi, *Sufi Music of India and Pakistan,* 119.

27. Saiyid Athar Abbas Rizvi, *A History of Sufism in India,* vol. 1, 326, describes Shaikh Qutubuddin Bakhtiyar Kaki (d. 1237), a spiritual descendant of Hazrat Khawaja Muinuddin Chishti; he was overcome while attending a powerful *samāʿ* performance and died a few days later.

28. Oriental Star Agencies website, "Ustad Nusrat Fateh Ali Khan," http://www.osa.co.uk (17 November 1999).

29. Ibid.

30. The late Alan Faqir (d. 2000), who claimed to be a *faqīr* of Shah Abdul Latif's shrine, told me in his interview that Sassi and Marvi in Shah's poetry also represent the land pillaged by conquerors and invaders. He claimed that when he sang Shah's poetry he did it with a passion that would convey the exploitation of the land.

31. The practice of non-Muslim devotees visiting Muslim shrines and vice versa is common when diverse religious communities coexist. This was especially so in undivided India before the partition of 1947. Islamic mysticism,

that is, Sufism, was a shared experience with the indigenous forms of mysticism. Mughal emperors such as Akbar encouraged the syncreticism. Akbar's great-grandson Dara Shikoh, a devotee of Hazrat Mian Mir, a Qadiriya Sufi mystic of Lahore, also patronized Hindu mystics (*saniyasis*). He was executed by his orthodox-Muslim brother Aurengzeb, who ascended to the throne of Delhi and was the last of the great Mughals.

32. See special editions of *Manushi,* nos. 50, 51, 52, on women Bhakta poets (New Delhi: Manushi Trust, 1989). There are several articles on women's roving-minstrel traditions in the journal. This tradition was strong among the Bhakta poets in India who were roving minstrels, especially women like Mira Bai, a Rajput princess who composed mystical poetry in the indigenous languages.

33. Nazir Jairazbhoy and Amy Catlin, *Musical Instruments of Kacch and Its Neighbors,* 1999, videocassette, shown at the forty-fourth Annual Seminar of the Society for Ethnomusicology at the University of Texas at Austin, 1999.

34. See Aziz Baloch, "Music Traditions of Lower Indus Valley," in *Folk Music of Sind,* ed. G. A. Allana (Jamshoro: Institute of Sindhology, 1982), 50–64; N. A. Baloch, "Developments in the Subcontinent: Evolution of the Music Tradition of Sind," in *Folk Music of Sind,* ed. G. A. Allana (Jamshoro: Institute of Sindhology, 1982), 17–26; N. A. Baloch, "Shah Abdul Latif: The Founder of a New Music Institution," in *Folk Music of Sind,* ed. G. A. Allana (Jamshoro: Institute of Sindhology, 1982), 27–37.

35. Encyclopedia Britannica website, "Bhakti Movement of Medieval India," http://www.britannica.co.in/spotlights/bhakti/pt01.htm (14 December 2000). The Bhakti started to emerge in the sixth century AD.

36. Also called Baba Farid.

37. Encyclopedia Britannica website, "Bhakti Movement of Medieval India." Additionally, see Saiyid Athar Abbas Rizvi, "The Interaction between Medieval Hindu Mystic Traditions and Sufism," in *A History of Sufism in India,* vol. 1, 322–96.

38. Ibid.

39. Tirathdas Hotechand, "The *Risālo:* Its Musical Compositions," in *Shah Abdul Latif: His Mystical Poetry,* ed. Abdul Hamid Akhund (Hyderabad: Shah Abdul Latif Bhit Shah Cultural Center Committee, 1991), 162.

40. This is a term created by Jacqueline Henkel of the Department of English at the University of Texas at Austin.

41. *Jamālī* mysticism is attained through intuition and creativity, such as by Shah Abdul Latif, a poet and musician. In contrast to this, *jalālī* mysticism is achieved through rigor and discipline. 'Ali, the fourth caliph, is known for his *jalālī* powers. Hazrat Lal Shahbaz Qalandar of Sehwan is also known for his *jalālī* or supernatural powers, and his shrine is called a *jalālī* shrine.

42. A Sufi epic based on three books. In Sindhi *risālo* means "the message." The *Risālo* narrative is based on thirty sections, each of which is built

around a *sūr* that is a form or mode of singing, a rhythm, or melody. Ten of the *sūrs* in the *Risālo* are built around female heroines (*sūrmis*) and thus are called *Sūr* Sohni, *Sūr* Sassi, *Sūr* Marvi, *Sūr* Mumal-Rano, *Sūr* Leela-Canesar, *Sūr* Sassi-Ma'azuri, and *Sūr* Sassi Desi. See Makhdoom website, "The Melodies of Harmonized Music," http://home.pacific.net/sg/~makhdoom/ sur.htm (30 December 2000).

43. M. Yakoob Agha, trans., *Shah Jo Risālo alias Ganje Latif*, vol. 2 (Hyderabad: Shah Abdul Latif Bhit Shah Cultural Center Committee, 1985), 945–50.

44. *Jogīs* (mendicants) have their ears pierced to wear large round rings in them. In mystical poetry in the indigenous languages there are numerous references to *jogīs* with slit ears, in other words, pierced lobes. Some wear several rings in their ears. Their identity is their orange robes, slit ears, the beads they wear around the neck, and a begging bowl.

45. Transliterated with some adaptations according to the conversation analysis system of Harvey Sacks, Emanuel A. Schegloff, and Gail Jefferson, "A Simplest Systematics for the Organization of Turn Taking for Conversation," in *Studies in the Organization of Conversational Interaction*, ed. Jim Schenkein (New York: Academic Press, 1978). I use a dash to represent a pause in speech.

46. A=Abbas, P=Abida Parvin, H=Shaikh Ghulam Hussain.

47. John Platts, *A Dictionary of Urdu, Classical Hindi, and Urdu*, 169. Although Platts gives the meaning of *banjārā* as grain carriers, the term is also applied to roving minstrels.

48. Translated and annotated by M. Yakoob Agha, *Shah Jo Risālo alias Ganje Latif*, vol. 1 (Hyderabad: Shah Abdul Latif Bhit Shah Cultural Center Committee, 1985), 23.

49. Ibid., 2:770.

50. Ibid., 772.

51. A native Sindhi informant corrected this term to mean a choir of mendicants who sing mystical poetry, but I retain the context in which I interviewed Baloch and Mirza.

52. *'Urs* celebrations usually go on for several days and can be observed at many levels. They are performed as part of popular culture when the caretakers of the shrine make arrangements to initiate the *'urs*, and the devotees participate in the rituals for several days. At the official level the party in power in the country shows its patronage of the event and sets its own time frame within the same *'urs* period to participate in the ritual. The party members, usually led by a governor or chief minister of the province, bring wreaths and perform rituals. As part of the celebrations the ruling party in government contracts with renowned musicians to sing at the shrines.

53. Lorraine H. Sakata, personal communication, forty-fourth Annual Seminar of the Society for Ethnomusicology, University of Texas at Austin, 1999.

54. She sang it at the Allama Iqbal Open University in 1985. Although key musicians perform at private concerts, they are additionally patronized by

state organizations like a university, a state-run arts council, or Lok Virsa, the Institute of Folk Heritage run by the state.

55. I have discussed the melody with both Muslim and non-Muslim informants and conclude that there is no fixed interpretation. The lyric is drawn cross culturally from the regional folklore.

56. They additionally sing around shrines in Multan and Sahiwal to earn a living.

57. A=Abbas, R=Reshma.

58. A vow made at a shrine.

59. I contacted the musician through the family of her *pir*, Gilani, after a year's effort.

60. M=Mirza, B=Baloch, A=Abbas.

61. I have changed the musician's name to protect her privacy.

62. Name changed for privacy.

63. Surraiya Multanikar, a Siraiki singer of Sufi poetry, in particular that of Khawaja Ghulam Farid, also confirmed in her interview with me that she is specially blessed by her *pir*, a Gilani Syed. She said that, because of his prayer, there is much *sūr* (melody) in her voice.

64. Another Sindhi informant's input about *maidānī* is that these women's voices are full throated and high pitched.

65. See n. 51.

66. Inam Muhammad, *Hazrat Lal Shahbaz Qalandar of Sehwan* (Jamshoro: Institute of Sindhology, 1999), 9–10.

67. Sakata, personal communication, 1999.

68. One who claims descent from the prophet Muhammad's family. He is chair of the English department at Sind University.

69. Name changed for confidentiality.

70. Q=Qalandar Shah; A=Abbas; K=Kubra, a Sidi female informant and musician.

71. Helene Basu, *Habshi-Sklaven, Sidi Fakire.* A portion translated by Amy Catlin (UCLA) is used in this book. The Hammerton Treaty of 1840 banned bringing African slaves to India. Many were freed in Bombay, 46.

72. R. W. Beachy, *Slave Trade in East Africa* (London: Rex Collins, 1976).

73. Kubra expresses the community's negative attitude toward women singing; among the peasant or working classes singing in public contexts even among women is sometimes taboo since dancing and singing are skills associated with courtesans.

74. Throughout the interview Kubra is reluctant to admit her identity as a musician. Ironically, she chants for me and provides the data for substantial discussion in this chapter.

75. Qalandar Shah confirms that Kubra's singing in public would be socially damaging for her husband's visible position as a functionary in the university. His male peers would taunt him.

76. This is a shrine linked with Bava Gor, the Sidi saint who was a follower of Hazrat Bilal. Details of Bava Gor follow in this chapter.

77. This is an Islamic *salwat* (prayer) that bestows blessings on the prophet Muhammad and his family.

78. Many Muslims in the subcontinent can read and recite Arabic because it is the sacred language of the Quran; they may not necessarily understand Arabic. Kubra's chant is simple and can be understood cross culturally.

79. Transliterated and adapted according to the conversation analysis system of Harvey Sacks, Emanuel Schegloff, and Gail Jefferson, in *Studies in the Organization of Conversational Interaction.*

80. Bava Gor.

81. Bava Gor is the Abyssinian saint of the Sidi in Gujrat in India, where a shrine is dedicated to him, his brother Bava Habash, and his sister Mai Misra.

82. See photographs.

83. Their spiritual mentor's death anniversary celebrations, called a *melā* or *'urs.* The death anniversary is celebrated as the anniversary of the saint's union with the deity.

84. The Mangopir shrine is associated with crocodiles and is dedicated to Bava Gor, the African Muslim saint.

85. Helene Basu, *Habshi-Sklaven, Sidi Fakire,* a portion of which is translated by Amy Catlin.

86. Ibid., 71–74. Hazrat Bilal was a follower of Muhammad the Prophet, and was liberated. His *āzān* (call for prayer) is legendary.

87. A reference either to Bilal or to the prophet Muhammad himself.

88. Helene Basu, *Habshi-Sklaven, Sidi Fakire,* research section translated by Amy Catlin.

89. Ibid.

90. Ibid.

91. *Jakat* or *zakat* is an obligatory annual charitable gift that a well-to-do Muslim must make. It is one of the pillars of Islam.

92. Non-Muslim migratory peasants who work on large landholdings in Sind and Indian Gujrat.

93. Helene Basu, *Habshi-Sklaven, Sidi Fakire,* 50–51.

94. Ibid., 51.

95. A Sufi mystic of Sind whose spiritual powers are renowned. He is called upon as a bestower of children.

96. See Judith Butler, *Bodies That Matter* (New York: Routledge, 1993), 57–91; Ferdinand de Saussure, *Course in General Linguistics,* eds. C. Bally et al. (New York: McGraw Hill, 1959); J. L. Austin, *How to Do Things with Words,* 2d ed. (Cambridge: Cambridge University Press, 1975).

97. Helene Basu, *Habshi-Sklaven, Sidi Fakire.*

98. See Della Pollock, "Performing Writing," in *The Ends of Performance,* eds. Peggy Phalen and Jill Lane (New York: New York University Press, 1998),

95, where she draws upon Austin's concept of performative utterances. She distinguishes between words that report or describe (constatives) and words that *do* what they say (performatives). She also draws upon Eve Sedgwick's example of Austin's distinction between the wedding announcement and the wedding vow.

99. For forty days the faithful mourn Hussain's death at Kerbala. *Marsiyās* and *nohās* that are litanies are sung in the segregated female and male assemblies.

100. The Sidis take great pride in joking, and this is a special quality in their interaction.

101. Helene Basu, *Habshi-Sklaven, Sidi Fakire.* Research portion translated by Amy Catlin (UCLA).

102. A stew made of rice and legumes.

103. Helene Basu's recording, trans. Catlin, 1999.

104. *Dhammāl* is a ritual ecstatic dance performed at the Sufi shrines or in contexts where Sufi texts are sung.

105. Helene Basu, *Habshi-Sklaven, Sidi Fakire.* Research portion translated by Amy Catlin.

106. Nazir Jairazbhoy and Amy Catlin, *Musical Instruments of Kacch and Its Neighbors,* 1999, videocassette.

107. Momin Bullo, "Zafar Kazmi: Alan Faqir's Foster Brother," *Friday Times Lahore* 11, no. 42 (Dec. 17–23, 1999).

108. Helene Basu, *Habshi-Sklaven, Sidi Fakire.* Research portion translated by Amy Catlin. There is evidence in South Gujrat of the Sidis of Ratanpur, who lived as *faqīrs* until this generation. They traveled from village to village, entertaining with their music and dance. The *faqīrs* received alms, which were their primary source of livelihood.

109. F=Alan Faqir; A=Abbas.

110. See chapter 4, "The Female Voice in Sufi Ritual," for more details on this interview.

111. Nusrat Fateh Ali Khan reportedly managed to have several of his nephews admitted to the University of Washington in Seattle where some of them perhaps follow the family's traditional musical trade of *qawwālī.*

112. See *Akhri Geet: Manganhar Musicians of Sind,* prod. Uxi Mufti, Institute of Folk Heritage, Islamabad 1999, videocassette.

113. *Roshni,* CD ROM Sound Master SMCD 146, produced by Irfan Kiani and distributed by Sadaf Stereo, Pakistan.

114. Sohni drowned as she tried to cross the river on an earthen pot to meet her beloved Mahival.

115. The barbers (*nāis*) communicated births and deaths in the community and were paid for their services; they performed male circumcision and cooked huge quantities of food for ritual celebrations; the potters (*kumhārs*)

traditionally were also the carriers of the bride's palanquin or small litter called a *ḍolī*. There are references to the potters (*kahārs*) in Hir's laments in Waris Shah's *Hir-Ranjha* narrative; I have observed this through my association with the landowning Syeds in Burewala, Multan. The family are politicians in the Pakistan Muslim League.

116. In the subcontinent of India and Pakistan, as also in the other former British colonies, the rulers created an administrative framework that employed the native-educated elite to assist the rulers in running the colonies. Even after more than half a century of independence these elitist social structures are still in place.

117. There is a stigma attached to women singing because this is a skill associated with courtesans.

118. This seems to be a class phenomenon. Rubina Qureshi, a renowned female singer of Sindhi Sufi poetry and a faculty member at Sind University, is reportedly the wife of a top official in the Sind government organization.

CHAPTER 2. ETHNOGRAPHICS OF COMMUNICATION

1. Dell Hymes, ed., *Language in Culture and Society* (New York: Harper & Row, 1964); Richard Bauman and Joel Sherzer, *Explorations in the Ethnography of Speaking* (New York: Cambridge University Press, 1989), 7.

2. Adam Nayyar, *Origin and History of Qawwālī* (Islamabad: Lok Virsa Research Center, 1988); Oriental Star Agencies website, "Ustad Nusrat Fateh Ali Khan and Qawwālī," http//:www.osa.co.uk (12 August 2001).

3. I bring out the verbal interaction among the *qawwāl* musicians in my transliterations through the conversation analysis system of Harvey Sacks, Emanuel Schegloff, and Gail Jefferson, in "A Simplest Systematics for the Organization of Turn Taking for Conversation," in *Studies in the Organization of Conversational Interaction*, ed. Jim Schenkein (New York: Academic Press, 1978).

4. Regula Qureshi, *Sufi Music of India and Pakistan* (Cambridge: Cambridge University Press, 1986), 103–31.

5. Ibid.

6. Nusrat Fateh Ali Khan, *Private Mehfil*, 1 and 2, Oriental Star Agencies, Birmingham, U.K., 1984, videocassette.

7. Ali Asani, "Propagating the Message: Popular Sufi Songs and Spiritual Transformation in South Asia," *Bulletin of the Henry Martyn Institute of Islamic Studies* 15, nos. 3–4 (1998): 5–15; Peter Manuel, *Cassette Culture* (Chicago: University of Chicago Press, 1993), 136–7.

8. Nusrat Fateh Ali Khan, *Private Mehfil*, 1 and 2, videocassette.

9. Amelia Maciszewski, interview by author, Austin, Tex., November 20, 2000.

10. Nusrat Fateh Ali Khan, *Private Mehfil,* 1 and 2, videocassette.

11. Roman Jakobson, "Closing Statement: Linguistics and Poetics," in *Style in Language,* ed. T. A. Sebeok (Cambridge, Mass.: MIT Press, 1960), 351.

12. Ibid.

13. Nusrat Fateh Ali Khan, *Private Mehfil,* 1 and 2, videocassette.

14. Here I use the transliteration system from conversation analysis to portray the dialogue among the performers themselves and the turn-taking that occurs as the discourse emerges. It can be seen that the narrative is not fixed and evolves within the performance context. A=Nusrat Fateh Ali Khan; B and C are two of the other lead musicians in the ensemble. The lines are numbered, and I have created the line according to the pause since there is a semantic pattern in the chant.

15. Mansur Hallaj (858–922 AD), glorified in the oral Sufi tradition for giving his head for a principle. He was executed in Baghdad for political reasons.

16. Richard Bauman and Joel Sherzer, *Explorations in the Ethnography of Speaking,* 7.

17. Oriental Star Agencies website, "Ustad Nusrat Fateh Ali Khan," http://www.osa.co.uk (17 November 1999).

Nusrat Fateh Ali Khan was born in Faisalabad in Pakistan in 1948 and was the son of Ustad Fateh Ali Khan, a renowned musician who had been trained in the classical traditions of the subcontinent. The family were a lineage of professional musicians linked to the singing of Sufi mystical texts for six centuries. After his father's death in 1964, Nusrat's paternal uncles Ustad Mubarik Ali Khan and Ustad Salamat Ali Khan took over his training, and the latter initiated him into singing *qawwāli.* WOMAD (the World of Music, Arts, and Dance; an organization founded by Peter Gabriel in 1980; WOMAD organizes festivals around the world and releases CDs through its own select descriptions) discovered Khan in the early eighties, and Oriental Star Agencies (OSA) in Birmingham later recorded a large number of his *qawwālī* performances in the United Kingdom. I used these as a database for my dissertation. I spent time at OSA to select intimate *mehfil* settings for studying the musicians' interactions with each other and with their audiences. The musician died from diabetes and multiple liver complications in 1997 in the United Kingdom. Lorraine Sakata reports that Rehmat Gramophone Company in Faisalabad contains an archive of the family's *qawwālī* repertoire of the Panjabi *ang* (style of singing *qawwālī*). That further explains the musician's vast repertoire of inherited Panjabi texts and the fact that he was a great linguist who could sing in the many varieties and dialects of Panjabi. His Panjabi texts are extensive.

18. Lorraine Sakata, personal communication, 1999. Sakata accompanied the musician to Pakpattan Sharif where he performed at the shrine. She observed the performance sitting behind a pillar where the men could not see her.

19. "*Beṭhi*" is the feminine marker in the text, indicating the act of sitting.

20. Roman Jakobson, "Closing Statement: Linguistics and Poetics," 351.

21. Regula Quereshi reports in *Sufi Music of India and Pakistan,* 128, that a famous couplet from the Persian mystic Ahmed Jam brought about this state for Shaikh Bakhtiyar Kaki, that continued for several days. The *qawwāl*s had to continue singing until finally the Sufis present asked the performers to end the singing on the first couplet, "for the martyrs of the dagger of submission," so that the saint would rest in final union with his beloved.

22. Richard Eaton, *The Sufis of Bijapur* (Princeton: Princeton University Press, 1978); Spenser Trimingham, *The Sufi Orders of Islam* (Oxford: Clarendon Press, 1971).

23. Tahir Lahori, "Auliya ke 'Urs," in *Sohna Shehr Lahore* (Lahore: Sang-e Meel Publications, 1994), 153–5.

24. See Regula Quereshi, *Sufi Music of India and Pakistan,* 231.

25. See Elizabeth Fernea's article "Saints and Spirits," in *Religious Expression in Morocco: A Guide to the Film* (Austin: University of Texas at Austin, 1979), which highlights the ritual among the *gnawa* in Morocco.

26. The opening verse of the Quran, Sura al-Fāteḥā, is recited ritually to pray for the dead.

27. The translation is contextual and not a word-for-word rendering. I have discussed the poetry with native Sindhi informants. "Lalan" can be a reference to Lal Shahbaz Qalandar, although the reference could also be to other indigenous beliefs about protectors of the cradle.

28. Ali Asani, "The Bridegroom Prophet in Medieval Sindhi Poetry," in *Studies in South Asian Devotional Literature: Research Papers 1989–91,* ed. F. Mallison and A. Erswistle (Delhi: Manohar, 1994), 213–25.

29. Nusrat Fateh Ali Khan, *Private Mehfil,* 1 and 2, videocassette.

30. "*vālā*" is an exact reproduction from the musicians' speech.

31. A=Abbas; K=Ustad Nusrat Fateh Ali Khan.

32. The translation is a poetic rendering in context, worked out with a native Siraiki informant, and is not a paraphrase. The transliteration is produced from the live performance, *A Musical Evening with Abida Parvin,* Allama Iqbal Open University, Islamabad, 1985, videocassette.

33. Notice that the form of her narrative is a monologue because she is a solo singer here.

34. The end word "*hū*" indicates Sultan Bahu's poetry. Born in the Panjab in 1631 AD, Sultan Bahu wrote 140 books on mysticism all of which are in Arabic and Persian except for his *ābīāt* and *sihārfī,* which are in Panjabi.

35. Muhammad the Prophet is buried in Medina in a part of the Masjid-e Nabawi.

36. Transliteration produced from live performance at the Open University, Islamabad, August 1985.

37. Overlap with the performer's singing.

38. M. Wahid Mirza, *Life and Works of Amir Khusrau* (1934; reprint, Lahore: Panjab University Press, 1962), 137.

39. Zia Jaffery, *The Invisibles: A Tale of the Eunuchs of India* (New York: Pantheon Books, 1996); Jamil Dehlavi, prod., *Immaculate Conception* (UK: Feature Film Company, 1992): a film about a *hijṛā* shrine in Karachi, Pakistan.

40. Taufiq Rafat, *Bulleh Shah: A Selection* (Lahore: Vanguard, 1982) and Lajwanti Ramakrishna, *Panjabi Sufi Poets* (New Delhi: Ashajanak Publications, 1973).

41. Taufiq Rafat, *Bulleh Shah: A Selection.*

42. Erving Goffman, "The Neglected Situation," in *Language and Social Context,* ed. Pier Paolo Giglioli (Harmondsworth, U.K.: Penguin, 1972), 133–6.

43. Ervin Goffman, "The Neglected Situation," and *Forms of Talk* (Philadelphia: University of Pennsylvania Press, 1981); Harold Garfinkel, "Remarks on Ethnomethodology," in *Directions in Sociolinguistics,* eds. John Gumperz and Dell Hymes (New York: Holt and Rhinehart, 1972); and Harvey Sacks, Emanuel Schegloff, and Gail Jefferson, "A Simplest Systematics for the Organization of Turn Taking for Conversation," in *Studies in the Organization of Conversational Interaction,* ed. Jim Schenkein (New York: Academic Press, 1978).

CHAPTER 3. FEMALE MYTHS IN SUFISM

1. See page 92–93 of this chapter for Hir's discourse.

2. I use Lilaram Watanmal Lalwani, *The Life, Religion, and Poetry of Shah Latif* (1889; reprint, Lahore: Sang-e Meel Publications, 1978) to discuss the myths in the Sindhi context.

3. Ibid., 75.

4. Ibid., 77.

5. Siraiki is a language found between the regions of Panjab and Sind. Unfortunately, Pathana Khan died in the summer of 2000.

6. The translation is in the context of live speech and is therefore not a paraphrase. The excerpt is transliterated from *A Tribute to Great Mystics: Bulleh Shah, Shah Hussain, and Khawaja Farid,* Institute of Folk Heritage, Islamabad, 1985, audiocassette.

7. M. Yakoob Agha, trans., *Shah Jo Risālo alias Ganje Latif,* vols. 1, 2, 3 (Hyderabad: Shah Abdul Latif Bhit Shah Cultural Center Committee, 1985).

8. Denzil Ibbetson, *Panjab Castes* (Lahore: Government Printing Press, 1916), 103. In some communities of India women practiced *satti* through burning themselves on their husband's funeral pyre. British colonial rule in the subcontinent (1857–1947) prohibited this custom.

9. C. L. Osborne, *The Adventures of Hir and Ranjha* (London: Peter Owen Ltd, 1973), 173.

10. Although the myth is several hundred years old, villagers in the district of Jhang do identify Hir's tomb to this day.

11. Sant Sekhon, *The Love of Hir and Ranjha* (Ludhiana: Panjab Agricultural University, 1978), 1.

12. S. Hamidullah Hashimi, *Syed Waris Shah* (Faisalabad: Majlis-e Panjabi Adab, 1978), 179.

13. There seem to be similarities to the Radha-Krishna myth.

14. Sant Sekhon, *The Love of Hir and Ranjha,* 2.

15. Abbas Jalalpuri, *Muqamat-e Waris Shah* (Lahore: Hamid Raza Press, 1972), 24–25.

16. *Hir,* Institute of Folk Heritage, Islamabad, 1987, audiocassette.

17. Private recording, Institute of Folk Heritage, Islamabad, 1987, audiocassette.

18. Abbas Jalalpuri, *Muqamat-e Waris Shah,* 118.

19. The *ḍolī* (palanquin) has a strong emotional context in Panjabi ritual, as a complex of emotions are associated with it.

20. In the socioeconomic caste system the potters traditionally carried the bride's palanquin.

21. Lilaram Lalwani, *The Life, Religion, and Poetry of Shah Latif,* 70–72.

22. Ibid.

23. Ibid., 71.

24. Ibid., 72.

25. Private recording, Institute of Folk Heritage, Islamabad, 1987, audiocassette.

26. John Platts, *A Dictionary of Urdu, Classical Hindi, and English* (London: Oxford University Press, 1982), 845. Platts has several meanings for *kuli.* In this context the meaning of *kuli* is "abode."

27. Margaret Mills, *Rhetoric and Politics in Afghan Traditional Storytelling* (Philadelphia: University of Pennsylvania Press, 1991), 15.

28. *Qawwālīes: Live in Concert,* Oriental Star Agencies, Birmingham, 1981, videocassette.

29. A. J. Alston, *The Devotional Poems of Mira Bai* (Delhi: Motilal Banarsidass 1980), 2.

30. Andrew Schelling, *For Love of the Dark One* (Boston: Shambala, 1993), 31.

31. Ibid.

32. Ibid., 11.

33. The musicians' speech is not very clear semantically, but they use a number of dialects that are Braj, Bhojpuri, and Purbi.

34. Notice the boundaries of speech and song here. The *qawwāls* use the colloquial speech form.

35. Supporter of the poor.

36. One of the *qawwāl* leaders is showing his appreciation of the story.

37. Saiyid Athar Abbas Rizvi, *A History of Sufism in India,* vol. 1 (New Delhi: Munshiram Manoharlal Publishers, 1978), 326.

38. Schelling, *For Love of the Dark One,* 23.

39. Mira's melismatic cry.

40. This is an adaptation from the *ṭhumrī* style, where the female begs the beloved to hold her arm.

41. Ibid.

42. Ganjavi Nizami, *Layla-Majnun* (Boulder: Shambala Press, 1966), 13.

43. Ibid., 64.

44. Ibid.

45. Ganajvi Nizami, *Layla-Majnun,* 104–5.

CHAPTER 4. THE FEMALE VOICE IN SUFI RITUAL

1. Within the shrine context Regula Qureshi, *Sufi Music of India and Pakistan* (Cambridge: Cambridge University Press, 1986) has discussed it adequately.

2. Abida Parvin sang the *qaul* "Mun kunto Maulā fā Alī-un Maulā" at the Marriott Hotel in Islamabad in concert in 1993; *Chants Soufis du Pakistan,* compact disc, Auvidis Distribution, 298492600038; Mehr Ali and Sher Ali sing the Persian *girah* "Haiderī-am, qalandar-am, mast-am" (I am a devotee of Haider, a *qalandar,* an intoxicated one), and "Bandā-e Murtaza Alī hastam" (I am a slave of Ali Murtaza), *Music du Monde: Music from the World,* Buda Music, Paris, CD-ROM 92611-2. Ghulam Kibria sang the same *girah* in *Qawwālīes,* Oriental Star Agencies, Birmingham, U.K., 1984, videocassette, transliterated in Shemeem Abbas's "Speech Play and Verbal Art in the Indo-Pakistan Oral Sufi Tradition" (Ph.D. diss., University of Texas at Austin, 1992), 94.

3. Regula Quereshi, *Sufi Music of India and Pakistan,* 121, 19, 24–27, 74–134.

4. Lajwanti Ramakrishna, *Panjabi Sufi Poets* (New Delhi: Ashajanak Publications, 1973); Annemarie Schimmel, *Mystical Dimensions of Islam* (Chapel Hill: University of North Carolina Press, 1975), *As Through a Veil* (New York: New York University Press, 1982), *My Soul Is a Woman* (New York: Continuum, 1997); Cristopher Shackle, *Fifty Poems of Khawaja Farid* (Multan: Bazm-e Saqafat, 1983) and *Sassi-Punnu* (Lahore: Vanguard, 1985); Regula Quershi, *Sufi Music of Pakistan and India;* Ali Asani, "The Bridegroom Prophet in Medieval Sindhi Poetry," in *Studies in South Asian Devotional Literature: Research Papers 1989–91,* ed. F. Mallison and A. Erswistle (Delhi: Manohar, 1994), 213–5, and "Propagating the Message: Popular Sufi Songs and Spiritual Transformation in South Asia," *Bulletin of the Henry Martyn Institute of Islamic Studies* 15, nos. 3–4 (1998): 5–15.

5. Saiyid Athar Abbas Rizvi, *A History of Sufism in India,* vol. 1 (New Delhi: Manshiram Manoharlal Publishers, 1978), 326. Rizvi maintains that *qawwālī* existed even before Hazrat Amir Khusrau, 1253–1325.

6. John Platts, *A Dictionary of Urdu, Classical Hindi, and English* (1930; reprint, London: Oxford University Press, 1982), 535.

7. *Encyclopedia of Indian Literature,* vol. 2, ed. Amaresh Datta (New Delhi: Sahitya Akademi, 1988–89), 1057–8.

8. Ibid.

9. M. Wahid Mirza, *Life and Works of Amir Khusrau* (Lahore: Panjab University Press, 1962), 136; Saiyid G. Samnani, *Amir Khusrau* (Delhi: National Book Trust, 1968), 61. The verses are translated to reinforce the poetic contexts and are not a word-for-word translation.

10. I break the complete Hindi verse to a poetic line for the translation.

11. Saiyid G. Samnani, *Amir Khusrau,* 61. Syed Akbar Haider, assistant professor of Urdu, Persian, and Hindi, Center for Asian Studies, University of Texas at Austin.

12. The *suhāg-rāt* (nuptial night) is an erotic metaphor in the poetry of the subcontinent.

13. John Platts, *A Dictionary of Urdu, Classical Hindi, and English,* 437: a ruddy goose in the subcontinent, commonly called the Brahmani duck, *Anas casarca.* The birds are romanticized in the folklore for being damned to separation in the night.

14. Ibid., 941–2.

15. Audiocassette. *Amir Khusrau: The Multifaceted Genius,* Gramophone Company, Calcutta, 1991; Mufti Shahabi and Dard Kakorvi, *Hazrat Amir Khusrau aur unka Urdu Kalām?* (Karachi: Daira al-Maraf Qurania, 1960), 72.

16. Regula Qureshi, *Qawwālī: Sufi Music of India and Pakistan,* 239. Qureshi affirms that "Rang" is the second principal ritual hymn sung at the Nizamuddin Auliya shrine, sung after the *qaul.*

17. An auspicious color in Islamic ritual.

18. Establishes the speaker's intimacy with the saint.

19. A female friend of a woman, and a favorite form of address in the Hindi *gīt.*

20. In a similar situation, "Merā pīyā ghar āyā o lālnī" (Celebrate thou, for my beloved has come home), composed by Bulle Shah, the Panjabi Sufi poet, for his mentor, Shah Inayat, is also sung as a wedding song.

21. M. Rehman "Affectionate Response to the Indian Environment," in *Amir Khusrau Memorial Volume* (Delhi: Ministry of Information and Broadcasting, 1975), 137. "*Basant*" is festival, which celebrates the start of the spring season. Children and grownups fly kites on the occasion. Yellow, the color of the mustard flower, which blooms in spring, is the dominant theme for "Basant."

22. Regula Quershi, *Sufi Music of India and Pakistan,* 240: *qawwālī* texts derived from Sufi invocations in Persian.

23. A semiclassical romantic song genre in the woman's voice; it is generally in Hindi.

24. Mufti Shahabi and Dard Kakorvi, *Hazrat Amir Khusrau aur Unka Urdu Kalam,* 73.

25. See *Brides of the Quran,* prod. Farah Durrani and Charles Bruce, BBC East, Pebble Mill, 1992, videocassette.

26. This could be due to his training in a *qawwāl gharānā* (lineage) from

whom he inherited his repertoire, but I also attribute it to his diverse, diasporic audiences. These were the large speech communities of Panjabi speakers in the United Kingdom and the Middle East who were the affluent patrons of his performances.

27. Khusrau's and Bulle Shah's mystical poetry is sung at weddings in Pakistan. *Arsi*, a *qawwālī* ceremony, is held in Nusrat Fateh Ali Khan's family in Faisalabad to celebrate the death anniversary of his father and uncles. Oriental Star Agencies website, "Ustad Nusrat Fateh Ali Khan," http://www.osa.co.uk (17 November 1999).

28. I use M. Rehman, "Affectionate Response to the Indian Environment," in *Amir Khusrau Memorial Volume*, 17, for the representation.

29. Persian.

30. Hindi.

31. Persian.

32. Hindi.

33. *Abdul Rahim and M Ali Faridi Qawwāl and Party*, Oriental Star Agencies, Birmingham, 1983, videocassette.

34. The gender markers for all the nouns are underlined in the transliteration.

35. *Encyclopedia of Indian Literature*, vol. 3, 1911.

36. Khawaja Ghulam Farid, *Kalām-e Farid*, ed. Kefi Jampuri (Multan: Bazm-e Saqafat, 1963), 32.

37. "*Kardi*" is the female form for the verb "to do."

38. Khawaja Ghulam Farid, *Kalām-e Farid*, 26.

39. *Musāg* is a thin branch of the nim tree chewed into a brush to clean the teeth.

40. A folk belief in the subcontinent that the crow forebodes the arrival of auspicious guests.

41. Khawaja Ghulam Farid, *Kalām-e Farid*, 158.

42. Carla Petievich, "Dakani's Radha-Krishna Imagery and Canon Formation in Urdu," in *The Banyan Tree: Essays in Early Literature in New Indo-Aryan Languages*, vol. 1, ed., Mariolo Offredi (New Delhi: Manohar Publishers, 2001), 113–30.

43. Ali Asani, "The Bridegroom Prophet in Medieval Sindhi Poetry," in *Studies in South Asian Devotional Literature: Research Papers 1989–91*, 214.

44. Wazir Agha, *Urdu Shāʿirī Ka Mizāj* (Lahore: Jadid Nashirin, 1965), 213.

45. F. Steingass, ed., *Persian-English Dictionary* (London: Kegan Paul, 1930), 387.

46. Carla Petievich, "The Feminine Voice in the Urdu Ghazal," *Indian Horizons* 39, no. 1–2 (1990): 25–41.

47. Ibid.

48. Personal communication at the forty-fourth Annual Meeting of the Society for Ethnomusicology, Austin 1999; Sharilee M. Johnston, "Poetics of

Performance: Narratives, Faith, and Disjuncture in Qawwālī" (Ph.D. diss., University of Texas at Austin, 2000), 363–8.

49. Joanna Liddle and Rama Joshi, *Daughters of Independence* (London: Zed Publications, 1986), 51–56.

50. M. Yakoob Agha, trans., *Shah Jo Risālo alias Ganj-e Latif*, vol. 1 (Hyderabad: Shah Abdul Latif Bhit Shah Cultural Center Committee, 1985), 361.

51. Ali Asani, "In Praise of Muhammad: Sindhi and Urdu Poems," in *Religions of India in Practice*, ed. Donald S. Lopez (Princeton: Princeton University Press, 1995), 159–86.

52. Tufail Niazi, *Hir*, Institute of Folk Heritage, Islamabad; 1987, audiocassette.

53. This is a ritual performed for an auspicious guest, especially a bridegroom. It is perhaps a Hindu custom, and the Jats were supposedly largely Hindu-Rajput converts.

54. Abbas Jalalpuri, *Muqāmāt-e Waris Shah* (Lahore: Hamid Raza Press, 1972), 127–8.

55. Hir's bringing the *cūri* to Ranjha seems to have a very romantic meaning in the discourse. *Cūri* is made from cream of wheat, mixed with sugar and pure animal fat. It is representative of a rural culture. It also has ritual connotations, as *cūri* is rolled into desserts called *ladoo*s for weddings in the subcontinent. They symbolize affluence in celebrations.

56. Ibid., 127.

57. "*Nī*" is an intimate, feminine-gender term in Panjabi, which women use to address one another. The fact that Waris Shah uses this in women's discourse reveals his sensitivity to feminine speech forms.

58. John Platts, *A Dictionary of Urdu, Classical Hindi, and English*, 177: Bhats are a mixed caste of minstrels and hereditary professional flatterers. Alternatively, the word can also mean *bhāṇḍ*, with the same connotation.

59. Ganjavi Nizami, *Layla-Majnun* (Boulder: Shambala Press, 1966), 191.

60. Nazir Jairazbhoy and Amy Catlin, *Musical Instruments of Kacch and Its Neighbors*, 1999, videocassette.

61. Michael Wood's film, *In the Footsteps of Alexander*, PBS Home Video, 1997, 1998, four videocassettes. The film portrays Sumeria, Iran, Afghanistan, and the Indus along the Baluchistan coast back through Persia as a route that seems to have been used for centuries. Aitzaz Ahsan, *The Indus Saga and the Making of Pakistan* (Karachi: Oxford University Press, 1996) posits a similar theory.

62. Joanna Liddle and Rama Joshi, *Daughters of Independence*, 53–54.

63. A=Abbas; F=Alan Faqir.

64. These are all Alan Faqir's political interpretations of the female myths in Shah Abdul Latif's *Risālo*.

65. The musician explained the politics of using the myths. Here, the reference is to the fact that Sind does not lead the land politically; here, Punnu

becomes the dispossessed prince who does not have his Kec, or land; he becomes identified with Sind. "Sind is not the amir" means that Sind is not in the position of leadership or amirship.

66. A name used for Sind in the poetic traditions.

67. He quotes the renowned Sindhi Sufi poet and author of the *Risālo*. Alan Faqir explains his interpretation of the female myths in Shah Abdul Latif's *Risālo*. He considered himself a *faqīr* (mendicant) of the Bhit Shah shrine of Shah Abdul Latif.

68. *Allāh hū* is essentially a *zikr* chant, or spiritual breathing exercise used by the Sufis.

CHAPTER 5. CLOSING THE CIRCLE OF THE MYSTIC JOURNEY

1. I have transliterated and translated a *qawwāli* about Kerbala that Aziz Mian and ensemble have sung. Shemeem B. Abbas, "Speech Play and Verbal Art in the Indo-Pakistan Oral Sufi Tradition" (Ph.D. diss., University of Texas at Austin, 1992. Ann Arbor: UMI, 1993, 3523537), 216–4.

2. A. Yusuf Ali, *The Meaning of the Holy Quran* (1946; reprint, Beltsville, Md.: Amana Publications, 1997), 1759, 1737.

3. Shemeem B. Abbas, "Speech Play and Verbal Art in the Indo-Pakistan Oral Sufi Tradition," 153–266.

4. A. Yusuf Ali, *The Meaning of the Holy Quran*, 1747, 1745.

5. Hindi Kanhyalal, *Tarikh-e Lahore* (1884; reprint, Lahore: *Majlis-e Tariqi-e Adab*, 1977), 315.

6. M. Latif Malik, *Auliya-e Lahore* (Lahore: Sang-e Meel Publications, 1992), 111.

7. Generally called "Data Sahib."

8. Ghulam Sarwar Mufti, *Tarikh-e Makhzan Panjab* (1887; reprint, Lahore: Maktab-e Nabawwiya, 1987), 96.

9. Both Nusrat Fateh Ali Khan and Reshma, musicians discussed in this book, claimed to be devotees of the Bibi Pak Daman shrine in Lahore.

10. Ismail R. al-Faruqi and L. L. al-Faruqi, *The Cultural Atlas of Islam* (London: Collier Macmillan, 1986), 295–304.

11. Margaret Smith, *Rabi'a: The Life and Work of Rabi'a and Other Women Mystics of Islam* (1928; reprint, Oxford: Oneworld, 1994).

12. Qamar Jahan Begam, *Princess Jahan Ara Begam: Her Life and Her Works* (Karachi: Library of Congress, CC no. 91-931192, 1991).

13. Muhammad Ibrahim, "Jahan Ara Begam kī ik ghair mā'ruf tasānīf," in *Sahibiyyā* (Ahmedabad: Oriental College Magazine, 1937), 3–13.

14. The sura *Yāsīn* is believed by the faithful to be the heart of the Quran. I have transliterated a *qawwāli* of Ghulam Kibria in which he sings about this: Shemeem Abbas, "Speech Play and Verbal Art in the Indo-Pakistan Oral Sufi Tradition," 198.

15. Qamar Jehan Begam, *Princess Jahan Ara Begam: Her Life and Her Works,* 46–48.

16. The mosque has recently been expanded and a huge structure built around the old mosque used by the Prophet and his Companions. Thousands of pilgrims can be accommodated in the building. Artisans from all over the world were engaged to recreate this breathtaking structure.

17. Muslims believe that the Black Stone in the Kaaba was laid by Abraham. Millions of pilgrims from the Islamic world perform the annual ritual of Hajj at the Kaaba and go around the structure. Hajj and its rituals are among the pillars of Islam, an obligation for Muslims who can afford it.

18. Shemeem Abbas, "Speech Play and Verbal Art in the Indo-Pakistan Oral Sufi Tradition," 155, 160, 168, 171.

19. Qamar Jahan Begam, *Princess Jahan Ara Begam: Her Life and Her Works.* Princess Jahan Ara donated Rs 40,000 to build a mosque in Kashmir for her spiritual mentor, Mulla Shah Badakhshi, and another Rs 20,000 for buildings attached to the mosque for his disciples, 68.

20. Muhammad Ibrahim, "Jahan Ara Begam kī ik ghair maʿruf tasānīf," *Sahibiyyā,* 3–19.

21. In Pakistan, the shrines are now under state control through the Auqaf Department.

22. Princess Jahan Ara Begam, *Munis ʿul Arwah,* ed. Qamar Jahan Begam (Karachi: Library of Congress, CC no. 91-931192, 1991), 7.

23. Princess Jahan Ara visited the shrine after she suffered severe burns.

24. Margaret Smith, *Rabiʿa: The Life and Work of Rabiʿa and Other Women Mystics of Islam,* 195–205.

25. Qamar Jahan Begam, ed., *Princess Jahan Ara Begam: Her Life and Her Works,* 106–7.

26. Ibid., 38.

27. For a detailed account of Amir Khusrau's early life, see M. Wahid Mirza, *Life and Works of Amir Khusrau* (1934; reprint, Lahore: Panjab University Press, 1962). The poet spent considerable time in Multan with Prince Muhammad.

28. A. Yusuf Ali, *The Meaning of the Holy Quran,* 33:35, 1067; Javed Nurbaksh, *Sufi Women* (London: Khaniqahi-Nimatullahi, 1990), 11.

29. A., *The Meaning of the Holy Quran,* 33:28–37, 1064–9.

30. Ibid. The verb in Arabic is *udhkurna,* feminine gender, as referring to the *azwaj* (the Prophet's consorts). *Udhkurna* means not only to "remember" but also to "recite," "teach," "make known," "publish" the Message that you learn at home from the Holy Prophet, the fountain of spiritual knowledge. The "Signs of Allah" refer specifically to the verses of the Quran, and Wisdom to the resulting instruction derived therefrom, 1067.

31. Pathana Khan, *A Tribute to the Great Mystics: Bulleh Shah, Shah Hussain, and Khawaja Farid,* IFH, 1985, audiocassette.

32. M. Yakoob Agha, trans., *Shah Jo Risālo alias Ganje Latif*, vol. 3 (Hyderabad: Shah Abdul Latif Bhit Shah Cultural Center Committee, 1985), 1399.

33. Nazir Jairazhbhoy and Amy Catlin, Aspara Media for Intercultural Education, Van Nuys, 1999, videocassette.

34. See Khusro Hussaini, "Bund Sama," *Islamic Culture* 44 (1970): 77–85.

35. Muhammad Ali Qazi, "Sindhi Music," in *Folk Music of Sind*, ed. Ghulam Ali Allana (Jamshoro: Institute of Sindhology, 1982), 65–84.

36. Pakistani and Indian migration to the United Kingdom started in the fifties.

37. See the primary sources used in this book.

38. Nasra M. Shah and Fred Arnold, "Pakistan," in *Handbook of International Migration*, eds. William J. Serow, Charles B. Nam, David F. Sly, and Robert H. Weller (London: Greenwood Press, 1990), 265.

39. Those in the major cities were audiences at the *qawwali* and *sufiānā-kalām* concerts.

40. U.S. Census Bureau website, "PCT004. ASIAN ALONE WITH ONE ASIAN CATEGORY FOR SELECTED GROUPS," http://factfinder.census.gov/servlet/ DTTable?ds_name=D&geo_id=D&mt_name=ACS_C2SS_EST-G2000_PCT004&_lang=en (4 September 2001).

41. See Khusro Hussaini, "Bund Sama," *Islamic Culture* 44 (1970): 77–85.

42. Shemeem B. Abbas, *The Storyteller* (Islamabad: UNICEF, 1994).

43. Aitzaz Ahsan, *The Indus Saga and the Making of Pakistan* (Karachi: Oxford University Press, 1996).

GLOSSARY

1. John Shakespeare, *Dictionary of Urdu-English* (Lahore: Sang-e Meel Publications, 1980), 230.

2. Regula Qureshi, *Sufi Music of India and Pakistan*, 243.

3. David Crystal, *Dictionary of Linguistics and Phonetics* (Oxford: Blackwell, 1997), 140. The term is first used in the preface.

4. The term is used in chapter 2.

5. See preface.

6. Qureshi, *Sufi Music*, 237.

7. Ibid., 239.

8. Ibid., 245.

9. Annemarie Schimmel, *As Through a Veil*, 147.

10. Qureshi, *Sufi Music*, 240.

11. Ibid.

Primary Sources

Abbas, Shemeem B. "Speech Play and Verbal Art in the Indo-Pakistan Oral Sufi Tradition." Ph.D. diss., University of Texas at Austin, 1992. Ann Arbor: UMI, 1993. 3523537.

———, ed. *Multimedia Assortments.* Hyderabad: Institute of Sindhology, 1999.

Ahmed, Masood. Personal interview. University of Texas at Austin, November 23, 1990.

Ali, Mehr, and Sher Ali. *Music du Monde: Music from the World.* CD-ROM. Paris: Buda Music 92611-2.

Ali, Syed Zulfiqar. Musician/composer. Personal interview. University of Sind, February 21, 1999.

Allah, Wasai. Musician. Audiocassette. Hyderabad: Institute of Sindhology, 1999.

Allana, G. Ali. Director-general, Sindhi Language Authority. Personal interview. Hyderabad, March 4, 1999.

Amina, Nur Jehan, Allah Bachai, and Parvin Akhtar. Manganhār musicians. Personal recordings and interviews. Massu Bhurgi Village, Sind, March 1999.

Anwar, Masud, dir. *Hir-Ranjha.* Videocassette. With Firduas and Ejas. Lahore: Evernew Studios, 1970.

Asif, Muhammad. Medical doctor and informant. Personal interview. Sehwan Sharif, February 28, 1999.

Attar, Hasan Ali. Media producer, Institute of Sindhology. Personal interview. Hyderabad, March 4, 1999.

Bai, Jeevni. Musician. GRAMOPHONE record/audiocassette. Hyderabad: Institute of Sindhology, 1999.

Bai, Muli. Musician. GRAMOPHONE record/audiocassette. Hyderabad: Institute of Sindhology, 1999.

Bakhsh, Muhammad. Musician. Personal interview. Bulle Shah shrine, Kasur, December 20, 1992.

Bali, Hinda Bai. Musician. GRAMOPHONE record/audiocassette. Hyderabad: Institute of Sindhology, 1999.

Baloch, Sikander. Director, Radio Pakistan. Personal interview. Hyderabad, March 2, 1999.

Bano, Nur. Musician. GRAMOPHONE record/audiocassette. Hyderabad: Institute of Sindhology, 1999.

Begum, Faqiriani. Manganhār musician. Audiocassette. Hyderabad: Institute of Sindhology, 1999.

Begum, Khursheed Paoli. Musician. GRAMOPHONE record. Hyderabad: Institute of Sindhology, 1999.

Behranwale, M. Ahmed Hassan Qawwal and Party. *Qawwalies.* Vols. 2 and 3. Audiocassette. Birmingham, U.K.: Oriental Star Agencies, 1986.

Bhagi, Mai. Manganhar musician. Audiocassette. Hyderabad: Institute of Sindhology, 1999.

Bhatti, Razia. Designer, Institute of Sindhology. Personal interview. Hyderabad, March 5, 1999.

Bhure Qawwal and Party. Audiocassette. Islamabad: Private collection, 1980.

Bhutto, Javaid. Personal interview. University of Texas at Austin, November 21, 2000.

Catlin, Amy. Ethnomusicologist. Personal interview. Forty-fourth Annual Meeting of the Society for Ethnomusicology, Austin, November 18, 1999.

Coupran, Susan. Personal interview. University of Texas at Austin, October 20, 1988.

Faqir, Alan. Musician. Personal interview. Hyderabad, February 26, 1999.

Faridi, Abdul. *Abdul Rahim, and M. Ali Faridi Qawwal and Party.* Videocassette. Birmingham, U.K.: Oriental Star Agencies, 1983.

Fernea, Elizabeth W. *Saints and Spirits: Religious Expression in Morocco.* Film and videocassette. Austin: University of Texas at Austin, 1979.

Firozee, Muhammad. Musician. Personal interview. Austin, November 11, 1999.

Haleema, Dai. Grassroots musician. Personal interview. Talagang, November 7, 1992.

Hir: Waris Shah. Vols. 1 and 2. Audiocassette. Islamabad: EMI Recording Co., 1987.

Jairazbhoy, Nazir Ali. Ethnomusicologist. Personal interview. Forty-fourth Annual Meeting of the Society for Ethnomusicology, Austin, November 18, 1999.

Jairazbhoy, Nazir Ali, and Amy Catlin. *Musical Instruments of Kacch and Its Neighbors.* Videocassette. Van Nuys: Apsara Media for Intercultural Education, 1999.

Jamaluddin, Muhammad. Folklorist. Personal interview. Umerkot, March 7, 1999.

Junejo, Abdul Qadir. Director. Personal interview. Institute of Sindhology, March 4, 1999.

Khan, Nusrat Fateh Ali. *Qawwāl*/musician. Personal interview. Islamabad, August 30, 1992.

Khan, Nusrat Fateh Ali. *Private Mehfil I: Birmingham.* Videocassette. Birmingham, U.K.: Oriental Star Agencies, 1984.

———. *Private Mehfil II: Birmingham.* Videocassette. Birmingham, U.K.: Oriental Star Agencies, 1984.

———. *Qawwalies.* Vols. 27 and 28. Audiocassette. Birmingham, U.K.: Oriental Star Agencies, 1985.

———. *Qawwalies.* Vols. 1 and 2. Audiocassette. Islamabad: Institute of Folk Heritage, 1987.

———. *Nusrat Fateh Ali Khan: En Concert à Paris.* Vol. 1. CD-ROM. Paris: Ocra, Radio France, 3 149025 003997.

Khan, Pathana. *A Tribute to Great Mystics: Bulleh Shah, Shah Hussain, Khawaja Farid.* Audiocassette. Islamabad: Institute of Folk Heritage, 1985.

———. *Great Musicians of Our Time.* Videocassette. Islamabad: Institute of Folk Heritage, 1987.

Khusrau, Amir. *The Multifaceted Genius: Lyrics.* Audiocassette. Hyderabad: Institute of Sindhology.

Kibria, Ghulam. *Qawwalies.* Vol. 2. Videocassette. Birmingham, U.K.: Oriental Star Agencies, 1984.

Lohar, Alam. *Maqbool Panjabi Qisse.* Vol. 2. Audiocassette. Karachi: Rita Recording Co., 1989.

———. *Qisse.* Vol. 2. Audiocassette. Karachi: Jugun Recording Co, 1989.

Maciszewski, Amelia. Personal interviews. University of Texas at Austin, 1999–2001.

Makha, Kasim. Associate director, Institute of Sindhology. Personal interview. Hyderabad, February 26, 1999.

Mastani, Taj. Musician. Personal interview. Hyderabad, February 14, 1999.

Mastani, Taj. *Aaj Taj Mastani.* Audiocassette. Hyderabad: T.M. Production, 1999.

Mehtani, Sushila. Musician. GRAMOPHONE record/audiocassette. Institute of Sindhology, 1999.

Mian, Aziz, and Party. *Qawwalies.* Audiocassette. Islamabad: Shalimar Recording Company, 1986.

Mira Bai. *Bhajans Sung by Lata Mangeshkar.* Audiocassette. Calcutta: Gramophone Co., 1981.

Mirza, Naseer. Music director, Radio Pakistan. Personal interview. Hyderabad, March 2, 1999.

Mufti, Uxi, prod. *Aakhri Geet: Art Video about Manganhar Musicians of Sind.* Islamabad: Institute of Folk Heritage, 1999.
Mughal, Gul Muhammad. Librarian, Institute of Sindhology. Personal interview. Hyderabad, February 14, 1999.
Multanikar, Surraiya. Musician. Personal interview. Multan, May 21, 1995.
Multanikar, Surraiya. *Kafian.* Audiocassette. Multan: Musician's personal collection, 1995.
Naqvi, Jaleel, and Khalida Naqvi. Custodians, Hazrat Pir Sabir Sharif shrine, Paran Kalyar. Personal interviews and fieldwork partners. Lahore, 1992–99.
Niazi, Tufail. *Hir.* Audiocassette. Islamabad: Institute of Folk Heritage, 1987.
Pakistan International Airlines. *Amir Khusrau.* Videocassette. Karachi: 1990.
Parvin, Abida. *A Musical Evening with Abida Parvin.* Videocassette. Islamabad: Allama Iqbal Open University, 1985.
———. *Chants Soufis du Pakistan.* Compact disc, Auvidis Distribution, 298492600038.
Parvin, Abida, and Sheikh Ghulam Hussan. Musicians. Personal interview. Islamabad, October 15, 1992.
Qureshi, Regula. Ethnomusicologist. Personal interviews. Forty-fourth Annual Meeting of the Society for Ethnomusicology, Austin, November 18–20, 1999.
Quereshi, Rubina. Musician. Audiocassette. Institute of Sindhology, 1999.
Ram, Prakash. Photography consultant, Institute of Sindhology. Personal interview. Hyderabad, March 4, 1999.
Reshma. Musician. Personal interview. Lahore, April 9, 1993.
Reshma. *Great Musicians of Our Time.* Videocassette. Islamabad: Institute of Folk Heritage, 1990.
Sabri, Ghulam Farid, and Maqbool Ahmed Sabri. *Qawwalies: Live in Concert.* Videocassette. Birmingham, U.K.: Oriental Star Agencies, 1981.
Saeeda, Asif. Informant. Personal interview. Sehwan Sharif, February 28, 1999.
Sakata, Lorraine H. Ethnomusicologist. Personal interview, Forty-fourth Annual Meeting of the Society for Ethnomusicology, Austin, November 20, 1999.
Shackle, Cristopher. Personal interview. School of Oriental and African Studies, University of London, June 10, 1988.
Shaikh, Saghir. Personal interviews. University of Texas at Austin, 1991–2001.
Sheedi, Khadija, and Karima Sheedi. Grassroots musicians. Personal interview. Karachi Mori Village, Sind, March 3, 1999.
Sheedi, Khadija, and Mohana fisherwomen. Musicians. Personal recordings and photography. Karachi Mori Village, Sind, March 3, 1999.
Shah, Qalandar. Chair, Department of English, Sind University. Personal interview. Karachi Mori Village, March 3, 1999.
Shah, Syed Ghulam Ali, and Nur Muhammad Shah. Bhit Shah musicians. Audiocassette. Hyderabad: Institute of Sindhology.

Shah, Waris. *Hir.* Edited by Ahmed Gujjar. Islamabad: Institute of Folk Heritage, 1992.

Solomon, Tom. Project partner, Language and Music course. University of Texas at Austin, fall 1987.

Tabish, Zulfiqar. Journalist. Personal interview. Lahore, April 10, 1993.

Valhab, Vali Ram. Associate director, Institute of Sindhology. Personal interview. March 3, 1999.

Wagha, Ehsan. Music director, Radio Pakistan, Multan. Personal interview. Islamabad, February 1, 1999.

Zaidi, Shamim. Director, Institute of Folk Heritage. Personal interview. Islamabad, January 30, 1998.

Zarina, Khatoon. Grassroots musician. Personal interview. Lahore, February 15, 1993.

BIBLIOGRAPHY

Aah, Safdar. *Amir Khusrau Bā Heseit Hindī Shā'ir.* Bombay: Alvi Book Depot, 1970.

Abbas, Shemeem B. "The Myth of Hir-Ranjha: The Female Voice." Paper presented at Fifth Annual South Asia Studies Conference on Race, Gender, and Ethnicity in South Asia, University of California, Berkeley, 1991.

———. "Speech Play and Verbal Art in the Indo-Pakistan Oral Sufi Tradition." Ph.D. diss., University of Texas at Austin, 1992. Ann Arbor: UMI, 1993. 3523537.

———. "The Power of English in Pakistan." *World Englishes* (University of Illinois) 12, no. 2 (1993): 147–56.

———. "Sufi Verbal Art." Paper presented at National Linguistics Conference, Quaid-e-Azam University, Islamabad, 1993.

———. *The Storyteller.* Islamabad: UNICEF, 1994.

———. "The Female Voice in Sufi Ritual." *The News* (Islamabad, March 23, 1995): 28.

———. "The Music Traditions of Ethnic Women." Paper presented at NGO Forum on Women, Beijing, 1995.

———. "Perspectives on a Grassroots Theory of Literary Orality and Esthetics." *Journal of Social Sciences* (Allama Iqbal Open University) 2 (autumn 1997): 1–9.

———. "ESL/EFL: State of the Art in Distance Education." Paper presented at the Annual Seminar of *World Englishes,* National University of Singapore, Singapore, 1997.

———. "Evaluating Core English Language Policies in Pakistan." In *Proceedings of the Annual International KELT Seminar.* Lahore: Kinnaird College, 1997.

———. "Primary Education in South Asia." *Journal of Social Sciences* (Allama Iqbal Open University) 2 (autumn 1997): 1–9.

———. "Primary Education in South Asia: Language Planning, Curriculum Design and Educational Management." *Proceedings of the Annual International KELT Seminar.* Lahore: Kinnaird College, 1998.

Abe, Isamu. "How Vocal Pitch Works." In *The Melody of Language*, edited by Linda Waugh and C. H. van Schoonveld. Baltimore: University Park Press, 1980.

Abu-Lughod, Lila. *Veiled Sentiments.* Cairo: American University Press, 1986.

Agha, M. Yakoob, trans. *Shah Jo Risālo alias Ganj-e Latif.* Vols. 1, 2, and 3. Hyderabad: Shah Abdul Latif Bhit Shah Cultural Center Committee, 1985.

Agha, Wazir. *Urdu Shā'irī kā Mizāj.* Lahore: Jadid Nashirin, 1965.

Ahmed, Aijaz. "Jameson's Rhetoric of Otherness and the National Allegory." *Social Text* (fall 1986): 3–25.

———. *In Theory: Nations, Literatures, and Classes.* London: Verso, 1992.

Ahmed, Imtiaz. *Caste and Social Stratification among the Muslims in India.* New Delhi: Manohar, 1978.

Ahsan, Aitzaz. *The Indus Saga and the Making of Pakistan.* Karachi: Oxford University Press, 1996.

Akhund, Abdul Hamid, ed. *Shah Abdul Latif: His Mystical Poetry. Proceedings of Shah Abdul Latif Conference on His 247 Urs Celebrations.* Karachi: Shah Abdul Latif Bhit Shah Cultural Center Committee, 1991.

Ali, A. Yusuf. *The Meaning of The Holy Quran.* 1946. Reprint, Beltsville, Md.: Amana Publications, 1997.

Ali, Mrs. Meer Hassan. *Observations on the Mussalmans of India.* 1832. Reprint, Karachi: Civil and Military Press, 1973.

Allana, G. Ali, ed. *Folk Music of Sind.* Jamshoro: Institute of Sindhology, 1982.

Alston, A. J., transl. *The Devotional Poems of Mirabai.* Delhi: Motilal Banarsidass, 1980.

Altorki, Soraya, and Camillia Fawzi El-Solh, eds. *Arab Women in the Field: Studying Your Own Society.* Syracuse, N.Y.: Syracuse University Press, 1988.

Amir Khusrau. *Memorial Volume.* Delhi: Amir Khusrau Publications Division, Ministry of Information and Broadcasting, Government of India, 1975.

Anzaldúa, Gloria. "Speaking in Tongues: A Letter to Third-World Women Writers." In *This Bridge Called My Back: Writings by Radical Women of Color*, edited by C. Moraga and Gloria Anzaldúa. Watertown, Mass.: Persephone Press, 1981.

Arberry, Arthur J. *An Introduction to the History of Sufism.* London: Allen and Unwin, 1942.

———. *An Account of the Mystics of Islam.* London: Allen and Unwin, 1956.

Asad, Talal, ed. *Anthropology and the Colonial Encounter.* London: Ithaca Press, 1975.

Asani, Ali. "The Bridegroom Prophet in Medieval Sindhi Poetry." In *Studies in South Asian Devotional Literature: Research Papers 1989–91*, edited by F. Mallison and A. Erswistle, 213–25. New Delhi: Manohar, 1994.

———. "In Praise of Muhammad: Sindhi and Urdu Poems." In *Religions of India in Practice*, edited by Donald S. Lopez, 159–86. Princeton, N.J.: Princeton University Press, 1995.

———. "Propagating the Message: Popular Sufi Songs and Spiritual Transformation in South Asia." *Bulletin of the Henry Martyn Institute of Islamic Studies* 15, no. 3–4 (1998): 5–15.

Atkinson, J. Maxwell, and John Heritage, eds. *Structures of Social Action: Studies in Conversation Analysis*. Cambridge: Cambridge University Press, 1984.

Bahu, Sultan. *Abiāt-e Bahu*. Edited by Maqbool Anwar Dawoodi. Lahore: Ferozesons, 1990.

Bakhtin, M. M. *The Dialogic Imagination*. Austin: University of Texas Press, 1981.

Baloch, Aziz. "Music Traditions of Lower Indus Valley." In *Folk Music of Sind*, edited by Ghulam Ali Allana, 50–64. Jamshoro: Institute of Sindhology, 1982.

Baloch, N. A. "Developments in the Subcontinent: Evolution of the Music Tradition in Sind." In *Folk Music of Sind*, edited by Ghulam Ali Allana, 17–26. Jamshoro: Institute of Sindhology, 1982.

———. "Developments under Islamic Civilization." In *Folk Music of Sind*, edited by Ghulam Ali Allana, 8–16. Jamshoro: Institute of Sindhology, 1982.

———. "Folk Musical Instruments of Mehran Valley." In *Folk Music of Sind*, edited by Ghulam Ali Allana, 104–27. Jamshoro: Institute of Sindhology, 1982.

Barani, Ziya'al Din. *Tarikh-e Firuz Shahi*. Translated by H. M. Elliott, edited by John Dawson. Lahore: Sind Sagar Academy, 1974. First English edition 1871, translated by H. M. Elliott.

Barthes, Roland. *A Lover's Discourse*. Translated by R. Howard. New York: Hill and Wang, 1978.

Bascom, William. "The Myth-Ritual Theory." *Journal of American Folklore* 70 (1957): 103–14.

Basso, Keith. "To Give Up on Words: Silence in Western Apache Culture." In *Language in Social Context*, edited by Pier Paolo Giglioli, 67–86. Harmondsworth, U.K.: Penguin Books, 1972.

Basu, Helene. *Habshi-Sklaven, Sidi Fakire: Muslimische Heiligenverehrung im westlichen Indien*. Berlin: Das Arabische Buch, 1995.

Bateson, Gregory. "A Theory of Play and Fantasy." In *Steps to an Ecology of Mind*. San Francisco: Chandler, 1972.

Baugh, John. *Black Street Speech*. Austin: University of Texas Press, 1983.

———. *Out of the Mouths of Slaves: African American Language and Educational Malpractice*. Austin: University of Texas Press, 1999.

Bauman, Richard. "Differential Identity and the Social Base of Folklore." In

Toward New Perspectives in Folklore, edited by Americo Paredes and Richard Bauman, 31–41. Austin: University of Texas Press, 1972.

———. "Verbal Art as Performance." *American Anthropology* 77 (1975): 290–311.

———. *Verbal Art as Performance.* Austin: University of Texas Press, 1977.

———. *Story, Performance, and Event.* New York: Cambridge University Press, 1986.

Bauman, R., and C. Briggs. "Poetics and Performance as Critical Perspectives on Language and Social Life." *Annual Review of Anthropology* 19 (1960): 59–88.

Bauman, Richard, and Joel Sherzer. "The Ethnography of Speaking." *An Annual Review of Anthropology* 4 (1975): 95–119.

———, eds. *Explorations in the Ethnography of Speaking.* 2d ed. New York: Cambridge University Press, 1989.

Beachy, R. W. Slave Trade in East Africa. London: Rex Collins, 1976.

Beck, Lois, and Nikki Keddie, eds. *Women in the Muslim World.* Cambridge: Harvard University Press, 1978.

Begam, Princess Jahan Ara. *Munis 'ul Arwah.* Edited by Qamar Jahan Begam. Karachi: Library of Congress, CC no. 91–931192, 1991.

———. *Sahibiyyā.* Edited by Muhammad Ibrahim. Ahmedabad: Oriental College Magazine, 1937, 1–19.

Begam, Qamar Jahan. *Princess Jahan Ara Begam: Her Life and Her Works.* Karachi Library of Congress, CC no. 91–931192, 1991.

Ben-Amos, D. "Toward a Definition of Folklore in Context." In *Toward New Perspectives in Folklore,* edited by Americo Paredes and Richard Bauman, 3–15. Austin: University of Texas Press, 1972.

Bullo, Momin. "Zafar Kazmi: Alan Faqir's Foster Brother." *Friday Times Lahore* 11, no. 42 (December 17–23, 1999).

Butler, Judith. *Bodies That Matter.* New York: Routledge, 1993.

Chand, Tara. *Amir Khusro aur Hindostan.* New Delhi: Amir Khusrau Academy, 1962.

Clark, H. Wilnerforce, transl. *A Dervish Textbook from the 'Awarifu-1 Ma'Arif: Written in the Thirteenth Century by Shaikh Shahabuddin Umar bin Muhammad Surhawardi.* London: Octagon Press, 1980.

Crystal, David. *An Encyclopedic Dictionary of Language and Languages.* Oxford: Blackwell, 1992.

———. *Dictionary of Linguistics and Phonetics.* Oxford: Blackwell, 1997.

Datta, Amaresh, ed. *Encyclopedia of Indian Literature.* Vols. 2 and 3. New Delhi: Sahitya Akademi, 1988–89.

Dehlavi, Jamil. *Immaculate Conception.* Film on *hijṛas* (eunuchs). U.K.: Feature Film Company, 1992.

Dil, Anwar, ed. *Language in Social Groups: Essays by John Gumperz.* Stanford, Calif.: Stanford University Press, 1971.

Dundes, Alan. "Who Are the Folk?" In *Frontiers of Folklore*, edited by W. R. Bascom, 17–35. Boulder: Westview Press, 1977.

Durrani, Farah, and Charles Bruce, prods. *Brides of the Quran*. Film. BBC East, Pebble Mill, 1992.

Dwyer, Daisy Hilse. "Women, Sufism, and Decision-Making in Moroccan Islam." In *Women in the Muslim World*, edited by Lois Beck and Nikki Keddie. Cambridge: Harvard University Press, 1979.

Eaton, Richard M. "Sufi Folk Literature and the Expansion of Indian Islam." *History of Religions* 14 (1974): 117–27.

———. *The Sufis of Bijapur*. Princeton, N.J.: Princeton University Press, 1978.

———. *Rise of Islam and the Bengal Frontier*. Berkeley: University of California Press, 1993.

Eglar, Zekye. *A Panjabi Village in Pakistan*. New York: Columbia University Press, 1960.

Elaide, Mircea. *Shamanism: Archaic Techniques of Ecstasy*. Princeton, N.J.: Princeton University Press, 1972.

Enayatullah, Anwar. "Muhammedan Music." *Grove's Dictionary of Music and Musicians*. Vol. 5, 817–18. 1954.

———. s.v. "Ghina." *Encyclopedia of Islam*. 1965.

Encyclopedia Britannica website. "Bhakti Movement of Medieval India." http://www.britannica.co.in/spotlights/bhakti/pt01.htm (December 14, 2000).

Ernst, Carl. "Lives of the Sufi Saints: A Woman Saint Bibi Jamal Khatun." In *Religions of India in Practice*, edited by Donald S. Lopez, 495–512. Princeton, N.J.: Princeton University Press, 1995.

———. *Shambala Guide to Sufism*. Boston: Shambala, 1997.

Esposito, J. L. *Women in Muslim Family Law*. Syracuse, N.Y.: Syracuse University Press, 1982.

Ewing, Katherine P. *Arguing Sainthood: Modernity, Psychoanalysis, and Islam*. Durham, N.C.: Duke University Press, 1997.

Fanon, Frantz. *The Wretched of the Earth*. Translated by C. Farrington. 1961. Reprint, New York: Grove Press, 1967.

———. *Black Skin White Masks*. Translated by Charles L. Markmann. New York: Grove Press, 1967.

Farid, Khawaja Ghulam. *Kalām-e Farid*. Edited by Kefi Jampuri. Multan: Bazm-e Saqafat, 1963.

———. *Naghmā-e Sehrā*. Translated by Kashafi Multani. Multan: Bazm-e Saqafat, 1963.

al-Faruqi, Ismail R., and L. L. al-Faruqi. *The Cultural Atlas of Islam*. London: Collier Macmillan, 1986.

Feld, Steven. "Linguistic Models in Ethnomusicology." *Ethnomusicology* 18 (1974): 197–217.

———. "Flow like a Waterfall: The Metaphors of Kaluli Musical Theory." *Yearbook for Traditional Music* 14 (1981): 15–23.

———. *Sound and Sentiment: Birds, Weeping, Poetics, and Song in Kaluli Expression.* Philadelphia: University of Pennsylvania Press, 1982.

———. "Communication, Music and Speech about Music." *Yearbook for Traditional Music* 16 (1984): 1–17.

———. "Wept Thoughts: The Voicing of Kaluli Memories." *Oral Tradition* 5 (1990): 241–66.

Fernea, Elizabeth W. *Guests of the Sheikh.* London: Hale, 1968.

———. *A Street in Marrakesh.* Garden City, N.Y.: Doubleday, 1975.

———. *Middle Eastern Muslim Women Speak.* Austin: University of Texas Press, 1977.

———. "Saints and Spirits." In *Religious Expression in Morocco: A Guide To the Film.* Austin: University of Texas at Austin, 1979.

———. *Women and Family in the Middle East: New Voices of Change.* Austin: University of Texas Press, 1985.

———. *In Search of Islamic Feminism: One Woman's Global Journey.* New York: Doubleday, 1998.

Fernea, Elizabeth W., and Robert A. Fernea, with Aleya Rouchdy. *Nubian Ethnographies.* Prospect Heights, Ill.: Waveland Press, 1991.

Fernea, Robert A., and Elizabeth W. Fernea. "Variation in Religious Observance among Islamic Women." In *Scholars, Saints, and Sufis: Muslim Religious Institutions in the Middle East since 1500,* edited by Nikki R. Keddie, 385–401. Berkeley: University of California Press, 1972.

Finnegan, Ruth. *Literacy and Orality: Studies in the Technology of Communication.* Oxford: Blackwell, 1988.

Fishman, J. A., C. A. Ferguson, and Das Gupta, eds. *Language Problems of Developing Nations.* New York: John Wiley, 1968.

Fishman, Joshua. *Readings in the Sociology of Language.* The Hague: Mouton, 1968.

———. *Oral Poetry.* Cambridge: Cambridge University Press, 1977.

Foley, John M. *The Theory of Oral Composition.* Bloomington: Indiana University Press, 1988.

Fox-Strangeways, A. H. *The Music of Hindostan.* Oxford: Clarendon Press, 1914; Oxford University Press, 1965.

Frazer, James G. *The Golden Bough: A Study in Magic and Religion.* London: Macmillan, 1911.

Frisbie, Charlotte. "Vocables in Navajo Ceremonial Music." *Ethnomusicology* 24, no. 3 (1980): 347–92.

Garfinkel, Harold. "Remarks on Ethnomethodology." In *Directions in Sociolinguistics,* edited by John Gumperz and Dell Hymes, 301–24. New York: Holt and Rinehart, 1972.

Geertz, Clifford. *Islam Observed: Religious Development in Morocco and Indonesia.* New Haven: Yale University Press, 1968.

———. *The Interpretation of Cultures.* New York: Basic Books, 1973.

———. "Art as a Cultural System." *Modern Language Notes* 91 (1976): 1473–99.

Giglioli, Pier Paolo, ed. *Language and Social Context.* Harmondsworth, U.K.: Penguin Books, 1972.

Goffman, Erving. *Behavior in Public Places.* New York: Free Press, 1963.

———. *Relations in Public.* New York: Harper and Row, 1971.

———. "The Neglected Situation." In *Language and Social Context,* edited by Pier Paolo Giglioli, 133–36. Harmondsworth, U.K.: Penguin, 1972.

———. *Frame Analysis.* New York: Harper and Row, 1974.

———. *Forms of Talk.* Philadelphia: University of Pennsylvania Press, 1981.

Grierson, G. A. *Linguistic Survey of India.* Delhi: Motilal Bonarsidass 1967–68.

Grima, Benedicte. *The Performance of Emotion among Paxtun Women: "The Misfortunes Which Have Befallen Me."* Austin: University of Texas Press, 1992.

Guha, Ranajit, and G. C. Spivak, eds. *Selected Subaltern Studies.* New York: Oxford University Press, 1988.

Gumperz, John. "Types of Linguistic Communities." *Anthropological Linguistics* 4 (1962): 24–40.

———. "Social Meaning in Linguistic Structures: Code-Switching in Norway." In *Language in Social Groups: Essays by John Gumperz,* edited by Anwar Dil, 274–310. Stanford, Calif.: Stanford University Press, 1971.

———. "The Speech Community." In *Language and Social Context,* edited by Pier Paolo Giglioli, 219–31. Harmondsworth, U.K.: Penguin Books, 1972.

———. *Discourse Strategies.* New York: Cambridge University Press, 1982.

Gumperz, John, and Dell Hymes, eds. *Directions in Sociolinguistics: The Ethnography of Communication.* New York: Holt and Rinehart, 1972.

Gupta, Das. *Language Conflict and National Development.* Berkeley: University of California Press, 1970.

Haider, S. N. Rizvi. "Music in Muslim India." *Islamic Culture* 15 (1941): 330–40.

Haq, Sirajul. "Samā' and the Raqs of the Dervishes." *Islamic Culture* 18 (1944): 111–30.

Hashimi, Hamidullah S. *Syed Waris Shah.* Faisalabad: Majlis-e Panjabi Adab, 1978.

al-Hashimi, Ali. *Woman in Pre-Islamic Poetry.* Baghdad: Matba'al al-Ma'arif, 1960.

Heritage, John. *Garfinkel and Ethnomethodology.* Cambridge: Polity Press, 1984.

Herndon, Marcia, and Roger Brunyate, eds. *Symposium on Form in Performance: Proceedings of a Symposium on Hard-core Ethnography.* April 17–19, 1975. Austin: College of Fine Arts, University of Texas at Austin, 1976.

hooks, bell. *Ain't I a Woman? Black Women and Feminism.* Boston: South End Press, 1981.

———. *Feminist Theory From Margin to Center.* Boston: South End Press, 1984.

———. *Talking Back.* Boston: South End Press, 1989.

Hotechand, Tirathdas. "The Risālo: Its Musical Compositions." In *Shah Abdul Latif: His Mystical Poetry,* edited by Abdul Hamid Akhund, 157–63. Hyderabad: Shah Abdul Latif Bhit Shah Cultural Center Committee, 1991.

Hussain, Shah. *Kafiān.* Translated by Abdul Majid Bhatti. Islamabad: Institute of Folk Heritage, 1987.

Hussaini, Syed Shah Khusro. "Bund Samāc." *Islamic Culture* (1970): 77–85.

Hymes, Dell. "Sociolinguistics and the Ethnography of Speaking." In *Social Anthropology and Linguistics,* edited by E. Ardner. Monographs 10 (1971): 47–93. London: Association of Anthropologists.

———. "Toward Ethnographies of Communication: The Analysis of Communicative Events." In *Language and Social Context,* edited by Pier Paolo Giglioli, 21–44. Harmondsworth, U.K.: Penguin Books, 1972.

———. "In Vain I Tried to Tell You." *Essays in Native American Ethnopoetics.* Philadelphia: University of Pennsylvania Press, 1981.

———. *Essays in the History of Linguistic Anthropology.* Philadelphia: John Benjamins Publisher, 1983.

———. *Ethnography, Linguistics, Narrative Inequality: Toward an Understanding of Voice.* London: Taylor and Francis, 1996.

Hymes, Dell, ed. *Language in Culture and Society.* New York: Harper and Row, 1964.

Ibbetson, Denzil. *Panjab Castes.* Lahore: Government Printing Press, 1916.

Ibn al-Arabi. *Sufis of Andalusia: The Ruh al quds and al-Darrah al-fakhirah of Ibn-Arabi.* Translated by R.W.J. Austin. Oxford: George Allen and Unwin, 1971.

Ibrahim, Muhammad, ed. "Jahān Arā Begam kī ik ghair mā'ruf tasānīf." *Sahibiyyā* (1937): 1–19. Ahmedabad: Oriental College Magazine.

Islamic Web website. "Population of Muslims around the World." http://islamicweb.com/begin/population.htm (December 14, 2000).

Jackendoff, Ray, and Fred Lerdah. *A Deep Parallel between Music and Language.* Bloomington: Indiana University Linguistics Club, 1980.

Jackson, Peter. *Delhi Sultanate: A Political and Military History.* Cambridge: Cambridge University Press, 1999.

Jaffery, Zia. *The Invisibles: A Tale of the Eunuchs of India.* New York: Pantheon Books, 1996.

Jakobson, Roman. "Closing Statement: Linguistics and Poetics." In *Style in Language,* edited by T. A. Sebeok, 350–77. Cambridge, Mass.: MIT Press, 1960.

———. "Poetry of Grammar and Grammar of Poetry." *Lingua* 21 (1968): 597–609.

———. *On Language.* Edited by L. R. Waugh and M. M. Burston. Cambridge: Harvard University Press, 1972.

———. "Musicology and Linguistics." In *Language in Literature,* edited by S. Pomorska and S. Rudy, 45–57. Cambridge: Harvard University Press, 1987.

———. "Quest for the Essence of Language." In *Language in Literature,* edited by S. Pomorska and S. Rudy, 413–27. Cambridge: Harvard University Press, 1987.

Jakobson, Roman, Krystyna Pomorska, and S. Rudy, eds. *Verbal Art, Verbal Sign, Verbal Time.* Minneapolis: University of Minnesota Press, 1985.

Jalal, Ayesha. "The Convenience of Subservience: Women and the State in Pakistan." *Women, Islam, and the State,* edited by Deniz Kandiyoti. Philadelphia: Temple University Press, 1991.

Jalalpuri, Abbas A. *Muqāmāt-e Waris Shah.* Lahore: Hamid Raza Press, 1972.

Jameson, Fredrick. "Third-World Literature in the Era of Multinational Capitalism." *Social Text* 15 (fall 1986): 65–88.

Johnston, Sharilee M. "Poetics of Performance: Narratives, Faith and Disjuncture in Qawwālī." Ph.D. diss., University of Texas at Austin, 2000.

Joshi, Barburao. *Understanding Indian Music.* Bombay: Asia Publishing House, 1963.

Jukes, A. *A Dictionary of the Jatki or Western Panjabi Language.* Lahore: 1900.

Kakar, Sudhir. *Shamans, Mystics, and Doctors.* Boston: Beacon Press, 1982.

Kanhyalal, Hindi. *Tarikh-e Lahore.* 1884. Reprint, Lahore: Majlis-e Tariqi-e Adab, 1977.

Kausar, Inamul Haq. *Tazkarā Sufiā-e Baluchistan.* Lahore: Markaz-e Urdu Board, 1976.

Keddie, Nikki R., ed. *Scholars, Saints, and Sufis: Muslim Religious Institutions since 1500.* Berkeley: University of California Press, 1978.

Keil, Charles. "The Concept of the Folk." *Journal of the Folklore Institute* 16 (3):209–10.

Keil, Charles, and Steven Feld. *Music Grooves.* Chicago: University of Chicago Press, 1994.

Kendon, Adam, ed. *Organization of Behaviour in Face-to-Face Interaction.* The Hague: Mouton, 1976.

Khan, M. Fahim. "Pakistan." In *Migration of Asian Workers to the Arab World,* edited by Godfrey Gunatilleke, 110–65. Tokyo: United Nations University, 1986.

Khan, Yusuf Hussain. "Sufism in India." *Islamic Culture* 30 (1956): 239–62.

———. *Urdu Ghazal.* Azamgarh: Matbua Press, 1957.

Kiani, Hadiqa. *Roshni.* Compact disc, Sound Master, SMCD 146. Produced by Irfan Kiani, distributed by Sadaf Stereo, Pakistan.

Kirshenblatt-Gimblett, B. *Speech Play: Research and Resources for Studying Linguistic Creativity.* Philadelphia: University of Pennsylvania Press, 1976.

Makhdoom website. "The Melodies of Harmonized Music." http://home.pacific.net/sg/ makhdoom/sur.htm (December 30, 2000).
Malik, Jamal. *Colonization of Islam: Dissolution of Traditional Institutions in Pakistan.* New Delhi: Manohar, 1996.
Malik, M. Latif. *Aulīyā-e Lahore.* Lahore: Sang-e Meel Publications (Institute of Folk Heritage Library, Pakistan), 1992.
Malinowski, Bronislaw. *The Dynamics of Culture Change: An Inquiry into Race Relations in Africa.* Edited by P. M. Kaberry. New Haven: Yale University Press, 1945.
———. *A Diary in the Strict Sense of the Term.* New York: Harcourt Brace, 1967.
Mandela, Nelson. *Long Walk to Freedom.* Boston: Little, Brown, 1994.
Mandelbaum, David G. *Women's Seclusion and Men's Honor: Sex Roles in North India, Bangladesh, and Pakistan.* Tucson: University of Arizona Press, 1988.
Manikpuri, Sahil. *Ghazal Pasmanzar.* Allahabad: Urdu Writers Guild, 1976.
Manuel, Peter M. *Cassette Culture: Popular Music and Technology in North India.* Chicago: University of Chicago Press, 1993.
Manushi. Special editions, "Women Bhakta Poets," nos. 50, 51, 52. New Delhi: Manushi Trust, 1989.
Marcus, George E., and M.M.J. Fischer. *Anthropology as Cultural Critique.* Chicago: University of Chicago Press, 1986.
Masica, Colin P. *The Indo-Aryan Languages.* Cambridge: Cambridge University Press, 1991.
Memmi, Albert. *The Colonizer and the Colonized.* Boston: Beacon Press, 1965.
Mernissi, Fatima. *Beyond the Veil.* Bloomington: Indiana University Press, 1987.
Meyer, Leonard B. *Emotion and Meaning in Music.* University of Chicago Press, 1956.
Miani, D. Singh. *Studies in Panjabi Poetry.* Delhi: Vikas Publishing House, 1979.
Mills, Margaret. *Rhetorics and Politics in Afghan Traditional Storytelling.* Philadelphia: University of Pennsylvania Press, 1991.
Milson, Menaham, trans. *A Sufi Rule for Novices: Kitab adab al-muridin of Abu al-Najib al-Suhrawardi* by A. Q. Ibn abd Allah al-Suhrawardi, 1097–1168. Cambridge: Harvard University Press, 1975.
Minault, Gail. *Secluded Scholars: Women's Education and Muslim Social Reform in Colonial India.* Delhi: Oxford University Press, 1998.
Minh-ha, Trinh T. "On the Politics of Contemporary Representations." In *Discussions in Contemporary Culture,* edited by Hal Foster. Seattle: Bay Press, 1987.
———. *Woman, Native, Other: Writing Postcoloniality and Feminism.* Bloomington: Indiana University Press, 1989.

Mirza, M. Wahid. *Life and Works of Amir Khusrau.* 1934. Reprint, Lahore: Panjab University Press, 1962.

Mufti, Ghulam Sarwar. *Tarikh-e Makhzan Panjab.* 1887. Reprint, Lahore: Maktab-e Nabawwiya, 1987.

Muhammad, Inam. *Hazrat Lal Shahbaz Qalandar of Sehwan.* Jamshoro: Institute of Sindhology, 1999.

Mujeeb, M. *The Indian Muslims.* Montreal: McGill University Press, 1967.

Mumtaz, Khawar, and Farida Shaheed, eds. *Women of Pakistan.* London: Zed Publications, 1987.

Murtaza, Syed. "Mazars, Malangs and Men." *Dawn* 2–8 (April 1991) 12–15.

Nadavi, Shah Muhammad J. *Islam aur Mausīqī.* Lahore: Institute of Islamic Culture, 1959.

Nair, Gopinathan P. R. "India." In *Migration of Asian Workers to the Arab World,* edited by Godfrey Gunatilleke, 66–109. Tokyo: United Nations University, 1986.

Naqvi, Syed Jaleel. *Tarikh-e Barvālā Sayyidin.* Lahore: Ganj-e Shakar Printers, 1989.

Nasr, Seyyed Hossein. "The Sufi Master as Exemplified in Persian Sufi Literature." *Studies in Comparative Religion* 4, no. 3 (1970): 140–49.

———. "Mysticism and Traditional Philosophy in Persia, Pre-Islamic and Islamic." *Studies in Comparative Religion* 5, no. 4 (1971): 235–40.

———. "The Influence of Sufism on Traditional Persian Music." *Studies in Comparative Religion* 6, no. 4 (1972): 225–34.

———. "Rumi and the Sufi Tradition." *Studies in Comparative Religion* 8, no. 2 (1974): 74–89.

———. "The Male and Female in the Islamic Perspective." *Studies in Comparative Religion* 14, nos. 1 and 2 (1980): 67–75.

Nayyar, Adam. *Origin and History of Qawwali.* Islamabad: Lok Virsa Research Center, 1988.

Nayyar, Adam, and Lorraine H. Sakata. *Musical Survey of Pakistan.* Islamabad: Lok Virsa Research Center, 1989.

Nayyar, Deepak. "International Labor Migration from India: A Macro-Economic Analysis." In *To the Gulf and Back,* edited by Rashid Amjad, 95–142. New Delhi: International Labor Organization, 1989.

Nazim, Bashir H. *Aulīyā-e Multan.* Lahore: Sang-e Meel Publications, 1992.

Nettl, Bruno. *North American Indian Musical Style.* Philadelphia: American Folklore Society, 1954.

Neuman, Daniel M. *The Life of Music in North India.* 2 vols. Detroit: Wayne University Press, 1979.

Nicholson, Reynold A. *The Mystics of Islam.* 1914. Reprint, London: Routledge, 1963.

———. *A Literary History of the Arabs.* Cambridge: Cambridge University Press, 1930.

Nizami, Ganjavi. *Layla-Majnun*. Boulder: Shambala Press, 1966.
Nurbakhsh, Javed. *In the Paradise of the Sufis*. London: Khaniqahi-Nimatullahi, 1983.
———. *In the Tavern of Ruin*. London: Khaniqahi-Nimatullahi, 1983.
———. *Sufi Women*. London: Khaniqahi-Nimatullahi, 1990.
Nyrop, Richard F. *Area Handbook for Pakistan*. Washington, D.C.: U.S. Government Printing Office, 1975.
Ochs, Elinor. "Transcription as Theory." In *Developmental Pragmatics*, edited by Elinor Ochs and Bambi B. Schiefflin, 43–72. New York: Academic Press, 1979.
Ong, Walter J. "African Talking Drums and Oral Noetics." *New Literary History* 8, no. 3 (1977): 411–29.
———. *Orality and Literacy: The Technologizing of the Word*. New York: Methuen, 1982.
Oriental Star Agencies website. "Ustad Nusrat Fateh Ali Khan." *http://www.osa.co.uk* (November 17, 1999).
Osborne, C. L. *The Adventures of Hir and Ranjha*. London: Peter Owen Ltd, 1973.
Osmani, S. R. "Bangladesh." In *Migration of Asian Workers to the Arab World*, edited by Godfrey Gunatilleke, 23–65. Tokyo: United Nations University, 1986.
Paredes, Americo, and Richard Bauman. *Toward New Perspectives in Folklore*. Austin: University of Texas Press, 1972.
Petievich, Carla. "The Feminine Voice in the Urdu Ghazal." *Indian Horizons* 39, no. 1–2 (1990) 25–41.
———. "Dakani's Radha-Krishna Imagery and Canon Formation in Urdu." In *The Banyan Tree: Essays in Early Literature in New Indo-Aryan Languages*, vol. 1, edited by Mariolo Offredi, 113–30. New Delhi: Manohar Publishers, 2001.
Platts, John T. A. *A Dictionary of Urdu, Classical Hindi, and English*. 1930. Reprint, London: Oxford University Press, 1982.
Pollock, Della. "Performing Writing." In *The Ends of Performance*, edited by Peggy Phalen and Jill Lane. New York: New York University Press, 1998.
Pritish, Nandy, trans. *The Songs of Mirabai*. New Delhi: Arnold-Heinemann, 1975.
Propp, Vladimir. "The Nature of Folklore." In *The Theory and History of Folklore*. Minneapolis: University of Minnesota Press, 1984.
Qazi, Muhammad A. "Sindhi Music." In *Folk Music of Sind*, edited by Ghulam Ali Allana, 65–84. Jamshoro: Institute of Sindhology, 1982.
Qureshi, Regula B. "Tarannum: The Chanting of Urdu Poetry." *Ethnomusicology* 13 (1969): 425–69.
———. "Indo-Muslim Religious Music: An Overview." *Asian Music* 3, no. 2 (1972): 5–23.

———. "Pakistan." *The New Grove Dictionary of Music and Musicians.* London: Macmillan, 1980b.

———. "Islamic Music in an Indian Environment: The Shi'a Majlis." *Ethnomusicology* 25, no. 1 (1981): 47–71.

———. "Qawwali: Making the Music Happen in the Sufi Assembly." In *Performing Arts in India: Essays on Music, Dance, and Drama,* edited by Bonnie C. Wade, 118–53. Berkeley: University of California Monograph Series 21, 1983.

———. *Sufi Music of India and Pakistan.* Cambridge: Cambridge University Press, 1986.

Qureshi, Samina. *Lahore: The City Within.* Singapore: Concept Media, 1988.

Rafat, Taufiq. *Bulleh Shah: A Selection.* Lahore: Vanguard, 1982.

Rai, Amrit. *A House Divided.* Delhi: Oxford University Press, 1984.

Ramakrishna, Lajwanti. *Panjabi Sufi Poets.* New Delhi: Ashajanak Publications, 1973.

Reddy, William. "Against Construction: The Historical Ethnography of Emotion." *Current Anthropology* 38, no. 3: 97.

Rehman, M. "Affectionate Response to the Indian Environment." In *Amir Khusrau Memorial Volume.* Delhi: Ministry of Information and Broadcasting, Government of India Publications, 1975. 117–42.

Richman, Bruce. "Did Human Speech Originate in Coordinated Vocal Music?" *Semiotica* 32, no. 3/4 (1980): 233–44.

Rizvi, Sayid Athar Abbas. *A History of Sufism in India.* 2 vols. New Delhi: Munshiram Manoharlal Publishers, 1978 (vol. 1), 1983 (vol. 2).

Rizvi, S.N.H. "Music in Muslim India." *Islamic Culture* 15, no. 3 (1941): 331–40.

Rizwani, Khan, ed. *Wasdiyan Jhokan: An Anthology of Siraiki Poetry, Folksongs, Folklore, Fiction, and Drama.* Multan: Siraiki Academy, 1974.

Rouget, Gilbert. *Music and Trance: A Theory of Relations between Music and Possession.* Chicago: University of Chicago Press, 1985.

Row, Peter. "The Device of Modulation in Hindustani Art Music." *Essays in Art and Humanities.* Vol. 6, no. 1 (March 1977): 104–20.

Russell, Ralph. "Some Problems of the Treatment of Urdu Meter." *Journal of the Royal Asiatic Society* (1960): 48–58.

Sabbah, Fatna A. *Woman in the Muslim Unconscious.* Translated by Mary Jo Lakeland. New York: Pergamon Press, 1984.

Sacks, Harvey, Emanuel Schegloff, and Gail Jefferson. "A Simplest Systematics for the Organization of Turn Taking for Conversation." In *Studies in the Organization of Conversational Interaction,* edited by Jim Schenkein, 696–735. New York: Academic Press, 1978.

Sadler, Albert W. "Visit to a Chisti Qawwali." *Muslim World* 4 (1963): 287–92.

Said, Edward. *Orientalism.* New York: Random House, 1979.

Sakata, Lorraine H. "The Sacred and the Profane: Qawwali Represented in the Performances of Nusrat Fateh Ali Khan." *The World of Music* 36, no. 3 (1994): 86–99.

Salt, John, and Reuben Ford. "The United Kingdom." In *Handbook of International Migration*, edited by William J. Serow, Charles B. Nam, David F. Sly, and Robert H. Weller, 325–40. London: Greenwood Press, 1990.

Samnani, Saiyid G. *Amir Khusrau*. Delhi: National Book Trust, 1968.

Sapir, Edward. *Language*. New York: Harcourt Brace, 1946.

de Saussure, Ferdinand. *Course in General Linguistics*. Edited by C. Bally et al. New York: McGraw Hill, 1959.

Sayyid, Najm Hosain. *Recurrent Patterns in Panjabi Poetry*. Lahore: Majlis Shah Hussain, 1968.

Schelling, Andrew. *For Love of the Dark One: Songs of Mirabai*. Boston: Shambala, 1993.

Schenkein, Jim, ed. *Studies in the Organization of Conversational Interaction*. New York: Academic Press, 1978.

Schimmel, Annemarie. *Mystical Dimensions of Islam*. Chapel Hill: University of North Carolina Press, 1975.

———. "The Marthiya in Sindhi Poetry." In *Ta'ziyeh: Ritual and Drama in Iran*, edited by Peter Chelkowski, 210–21. New York: New York University Press, 1979.

———. *As Through a Veil: Mystical Poetry in Islam*. New York: Columbia University Press, 1982.

———. *My Soul Is a Woman: The Feminine in Islam*. Translated by Susan H. Ray. New York: Continuum, 1997.

Schoun, Frithjof. "The Mystery of the Veil." *Studies in Comparative Religion* 112 (1977): 66–81.

Sekhon, Sant S., trans. *The Love of Hir and Ranjha*. Ludhiana: Panjab Agricultural University, 1978.

Sethi, V. K. *Mira: The Divine Lover*. New Delhi: Radha Soami Satsang Beas, 1979.

Shackle, Cristopher. *The Siraiki Language of Central Pakistan: A Reference Grammar*. London: School of Oriental and African Studies, 1976.

———. *Fifty Poems of Khawaja Farid*. Multan: Bazm-e Saqafat, 1983.

———. *From Wuch to Central Lahnda: A Century of Siraiki Studies in English*. Multan: Bazm-e Saqafat, 1983.

———. *Urdu and Muslim South Asia: Studies in Honor of Ralph Russell*. London: School of Oriental and African Studies, 1989.

Shackle, Cristopher, ed. *Hasham Shah: Sassi-Punnu*. Lahore: Vanguard, 1985.

Shafi, Maulvi Muhammad. *Auliya-e Kasur*. Lahore: Panjab University, 1972.

Shah, Abdul Latif. *Risālo*. Hyderabad: Institute of Sindhology, n.d.

Shah, Bulle. *Kafian*. Edited by Muhammad Sharif Sabir. Lahore: Syed Ajmal Hussain Memorial Society, 1991.

Shah, Hussain. *Kafian Shah Hussain.* Edited by Maqbool Anwar Dawoodi. Lahore: Ferozesons, 1987.
Shah, Nasra M., and Fred Arnold. "Pakistan." *Handbook of International Migration,* edited by William J. Serow, Charles B. Nam, David F. Sly, and Robert H. Weller, 261–85. London: Greenwood Press, 1990.
Shahabi, Mufti, and Dard Kakorvi. *Hazrat Amir Khusrau aur unka Urdu Kalām.* Karachi: Daira Al-Maraf Quarania, 1960.
Shakespeare, John. *Dictionary of Urdu-English, English-Urdu.* Lahore: Sang-e Meel Publications, 1980.
Sharar, Abdul H. *Lucknow: The Last Phase of an Oriental Culture.* Translated by E. S. Harcourt and Fakir Hussain. Boulder: Westview Press, 1975.
Sharif, Ja'far. *Islam in India or The Qanun-e Islam.* Translated by G. A. Herklots. New Delhi: Oriental Books, 1972 (first published 1832).
Sherzer, Joel. "Verbal and Nonverbal Deixis: The Pointed Lip Gesture among the San Blas Kuna." *Language in Society* 2 (1973): 117–31.
———. "Play Languages: Implications for Sociolinguistics." In *Speech Play: Research and Resources for Studying Linguistic Creativity,* edited by Barbara Kirshenblatt-Gimblett. Philadelphia: University of Pennsylvania Press, 1976.
———. *Kuna Ways of Speaking.* Austin: University of Texas Press, 1983.
———. "A Discourse-Centered Approach to Language and Culture." *American Anthropologist* 89, no. 2 (1987): 295–309.
———. *Verbal Art in San Blas: Kuna Culture through Its Discourse.* 2d ed. Albuquerque: University of New Mexico Press, 1998.
Sherzer, Joel, and Regna Darnell. "Outline Guide for the Ethnographic Study of Speech Use." In *Directions in Sociolinguistics,* edited by John Gumperz and Dell Hymes, 548–54. New York: Holt and Rinehart, 1972.
Sherzer, Joel, and Greg Urban, eds. *Native South American Discourse.* Berlin: Mouton De Gruyter, 1986.
Sherzer, Joel, and A. Woodbury, eds. *Native American Discourse.* New York: Cambridge University Press, 1987.
Silko, Leslie M. *Ceremony.* New York: Viking Press, 1977.
———. *Storyteller.* New York: Seaver, 1981.
Slawek, Steven. "Popular *Kirtan:* Some 'Great' Aspects of a Little Tradition." *Ethnomusicology* 32, no. 3 (1988): 249–64.
———. "Ravi Shankar as Mediator between Traditional Music and Modernity." In *Ethnomusicology and Modern Music History,* edited by Stephen Blum, Philip Bohlman, and Daniel Neuman, 161–80. Urbana: University of Illinois Press, 1990.
———. "The Study of Performance Practice as a Research Method: A South Asian Example." *International Journal of Musicology* 3, no. 9 (1994): 22.
Sleeman, W. H. *A Journey through the Kingdom of Avadh.* London: Richard Bentley, 1858.

Smith, Margaret. *Rabi'a: The Life and Work of Rabi'a and Other Women Mystics of Islam.* 1928. Reprint, Oxford: Oneworld, 1994.

Sorley, H. T. *Shah Abdul Latif of Bhit.* Delhi: Ashish Publishing House, 1984.

Steingass, F., ed. *Persian-English Dictionary.* London: Kegan Paul, 1930.

Stern, Theodore. "Drum and Whistle Languages: An Analysis of Speech Surrogates." *American Anthropologist* 59 (1957): 487–506.

Subhan, John A. *Sufism, Its Saints and Shrines: An Introduction to the Study of Sufism.* Lucknow: Lucknow Publishing House, 1960.

Tabatabai, Syed M. H. *Shi'ite Islam.* New York: University of New York Press, 1977.

Tannen, Deborah, ed. *Analyzing Discourse: Text and Talk.* Washington, D.C.: Georgetown University Press, 1981.

Titus, Murray T. *Islam in India and Pakistan.* Calcutta: YMCA Publication, 1959.

Trimingham, Spenser. *The Sufi Orders of Islam.* Oxford: Clarendon Press, 1971.

Trix, Frances. *Spiritual Discourses: Learning with an Islamic Master.* Philadelphia: University of Pennsylvania Press, 1993.

Trudgill, Peter. *Sociolinguistics.* New York: Penguin, 1983.

Trumpp, Ernst. *Shah Jo Risālo.* 1866. Reprint, Hyderabad: Institute of Sindhology, 1999.

Turkish Tourism Office. *La Samāʿ Danse Mystique des Dervishes.* Videocassette. Held at the University of North Carolina, 1999.

Tyler, Stephen A. "Post-Modern Ethnography: From Document of the Occult to Occult Document." In *Writing Culture: The Poetics and Politics of Ethnography,* edited by J. Clifford and George Marcus, 122–40. Berkeley: University of California Press, 1986.

Umiker, Donna J. "Speech Surrogates: Drum and Whistle Systems." *Current Trends in Linguistics* (The Hague) (1974): 476–536.

U.S. Census Bureau website. "PCT004. ASIAN ALONE WITH ONE ASIAN CATEGORY FOR SELECTED GROUPS." http://factfinder.census.gov/servlet/DTTable?ds_name=Dandgeo_id=Dandmt_name= ACS_C2SS_EST-G2000_PCT004and_lang=en (September 4, 2001).

———. "Confidentiality Protection." http://factfinder.census.gov/home/en/datanotes/exp.c2ss.html (September 4, 2001).

Usborne, Ch. Fredrick, L. Rama Krishna, and A. R. Luther. *Bulle Shah: A Mystic Poet of Panjab.* Lahore: Abdul Mauli Printer, 1982.

Utas, Bo, ed. *Women in Islamic Societies.* New York: Olive Branch Press, 1983.

Visweswaran, Kamala. *Fictions of Feminist Ethnography.* Minneapolis: University of Minnesota Press, 1994.

Wade, Bonnie. "Prolegomenon to the Study of Song Texts." *YIFMC* 8 (1976): 73–88.

———. *Music in India: The Classical Traditions.* Englewood Cliffs, N.J.: Prentice Hall, 1979.

———. *Imaging Sound: An Ethnomusicological Study of Music, Art, and Culture in Mughal India.* Chicago: University of Chicago Press, 1998.

Wasi, M. Abdul. *Divān-e Farid Maʿ Dhorājāt.* Multan: Qadimi Kutab Khana, n.d.

Weinrich, Uriel. *Languages in Contact.* The Hague: Mouton, 1979.

Werbner, Pnina, and Helene Basu, eds. *Embodying Charisma: Modernity, Locality, and the Performance of Emotion in Sufi Cults.* London and New York: Routledge, 1998.

Whorf, Benjamin. *Language, Thought, and Reality.* Edited by J. Carroll. Cambridge, Mass.: MIT Press, 1956.

Wilson, J. *Grammar and Dictionary of Western Panjabi as Spoken in the Shahpur District.* Lahore: Panjab Government Press, 1899.

Wood, Michael. *In the Footsteps of Alexander.* Four videocassettes. PBS Home Video, 1997, 1998.

Zaehner, Robert C. *Hindu and Muslim Mysticism.* London: Athlone Press, 1960.

———. *Mysticism: Sacred and Profane.* London: Oxford University Press, 1961.

Zaman, Mukhtar. "Qawwālī: Mystical Music." *Dawn* 2–8 (April 1991): 10–11.

Index

www.ingramcontent.com/pod-product-compliance
Ingram Content Group UK Ltd.
Pitfield, Milton Keynes, MK11 3LW, UK
UKHW031840110225
454967UK00001B/85

9 780292 725928